GRANTA 86, SUMMER 2004
www.granta.com

EDITOR *Ian Jack*
DEPUTY EDITOR *Matt Weiland*
MANAGING EDITOR *Fatema Ahmed*
ASSOCIATE EDITOR *Liz Jobey*
EDITORIAL ASSISTANT *Helen Gordon*

CONTRIBUTING EDITORS *Diana Athill, Sophie Harrison, Gail Lynch, Blake Morrison, Andrew O'Hagan, John Ryle, Sukhdev Sandhu, Lucretia Stewart*

ASSOCIATE PUBLISHER *Sally Lewis*
FINANCE *Geoffrey Gordon, Morgan Graver*
SALES *Frances Hollingdale*
PUBLICITY *Louise Campbell*
SUBSCRIPTIONS *John Kirkby, Anna Tang*
PUBLISHING ASSISTANT *Mark Williams*
ADVERTISING MANAGER *Kate Rochester*
PRODUCTION ASSOCIATE *Sarah Wasley*

PUBLISHER *Rea S. Hederman*

Granta, 2–3 Hanover Yard, Noel Road, London N1 8BE
Tel 020 7704 9776 Fax 020 7704 0474
e-mail for editorial: editorial@granta.com

Granta US, 1755 Broadway, 5th Floor, New York, NY 10019-3780, USA

TO SUBSCRIBE call 020 7704 0470 or e-mail subs@granta.com
A one-year subscription (four issues) costs £26.95 (UK), £34.95 (rest of Europe) and £41.95 (rest of the world).

Granta is printed and bound in Italy by Legoprint. The paper used in this publication meets the minimum requirements of American National Standard for Information Sciences—Permanence of Paper for Printed Library Materials, ANSI Z39.48-1984.

Design: Slab Media.

Back cover: storyboard from 'Taxi Driver', courtesy of Martin Scorsese collection and Sikelia Productions, sketch for 'Akira Kurosawa's Dreams', © Kurosawa Production, Inc. Licensed exclusively by HoriPro Inc., woodcut from 'Pather Panchali', courtesy of Sandip Ray

Acknowledgements are due to the following publishers for permission to quote from: 'Musée des Beaux Arts' from 'Collected Poems' by W. H. Auden, reprinted by permission of Faber and Faber Ltd and Random House, Inc.

ISBN 0-903141-69-8

FEATURING:

Allison Anders
Susanne Bier
Clare Binns
Rosa Bosch
Denise Breton
Lisa Cholodenko
Pauline Kael
Anna Karina
Katia Lund
Frances McDormand
Heather McGowan
Rebecca Miller
Emily Mortimer
Ramona Sanchez
Libby Savill

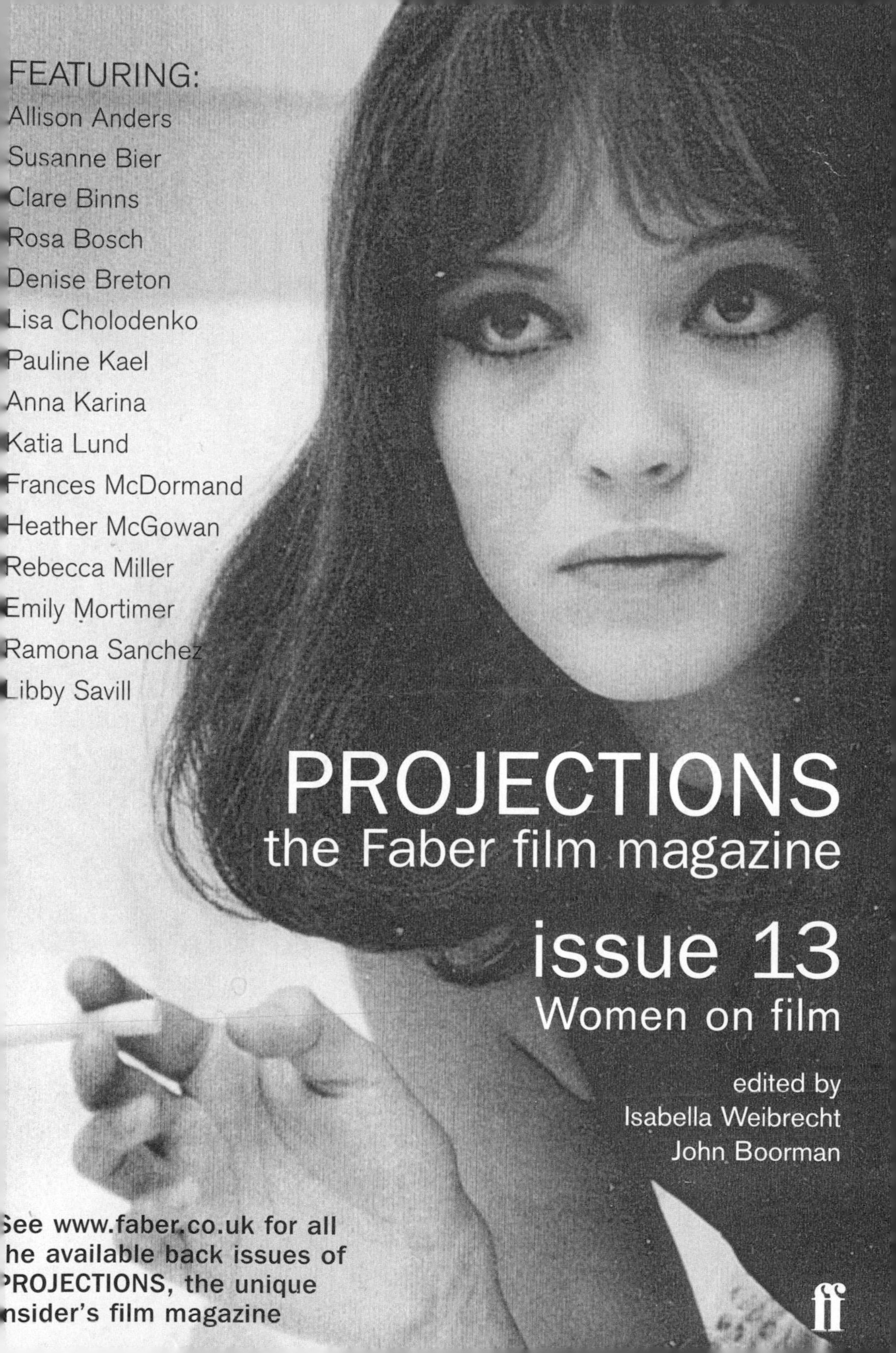

PROJECTIONS

the Faber film magazine

issue 13

Women on film

edited by
Isabella Weibrecht
John Boorman

See www.faber.co.uk for all he available back issues of PROJECTIONS, the unique nsider's film magazine

ff

'Set in a coolly
evoked city landscape,
An Empty Room
perfectly encapsulates
the confusions and
mistakes of a young adult
and tells us something
significant about the
furies and hurts
of first love'
Elizabeth Buchan

'Written with honesty
and an element of
wistfulness which
combine in a voice
that is clear and true'
Raffaella Barker

AN EMPTY ROOM

TALITHA STEVENSON

'So lucent, so resonant, so exquisitely written and, above all, so engaging'
Tim Lott, *Evening Standard*

PUBLISHED IN VIRAGO

Film

THE FRENCH LIEUTENANT'S DIARY

John Fowles

Meryl Streep in 'The French Lieutenant's Woman'

In 1966 John Fowles and his first wife Elizabeth moved from London to a farmhouse near Lyme Regis on the Dorset coast. Two years later he moved to the town itself—a town with literary antecedents, because it was from the steps on Lyme Regis's old stone pier known as the Cobb that Louisa Musgrove jumped in Jane Austen's Persuasion. *By the beginning of 1967, Fowles had written two novels,* The Collector *(1963) and* The Magus *(1966). The first of them had been successfully filmed by William Wyler with Samantha Eggar and Terence Stamp in the principal roles.*

January 25, 1967 *The French Lieutenant's Woman.* I started this today. Not so much with a plot as a mood and a language I wanted to use. It was really just one visual idea: a woman standing at the end of the Cobb and staring mysteriously out to sea.

February 11 Lelouch—*Un Homme et une Femme.* A very fine film. We saw it on the same day as a really bad English one, which has received splendid reviews in every direction: *Accident.* A masterly symposium of all that is pretentious and third-rate about the English avant-garde. In this sort of work (not in his own, of course) Pinter is a shyster; relying on pointless pauses to give some profound metaphysical content to banal dialogue. Acting and camerawork to match.

The sheer standardless silliness of the London reviewers is beyond belief. Some madness eats that town.

May 20 A remark of McLuhan's (in this month's *Encounter*) to the effect that literature really had no ability to convey all the realities of words—that it's always a narrowing of the potential, a thin artifice compared to the full 'nature' of all language. I am writing *The French Lieutenant's Woman* at the moment; and reading Mrs Gaskell's *Mary Barton* at the same time. Her dialogue is much more 'modern' than mine—full of contractions, and so on. Yet in order for me to convey the century that has passed since the time of my book I am right to invent dialogue much more formal than the Victorians actually spoke. This gives the illusion better. In a sense an absolutely accurate Victorian dialogue would be less truthful than what I am doing. I don't know if McLuhan is attacking the novel for this 'perversion' of reality. If he is, I don't agree with him. But a novel is really a kind of metaphor, a poem about reality rather than a report of it. And even with novels far more overtly reality-reflecting than mine.

In 1967 Fowles had adapted The Magus *for a film directed by Guy Green and starring Michael Caine, Anthony Quinn and Candice Bergen. Shooting began that autumn.*

September 6–20 The boredom of location shooting—orthodoxly made films like this require such an enormous amount of apparatus. Each small scene takes at least half an hour to set up; so much fiddling with the 'brutes' and the 'flags', so much shouting to 'lose' people in the backgrounds, and so little time spent on the actual acting. It's absurd, really; as if the frame mattered more than the painting.

Mike Caine on his first day of shooting. He brings a nice presence to what he does; a matter-of-factness the amateur always lacks. They made me play a little scene with him, so I am an authority now. It's not that I don't know exactly what I ought to do; but doing it 'on camera' is something else. Mike Caine said afterwards: 'You're always going to seem and sound artificial to yourself. It's finding the area where you can kid the audience into believing you're being natural.' He's very far from being a fool about his job; and his behaviour between takes, when he is endlessly bothered for autographs and snapshots, is exemplary.

October 14 *The French Lieutenant's Woman.* I'm now about three quarters of the way through and full of the usual doubts. That is, that I'm trying to do too much. I am split between writing out of my Englishness and against it.

January 6–23, 1968 Eliz has been away. I meant to get on with the final stages of *The FLW*, but a thriller story ['Somebody's Got to Do It'] I have toyed with for some time suddenly seemed to demand to be written. So I've written it, about 110,000 words, in seventeen days flat. I've gobbled down one meal a day, but otherwise worked from nine to one or two the next morning. In a sense it's been a reaction from the third-person cerebrality of *The FLW*. Not meant to be serious: just a headlong love-and-mystery story.

March 5 Jud [Kinberg, a film producer] has returned from Hollywood from the showing of the rough cut [of *The Magus*] to Zanuck and the other Twentieth Century moguls. He says they are delighted—which wouldn't mean much in my ears, if they hadn't also signed Guy Green for this summer's big picture and asked for the last scene (the happy ending in London) to be cut, as I've always wanted. Release 'in the fall'.

March 7–9 In London to see the rough cut of *The Magus*. We saw it alone with Jud and Max, the cutting editor. A terrible feeling of disappointment, after the new hope I'd foolishly drawn from the Hollywood reaction. Quinn has done well, and the two girls quite well; but Caine is really excruciatingly bad, totally incredible as an English graduate, however proletarian in origin. Just Caine, the best paid European film star, drifting through a role he doesn't understand. He seems to have no notion of how to react, let alone act. Guy Green is to blame, of course—only Quinn has the ability to rise above the general ambience of non-direction. No poetry, no mystery. And to make matters worse, they've cut it razor-sharp—the scenes skid and jump on so fast that there's no sense of space or even the briefest rest. The worst thing about Caine's failure is that it pervades the whole picture; the one part we couldn't afford to go wrong.

I saw it a second time two days later, reel by reel, and it didn't seem so bad, even though we'd seen a brilliant film (*Shakespeare Wallah*) in between—a film that had everything we lack...love, art, humanity. We agreed on a number of new cuts and restorations of footage and other changes.

June 6 Assassination of Robert Kennedy. In the city and on the day *The Magus* was to be shown in public for the first time. They cancelled the showing, of course. It seems to me a classic example— but then so was Oswald's story—of the effect of the nemo. I don't believe Sirhan can be explained by his reason; believing Kennedy was pro-Israel and so on. His motive was much more that of the nineteenth-century anarchists: to get his name into the history books, to do something about his nothingness. His only statement beyond yes or no in the first trial was apparently to tell the judge how to pronounce his name; just what one would expect. From now

John Fowles

on, Sirhan survives, whatever happens to his body. Several women rushed to the police when it was announced that he might have had a female accomplice. All this happens in America, of course, because there the nemo can be most brilliantly defeated by the successful and most totally felt by failures.

July 23 Eliz has read *The FLW*; doesn't like the ending or the Carroll episode. I had doubts about them myself, so now I am changing them. Characters, thank heaven, are endlessly manipulatable at this stage in a manuscript.

July 30 The film of *The Magus*. We went to see a showing—an audience of movie business friends of John [Kohn, screenwriter] and Jud. I thought there were distinct signs of a non-sale. It has turned out to be just about as vulgar as we feared. I suppose there is a certain slickness in the camera and cutting; but the music now added is repulsively banal. Caine's performance, in spite of all the cuts that have been made in it, remains wooden and hopelessly without depth. It's really the appalling hollowness and shallowness of the finished product that disgusts me. I am partly to blame—completely, where the script is just bad, and unconsciously, where I didn't foresee the danger of overwriting with someone like Guy Green. I understand better now why he wanted all the literary lines cut: he simply doesn't know how to direct them. All the dialogue is spoken at snail's pace and every meaningful line is atrociously over-stressed, both in delivery and in the killing pause that precedes it. I couldn't pretend, afterwards; which hurt Jud, the one person I didn't want to hurt in all this.

August 25 *The FLW*. Third revision and new ending completed.

September 5 *The FLW* sent to Tom Maschler [his publisher at Jonathan Cape]. With less trepidation than usual, though I expect him not to like it as well as the first two. But I know it is more or less what I intended.

On September 9, Maschler sent a telegram to Fowles at Underhill Farm: 'The French Lieutenant's Woman *is magnificent, no less. Congratulations.*'

October 1 Meeting with Tom Maschler. He wants the two endings switched, the 'author' suppressed, from *The FLW*; otherwise only very minor changes. Our relationship may go beyond the literary. He's all set to become a film producer now and he wants to use *The FLW* as his first step in the field—somehow he's managed to spirit the book away from Cape and get it to Karel Reisz, who Tom claims is a 'very close friend'. I admire Reisz, so I play along for the time being; and then all Tom's useful qualities, his force, might make him as good a film man as he is a publisher.

December 8 To London, to fetch Eliz and meet Oscar Lewenstein [a producer], whom Tom has 'interested' in *The FLW*. He's gentle-bright, very understated, a robin—a dunnock, rather. One sees him slipping quietly through the movie undercopse, getting his ends. The last man, really, at first look, to achieve what he has done in the cinema. He lives in the spendid Gothick house in Belsize Lane.

He is fairly optimistic, seems to see the difficulties on a script-style level well. But where my choice would really be Ken Russell, his is Dick Lester—mainly because the latter is 'easy to finance' and has a firm relationship with Lewenstein. We settle finally for a list of three top choices: Lester, Russell and Lindsay Anderson. Tom has complicated matters by trying to get Freddy Raphael interested as well—but he's cabled back from Jamaica to say that he's only interested if he can also direct. We can't tell Lewenstein this.

December 25 Quite good reviews of the film of *The Magus* in the *New York Times* and in *Time* magazine; two bad ones elsewhere. The good ones are absurd, the bad ones correct. I am beginning to feel like not selling film rights again.

April 24, 1969 To London, to meet Lindsay Anderson, whom Oscar has interested in the film. He's a curious mixture of aggression and shyness. A huge Cyrano nose, that scents for trouble; and he sits in all sorts of odd contorted positions, as if to suggest he is at ease, when the reverse is true. I rather favoured making more of the author-figure as narrator; but the others didn't like that. The general feeling seems to be that a voice-over commentary on the historical sidelights would be best. It wasn't a very conclusive meeting; Anderson managed to

John Fowles

convey the feeling that he was interested, but rather like the toreador
in the first rituals of the bullfight: not his time yet. It was decided
to approach David Storey to do the script—Anderson has just
produced a play of his. Tom and Oscar seemed very pleased—as I
will be, if it works. But now I think everything hinges on Storey. If
he says yes, we have Anderson; if not...

Lovely to get back to Lyme, and peace, interrupted only by a phone
call from Paul Newman in Hollywood, who wants a look at the
book. The garden gallops into its jungle phase now. A robin has
nested in the stable, between the wire-meshed inner door and wall;
absurdly in full view, but shrewdly unattainable by cats. There are
three black-hair nestlings. The parents fly in and out without any
concern; will even sit on the nest and stare at human eyes a foot away.

May 3 A letter from the 'Literature Director' of the Arts Council,
asking me if I'd like to lecture on my books. It irritated me greatly
by having a cyclostyled signature. The one world where bureaucracy
must be stamped out on sight is that of letters.

The French Lieutenant's Woman *was published in the United States
in autumn 1969.*

November 29 A curious note in many of the American reviews; a
sort of surprise that *The FLW* is both enjoyable and serious, of its
kind. I think this is a by-product of the death of religion. The novel—
along with other art-forms—has to stand in for the sermon. Thus a
serious work of art can supposedly be told by its excessive length
(or size), dullness, self-preoccupation and so on.

In a happy world, there would be no art. I retreat too often into
my imagination. In a happy world, the experience of reality would
be enough.

December 4 The film of *The Magus* has been offered to the British
public in our absence. It got what it deserved: universal damnation,
I'm happy to say.

December 18 To see Sidney Lumet's *The Seagull*. (Lumet wants to
make *The FLW*.) It's not very good, the cinema abhors the theatre;

and badly lit, shot on poor stock. We (Eliz and I) went on from there to the Cape party. Once again Tom and Fay Maschler and Tom's father; we speak to no one else. I told him I didn't want to go, so I suppose it's Tom's revenge. The other Cape directors ignored me completely once again. I felt frozen dead. Even allowing for American over-enthusiasm and extra honour given to foreigners, I can't forgive Cape for being such a cold-fish house... so lacking in warmth, such a poor comparison to Little, Brown in Boston. I feel certain now that everyone in Cape bar Tom thinks my reputation vastly inflated; I need cutting down to size. So. I am cut.

This sounds as if I just want lionizing. I don't. Just the humanity of a 'hallo'.

December 19 Oscar, Tom and I sat and made a list of directors, in order of preference: Lindsay Anderson, Tony Richardson, Zeffirelli, Polanski, Peter Brook, Zinnemann, Lumet, Jack Clayton, Joe Losey. Anderson, it seems, is still not quite firm with his refusal. Richardson, who we thought wouldn't be interested after his Crimea film, is—or may be. I outrage Tom and Oscar by saying I'd like Richardson because he's from Oxford. They kept hopping back to it when they mentioned other names: Of course, *he's* not an Oxford man. I didn't dare point out that my motives were really Marxist: an Oxford man knows more about English class, accent and alienation than anyone else—given equal talent in other directions. Richardson has apparently driven his ex-wife Vanessa Redgrave to read the book double-quick. He has always been high on my list—and she, if not visually perfect, is so far ahead in every other ability from our other toyed-with names (Sarah Miles, Glenda Jackson) that I pray we get them.

I came back to Lyme, Eliz staying up in town. I can't settle or enjoy anything at the moment, I want to write a piece about the United States—its lack of poetry, the errors in the cultural and social grammar, and so on. And the three scripts, but don't know which. I seem to have an endless capacity for planning these days, which is a function of depression, I think, not the creativity it might seem. Then the Hollywood–England novel, the Robin Hood novel. I want to do them all at the same time.

December 20 I think, too, I begin to want to direct films—it's partly

John Fowles

the collapse of Hollywood; the bankruptcy, literal and metaphorical, of the studios there. I mean, there is space now for the film as literature, for the writer as visualizer.

March 25, 1970 Oscar has been these last ten days in New York; trying to set up the film—and without success. The problem is not really lack of interest, but lack of direction in the backers. They want to pay for an extension of the option, no more. The whole industry is waiting at the moment to see which way the fickle public cat will jump. What will make money next. The book is still top of the [best-seller] list. Up to a year ago we could have asked for anything we wanted, and got it. Personally, I am quite indifferent. In a way, I should be happier if the film came to nothing, since the book has already come to something like everything.

May 4 Slipped at long last. Now second in *Time*. 130,000 copies sold.

May 9 London, to meet Dick Lester, the latest candidate for director. He looks and behaves rather like a distinguished Jewish-Viennese composer of the last century. Mendelssohn, perhaps. The language is hip, of course; and the clothes. But the dandyism, the bald brown head, long sinuous gestures, aggressive-defensive eyes, always testing, probing, doubting you. I could see he dazzles Oscar and he very swiftly dazzled Tom Maschler (who's been against him from the beginning)—in fact he was obviously a little bit what Tom wishes he was. For the first time Tom sounded faintly ashamed of publishing—a strange tone, almost of apology for being involved in such a square old profession. I think we only have Lester because of the sick situation over financing in the industry at the moment. He was as sour as a Morello cherry (with justification, apparently) about the studios. 'Why don't we go to the banks and get a loan?' Oscar, thank God, has more sense than that. I think I really don't want Lester; he's too much of a dark horse.

July 3 Now Oscar wants to withdraw if I decide to go forward with Sydney Pollack and ABC. I have decided to do so; I couldn't tell him, but his wanting to pull out made the decision even firmer. First, I think the novel is damned as source material for films and it cannot be

16

translated—one must always end with some kind of travesty. Second, the movie gets the book read and reread, and I don't think that it makes any difference if it is 'good' or 'bad'—the 'good' film satiates and one loses as many readers that way as one does by the bad film's repellent effect. Third, I am getting very tired of Tom's and Oscar's high standards...especially as they seem to be so anti-American; I don't really share their infallibility as regards artistic sheep and artistic goats. Pollack is a gamble; he may be very bad; but there's at least a chance that he may be very good. All this may add up to a general bad motive, a kind of spite against them and English fastidiousness in general. But I made my existentialist choice some weeks ago; and I shan't renege.

All I've asked is that he should at least do the deal before he backs out; and he's agreed to give Pollack a chance. Meanwhile, it remains to be seen if there is still a deal to negotiate. We haven't heard from ABC for over a month now, though they say they are still 'interested'.

July 15 Not being able to write poetry because you see too much of it every day. All the poetries in this garden; words are like throwing stones at swallows. Mean and futile.

August 20 Another round of absurd intrigue over the film of *The FLW*. Oscar's option fell in on the 7th. Since ABC still haven't made up their minds, I gave him an extra month. Now John Calley [a producer] from Warner has come through with an offer of $20,000 if I will organize a script. A week ago United Artists did exactly the same thing. Tom Maschler has been working on their London man— a gentleman I didn't take to at all. Both are anxious to go behind Oscar's back, of course. Owing to some absurd confusion, Pollack has told Oscar that Warner are interested, when the truth is that they are interested only if Oscar is dropped from the proceedings and so don't want him to know they are sniffing around. The situation is now quite watertight: everyone has to lie to everyone else. It needs a Marivaux.

August 21 A letter to John Calley. The thing I really haven't said is that Pollack's peculiar behaviour is probably not absurd confusion but calculated horse-playing: I suspect he is trying to pressure ABC into closing. 'You'd better hurry, or Calley will snatch the golden apple.' Now he's neatly got Calley snatching it, whether hungry or not.

August 25 Now David Susskind [a producer for ABC] has made an offer: a co-production deal and $50,000 for script development.

November 22 To London, to meet Franklin Schaffner and his producer Lester Goldsmith. Dinner with them, and Tom and Fay, in some supposedly Greek restaurant off Bond Street. Not a success. Schaffner is grey-haired, one of those directors who might have been US ambassadors; a lot of fencing. I'd have done much better to meet him alone somewhere. But he seems keen to do the picture after he has finished *Papillon*, which starts shooting next spring.

We went the next morning to the preview of *Nicholas and Alexandra*, Schaffner's latest, at the Leicester Square Odeon. Tony Richardson was there, David Niven, Sam Spiegel (who produced) mournfully and impatiently shepherding people about. It's not a great film by any stretch of the imagination; fairly good by David Lean tasteful-epic standards. Whether we 'go' with Schaffner is academic now, really; we have to snatch at a man of his 'bankability'. Whether Columbia backs the film depends entirely on whether he convinces them he wants to do it. So the die is cast.

May 1, 1971 Schaffner, James Goldman [a screenwriter] and mistress, Lester Goldsmith and Tom Maschler come down from London. I take them out to Underhill Farm and then they insist on going out over the cliffs. So I march them down through the jungle and along Pinhay Warren above the bay, then back to the path. In their dapper clothes. They flop and wallow and fall about, get stung by nettles (what is that goddam plant?) and torn by brambles. It becomes sadistic. I smell an American version of Guy Green in Schaffner—the same insecurity deep down and disinclination to take risk. He plays the percentage game, I suspect. Goldman is bearded and genial, a nice man but no flair or fire, at first meeting. Little Lester G. is like a small white owl or toad; says nothing. The only time he sounded in his element was during some interminable call to Los Angeles on some financial matter. That is what is so distressing about these 'international' film people. One feels they are only really at home in a jet, or on a long-distance phone line, or in the latest 'great' restaurant. Most of each of them is always somewhere else. Neither Schaffner nor Goldman would talk about the script at all; or casting. I have a feeling that they have made up their minds already and what they want; and want no argument from Tom or myself. Tom is still optimistic and I feel he is naive.

May 2 Committed now, anyway. I went up to London and swore the documents with Goldsmith at the American Embassy.

September 27 Robert Bolt has declared renewed interest in doing *The FLW* script—Tom swears he wants to do it, it's merely finding the time.

A Chabrol film, *Ten Days' Wonder*, which is bad and amusing; and a Truffaut, *Anne and Muriel*, which is just rather bad. They both have a sort of style, a rhetoric of images; content, none. Much better was De Sica's *The Garden of the Finzi-Continis*, a return to his old depth and humanism.

November 20 Tom and Fay for the weekend, because Bolt is coming—not to do the script, that's certain now, but out of respect for book and author. We had a business-type talk before the dinner, what we should do with the script and all that, and he put on a big-time director persona that I didn't like. One senses that he is a bit dazzled by his work for Lean, Spiegel and the rest; by his own rise to fame, in fact. He knows he has all the middle-of-the-road virtues; solid craftsman and the rest; but apparently confuses them with what true art is about—in the cinema, at any rate.

I liked Bolt better when the Maschlers went to bed. He would sit up and drink and talk—about his father, a second-hand furniture-dealer, Methodism, his life, his money ('I've got £80,000 in the world, including my house'—a figure none of us could believe, but he seemed so anxious to take on my own kind of cryptic colouring). At three a.m. we walked down to the end of the Cobb, at his insistence. A curious and finally rather likeable man.

He has 'given' us one good idea for the script, also: to make the author-figure Charles as well (the same actor).

None of the proposed producers and directors managed to make a film of The French Lieutenant's Woman, *and Fowles spent the next few years writing* The Ebony Tower, *which appeared in 1974, and beginning* Daniel Martin.

John Fowles

February 21 The film of *The FLW* stalks the streets again, dreaded phantoms. Now Tom Maschler has sent the book to Fred Zinnemann. Lester Goldsmith is back in town, claiming he has the money if we can come up with a director and writer.

March 11 Fred Zinnemann and Tom Maschler appeared just after midday, having trained down from London. Zinnemann is a slight little man—he's sixty-eight years old—blue-grey eyes in a rather wizened face, a swollen vein on one temple; very polite and deferential, he might be a Jewish watchmender. It turns out he's a great friend of the director George Stevens, who died earlier this week; as also of Willie Wyler. It was a grey day, but I took them out round the town for an hour. Z. seemed pleased, in spite of all the problems; kept on turning to me: would that angle pass as Victorian, would that?

A nice lunch, he told us stories about Gary Cooper in their famous Western, *High Noon*; how as soon as he tried 'to emote', or to act, he was hopeless. Then working with Spencer Tracy, how Z. would watch him mumble his way through a scene and fear the worst— and how it all looked ten times better, a fine performance, in the rushes. He told us this when we were discussing a casting for Sarah. The enormous difficulty of finding faces that 'worked' on screen— and how it had nothing to do with stage acting ability. He cited Robert Stephens, and Olivier, as examples of fine theatre actors who couldn't ferry across.

On Sarah, we discovered that we both had a liking for Gemma Jones in the part, but Z. warned me that a studio might not wear such an unknown in box-office terms. On the studio, he wasn't against going with Warner but he wanted the picture in the 'right all-over production frame'—that is, not to be edged out by bigger projects; and he thought we might have to settle for Twentieth Century Fox on those grounds.

An impressive, humane man, and he fills me with hope; though much still remains to dash it. For a script we, or he, shall first go to Pinter, then to Stoppard.

April 12 I went to talk with Fred Zinnemann in his Mount Street office; a rather old-fashioned and unostentatious penthouse. He is his usual gentle and soft-spoken self. He has seen Gemma Jones and

Kate Nelligan; both are keen to do the part. He wants Orson Welles to play Mr Freeman. We discuss a fit actor for Charles—perhaps Robert Redford, even though he is so expensive, a million dollars or more (which of course he earns back in box-office receipts). Fred Z. rates him third in this faculty for pulling in audiences, after McQueen and Nicholson; then Redford; Paul Newman next. I am anxious about his accent. But it seems Warner positively want it. Fred has already been told to make sure the voices are 'mid-Atlantic'. He says this is an increasing problem—American audiences complained in his last picture (*The Day of the Jackal*) of Edward Fox's voice in the assassin role. This appears to be a new tyranny of the medium; and yet one more death-blow to a native cinema.

Rather to my alarm Fred told me exactly the same stories about Spencer Tracy and Gary Cooper as last time; I do not like such anecdotage.

Then he wants to start the film with Sarah's past, the shipwreck of the French lieutenant. I foresee difficulties getting a convincing sea, but he dismisses that. They can do miracles in the tank, these days. I don't have the courage to tell him that they don't for this cinema-goer.

April 15 Fred Zinnemann rings. He has got on well with David Picker [a producer], but Warner still insist on the option deal. He has refused, and decided to fly to California to sort out the other possibilities.

We returned to Lyme; another huge pile of mail. This endless talk of film business, meeting people I don't really want to meet, vile and endless fussing about nothing. My poor book [*Daniel Martin*]—everything seems to tear me away from it.

April 24 A cable from Paramount in California. They are backing the film. Then Fred Zinnemann rings. He seems pleased. Apparently we were lucky, they were looking for a serious major project. I am to get $15,000 dollars on signing, $85,000 if Fred is satisfied with the script, $75,000 deferred; all depends on a viable script and Fred's health, in effect.

April 27 I've given up hope of going back to *Daniel Martin* before we leave. The film, the endless calls about financial details.

John Fowles

By the spring of 1975, the film was at last under option to Paramount Pictures, with Fred Zinnemann to direct. Dennis Potter was hired to write the screenplay.

July 14 We went in the evening, Eliz and I, to see Antonioni's latest film, *The Passenger*; hilariously silly at all its deeper levels, exploiting the fancy pessimisms of the spoilt bourgeoisie...all this side of twentieth-century European art grows more and more like the narcissistic wild shores of the Romantic movement. Beckett is our Chateaubriand. But the film is very agreeable on the surface; very cool, inconsequential, contemptuous of plausibility and of plot...in fact connects so well there, in contrast to its would-be general theme of disconnection, that the game is given away. Alienation and despair, used like this, become one more form of dandyism. The thing is beautiful, in short, as dandies are beautiful; and as shallow in its philosophy as theirs.

July 15 I went to see Fred Zinnemann in the afternoon. He was looking very fit and alert, as affable as ever, if one discounts the rather steely grey-blue eyes. He suggested recently a new ending in the British Museum reading room, and asked my opinion, and I wrote him a little screed on the pro's and con's—about which he was very complimentary. 'Like being in a Rolls-Royce after a Cortina,' he said, rather unkindly to poor Dennis Potter. He let me glance at Potter's script, which is in longhand, laid out like a TV scenario; but I'm not to read it yet (or Tom Maschler, which is causing trouble).

September 13 The full script of *The FLW* arrives. It isn't perfect, it lacks countless echoes and historical depths in the book, it's basically just the love story; but it is something of a feat of condensation and has a good deal of dramatic strength. Eliz doesn't like it, nor Tom, who from finding the first twenty pages 'terrific' now seems full of gloom. I think the schism is between non-creators and creators. I know Fred is full of doubts and anxieties, and it is quite pointless adding to them at this stage by being highly critical; as bad as damning babies at birth. Nine-tenths of the problem is dialogue, anyway. Potter, so astute and temperate in his own contemporary television plays, has an oddly deaf ear at times.

September 21 More trouble over the script—I spent last week going over the dialogue in detail; making a few suggestions; pointing out the three major areas of weakness, Grogan's character (too weak now), Sarah's lack of development, the general absence of deeper 'historical' background…the relevance of Darwin, etc.

September 27 I gave Jud Kinberg the script of *The FLW* to read in the morning. It produced an expectable reaction. It was appalling, shit, a failure from beginning to end; no drama, you weren't made to care for anyone—'care' is his current script word, one must make audiences 'care' for one's characters. As usual some good ideas came floating amid the abuse. He nearly got very angry, because he could see I wasn't taking all this too seriously, was playing 'English'. It also angers him that 'I pretend' not to care very much what happens over the film—'why should you worry, you don't care anyway' and similar sarcasms. All of which made me smile inwardly.

The afternoon with Tom Maschler at Chalcot Gardens, concerning our own criticism of the script. It was a relief to be with someone moderate and practical again. I hold, through all this, by my view that Mr Z. and an eventual production still remain far from certain.

October 7 The grand script conference, which turned out to be a near-disaster. Potter was there when I arrived, cinnamon-haired, freckled, crippled hands, suit and tie, dapper and polite—an impression of ginger and indigo. Fred Z. claimed he didn't want to run the discussion, whereupon Potter jumped in and said he felt he must make some general observations. My—or Tom's and my—suggestions had 'cast him into deep dejection'. We had signally failed to understand what he was aiming at. There followed a sermonette on the difference between drama and the novel. I kept my mouth shut, as did Tom after a few minutes of this. It grew more and more peculiar. We must observe 'areas of sovereignty', an ominous phrase he kept using. Then there came a speech defending Fred himself from us wicked tamperers with the Gospel. Discussion of the script would only 'upset' Fred, 'confuse issues'; it was 'counterproductive'. We were left finally very nearly speechless. Fred tried to intimate that he could look after himself, but even there Potter gave the impression that he knew better. Tom tried to get a discussion going on Ernestina's character, since she strikes us, as Potter has written her, as unnecessarily silly. But Potter killed that at once: she was 'charming', 'delightful', we weren't 'reading between the lines'. What little discussing we did achieve was all wrecked on this rock: we weren't reading what Potter had meant. He did at one point admit that he was 'behaving like a thug', but 'only because I know the approach is right'.

And I forgot, he began all this by saying to me that he had 'until this moment' regarded me as dead and non-existent. It was very clear by the end that he wished me so, also.

Potter, because of his hands, won't eat in public, so he did disappear just after noon. We managed to get some work done during the rest of the day. Fred was more amenable, if obstinate, over a number of points; but this was in a reasonable way. Potter was beyond dealing with. Fred kept saying, 'Yes, I'll see it is shot like that, but I won't bring it up with Dennis.' (They are to meet next week to discuss the rewrites.) Somehow he has let the man, or his sad physical condition, brainwash him. It's the first time I've ever heard a director pursue the line that one can't be frank with a scriptwriter because it might hurt him.

I was offered the Karl Marx role again; and turned it down.

Later that day we went to see *The Night Porter* in Audley Square—Fred had it run for us so that we could see Charlotte Rampling. A very sick film; playing on female bondage and Nazi sadism—the others would have walked out, but I took a sort of natural historical interest in it, since so many wrong values were being trotted out. The girl herself has a very striking face, slightly gaunt, with bruised eyes. I can grasp what Fred sees in her. But there is no evidence that she can act.

On the way out I talked with the manager of the place, who said Fred had been running his 'shots of ponds' a few days before. Ponds? Yes, with all the swans and things, down at Winston Churchill's place (Chartwell). That came as a shock to Tom and myself, since we had attacked the repeated black swan symbol in the script all through the afternoon, and not a murmur from Fred that he had actually done some test-shooting on the theme. He plays his cards ludicrously close to his chest.

October 8 Fred Z. telephones, full of apologies for yesterday's meeting. 'I'm only a bus driver,' he said at one point. I said I thought he could promote himself, metaphorically, at least to ship's captain. 'No, no, I am a very modest man. It is simply I must get my bus to its right destination.' He was only half joking. I think he is less modest and more acutely afraid of seeming a Hollywood tyrant, like Willie Wyler.

October 9 In the afternoon I went to see Fred Z. on my own—Tom having departed for the Frankfurt Book Fair. He was all milk and honey. He wanted my help, he wanted me to know everything that was going on. He was much franker, and persuaded me that he wants to make the film (sent me to talk with Tom Pevsner at the end, who had the production schedule laid out upstairs); the obstacles remain the budget and the casting. Paramount are muttering now about the film not being commercial. Fred is still far from sure about Sarah's role—will test Gemma Jones and Rampling, possibly Francesca Annis. Redford has just been given the script, but Fred was obviously fed up with all the indecision there... The hanging on a whim that such castings entail, the absurd money the Redfords now demand— a million dollars minimum plus a huge percentage. He is thinking of Richard Chamberlain for the part—he has said he is 'very interested'.

Fred also complained once more about Tom's 'aggression'. There has been an argument over whether he can be allowed to see the rushes, and Fred is hurt that Tom won't take no for an answer. I foresee mounting trouble there.

But things seem all right between Fred and myself; and the production schedule, those endless lines of lemon, pink, pale green cardboard—black for the holidays—were better proof than words.

We went to see Kobayashi's *Kaseki* after that, three and a half hours of it. The story is thin; a Japanese industrialist's realization, under the threat of death, of deeper values than commercial ones. The film is not as good as Kurosawa's more overtly humanist *Living*. But a considerable effort, for all that, and beautifully photographed, with constant echoes of the Zen view of art. A lovely opening minute, very Japanese; and some fine scenes in France...and it also demonstrates the value of this length of film. The gradual immersion into a man's nature, so that at the end he hardly needs to speak, one knows him so well.

The cinema was empty—only three or four other people besides us; and I had the sad thought that every friend we have in London would have walked out during the first hour. The curse of the Americo-European cinema is its need to package, to sell something, so that true aesthetic judgement becomes a valuation of whether the packaging is slickly enough done. *Kaseki* sells nothing; it simply is, which is why, profoundly (and even explicitly, in one sequence), it is a Zen work. Its very slowness is its speed.

November 1 Two depressing phone calls from Fred Zinnemann: the Paramount audience-reaction man doesn't like the script, 'you' don't know whose side you're on at the end, the only person you identify with (if you're a nice ordinary American) is Freeman, and so on; at least it seems to have convinced Fred that a new writer is necessary. But he's used up his $150,000 exploratory budget, has to ask for more money to pay a new pen, so if Paramount want to pull out...

November 18 More anguish from Fred Zinnemann over the film: apparently the Paramount people are over to settle its hash one way or another. James Costigan [a screenwriter] thinks the Potter script 'lacking'—young American audiences won't understand what's going on, Sarah is too mysterious, etc. So all depends on whether Paramount are prepared to provide more money. The tests were also disappointing, it seems. Gemma Jones was best, but photographs badly; Nelligan and Annis failed in other ways. Neither of the men was any good.

Now Fred talks of delaying the production, even if it isn't cancelled outright. How he can't work with 'second-class' people (Annis and Nelligan). I once again tried to get him to look at [Helen] Mirren; with no more success.

A pox on all of it

November 23 The film is definitely postponed. Paramount are prepared to pay Costigan, but it can't be done in time. They will shoot locations in Lyme next September now—if at all. Fred Z. kept assuring me that he would pursue the project; but he said 'God bless you' at the end of our call, and it sounded to me like a farewell.

December 11 Fred Zinnemann rings. Paramount have agreed to hire Costigan to do an entirely new script. He's flown to London, and hopes to have it finished by February.

February 11, 1976 Fred Zinnemann rang, to say the Costigan script is no good, and that Paramount feel they can't put any more money in. He sounded sincerely sad about it, perhaps because he fails to understand how unsurprised I am, and how indifferent. Of course he has also failed throughout to see that the book is too complex for the medium, especially when it has to be put over in two hours.

February 12 Tom Maschler rang (having written our 'farewell' letter of thanks to Fred yesterday) to say that Fred's just telephoned: we mustn't think all hope is gone, David Picker is still very keen, etc., etc. He baffles us both at times like these.

Later that year, Paramount allowed their option to expire and Zinnemann dropped out. Fowles turned to completing Daniel Martin.

January 17, 1977 Eliz and I went up to town; I straight to Anthony Sheil's, to deliver *Daniel Martin*, all 1,108 pages of it. While I was there, Tom Maschler rang: quite extraordinary, since a week or so ago Christopher Bigsby of the University of East Anglia wrote, on behalf of himself and Malcolm Bradbury, to suggest they try a TV adaptation of *The FLW*; which I had come to London to second, but now Tom announces that the producer of the vogue film of last year, *One Flew Over the Cuckoo's Nest*, has appeared and declared himself interested. A Mr Saul Zaentz.

January 18 I went into Tom's office and met Zaentz. An alert, no-nonsense man, in his fifties; a grey-white beard, shrewd eyes. He's made a fortune in the world of pop and jazz records; financed the Forman film himself, would do the same with us. A curious blend of ignorance and positiveness. He sold himself to us. He'd like Louis Malle to direct, David Mercer possibly to script.

Tom on top form; he'd put every agent in the world out of business, if he took that up.

February 8 Anthony rings to say that Little, Brown will offer a minimum of $250,000 for *Daniel Martin*. I think he felt I lacked sufficient enthusiasm. He doesn't realize how deeply I have quelled that demon.

February 11 And Tom, or Jonathan Cape, proposes a £25,000 advance. On top of everything else Zaentz has written to Roger Burford [a film agent]: he seems to mean business over filming *The FLW*. The deal is a $25,000 option, $75,000 on first day of shooting, $100,000 deferred, and five per cent. Half a million dollars in one week. I feel like Midas; more exactly than most people could ever realize.

March 10 Roger Burford says Zaentz continues interested. He flies soon to London to tie things up.

Eliz and I went to the new Satyajit Ray film, *The Middleman*. He grows and grows in stature. It occurred to me, watching it, that he may be like Jane Austen: someone whose true importance doesn't emerge until many years later. His own six inches of ivory have just that central morality we now see in her; the same accuracy; universality concealed in the remote and small. I made a note for *Daniel Martin*—to cross out Fellini's name, and put Ray's in its place.

March 22 Back in London. Ten days of doing the last changes and rewrites for *Daniel Martin*. A seemingly endless task, with a manuscript this size. Dealing with repetition rashes: the criminals this time were 'little', 'faintly' and 'silent'. It is difficult to write about the English without them. I can see why the diminishing adjectives and adverbs crept in; it's the paucity of verbs and adjectives in describing micro-behaviour—or the over-strength of what few there are. I also used 'grimace' and 'pull a face' too much; in reality there are dozens of variations of this expression—but only two or three words and phrases to notate it. Worst of all is everything to do with irony or dryness; half of any educated private Englishy conversation employs it facially or in attitude—i.e., not verbally, which means one can't (or certainly can't always) put the irony in the dialogue.

B. S. Johnson argued that this is why the visual media have made the descriptive side of the novel obsolescent. A good actor gives the most delicate nuance in a second; on top of that the novelist keeps on having to repeat tedious descriptions. But that is absurd. It's at least equally advantageous not to have to give the whole, as vision must. It is precisely why, on the contrary, the novel is much better adapted to moral and psychological discrimination. The flesh, or its image, is not always there to screen such matters out.

March 23 Tom and I went to meet Zaentz, who's flown back to London, in Roger Burford's office. I continue to like him; he manages to be jovial, crisp, amused; and clear what he wants. We think of trying David Mercer for the script. Settle a mutually acceptable clause over directors. He will be in touch.

Back in Lyme this evening, we saw him win all the prizes at the British Film Academy annual award gala. I didn't like him so well being grateful for the gilded merde. His friend Milos Forman was also out there on the podium. Zaentz has given him *The FLW* to read, but thinks it unlikely that 'Milosz' will fall for the subject. I'd just as sooner he didn't, good director though he is. His forte is contemporary wry humour.

Finally, the movie was undertaken with backing from United Artists. Karel Reisz would direct, Leon Clore produce, and Jeremy Irons and Meryl Streep star. Harold Pinter was hired to write the screenplay, and shooting began in autumn 1980.

October 22, 1980 Our evening with Karel and Betsy [his wife]. From being neutral about him (as a person) before the filming, I have come to like him. He is strangely oriental, Buddha-like, and not only in looks; endlessly patient and optimistic, and funny. We watched the Liverpool–Aberdeen match on the telly, while Betsy and Eliz talked upstairs. He has been offered Malraux's endlessly attempted (at production stage) *La Condition Humaine*, and thinks he will do it— his 'last picture', he says. We drink tea upstairs, and talk about Harold and Antonia's wedding, to which we were supposed to go. Harold's script is to be published, I have done a little introduction to it: honest in everything but my inward indifference to seeing my books filmed.

It's not that I didn't enjoy most of the filming at Lyme; or what little watching I did of it. Karel and Betsy and Jeremy Irons rented

John Fowles

our old house, Underhill Farm (Meryl Streep stayed at Haye House). Lyme itself made more general hay while the sun shone. Financially, the weather was appalling and contrary throughout—except for one day when a little storm blew up (something I had assured Karel wouldn't happen) and they were able to shoot the scene (scheduled for autumn) at the end of the Cobb.

I suspect the only person who didn't enjoy it was Tom Maschler, who was put in charge of publicity, and managed to get everyone's back up in one way or another—even the equable Meryl's, when she had to sacrifice one of her rare free days to implement one of his coups. She walked out on a session with Snowdon [Lord Snowdon, photographer, then married to Princess Margaret], he took so long making up his mind. I had to take Snowdon round all the locations; not a very impressive human being, though he is polite and 'interested'—I ended up by feeling a little sorry for him, his limp, the way he is endlessly stared at and photographed himself, poor devil. Some stupid woman stood in his path with an idiot smile and demanded to know how his children were, why he hadn't bought them to Lyme. 'I sincerely hope they're working hard in class,' says Snowdon, looking at his watch. One can't blame royalty, it's the high proportion of morons among their subjects who make them what they are.

Great precautions were taken to see that no one knew about the past and modern aspects of Harold's script, though one paper leaked it. Even the crew seemed a bit puzzled. There was a nice story from Freddie Francis, the lighting man, after they had shot one of the rehearsal scenes, in which Jeremy and Meryl have a misunderstanding. It went well. Later that evening Freddie saw one of the grips in town. 'Everything okay, then?' says Freddie. 'Except that scene this afternoon,' says the grip. 'I mean it's really bloody marvellous, innit? They're supposed to be stars, supposed to have been working together for three weeks now. And all they can do is start spatting on camera.'

Another story went round on the first day of the shooting. One of the electricians said to his mate, 'Who are those two geezers over there?' 'Wake up. That's the bloke who wrote the book and the scriptwriter.' 'Well, I realized the bearded git was a writer. That other one looks like a second-hand car salesman.' Harold does dress with some sharpness, and never informally.

We got to like him, too, once we had adjusted to his neuroses. He has to drink a lot, but is funny once he is relaxed; beautifully phrased anecdotes, rehearsed and timed, I suspect, but none the worse for that. Tom and I went off into the backlands with him and Antonia. She fell asleep at the table afterwards, apparently a common habit, and Harold told us of their first night of love, when the decision to start the celebrated affair was taken. He decided to do it in style, and that there could be no better way to express the depth of his feeling than by reading her some of his poems. Antonia arrives, sits in an armchair, Harold reads his carefully selected poems with the most painstaking attention to tone and phrasing and effect. After a few minutes he looks up. Antonia is fast asleep.

Two other stories about Harold. There was trouble with the proposal scene, and one day Karel rang me up to see if I could help— he felt it was too curt and quick. 'Harold says he'll do anything, but he simply can't write a happy scene.'

When he came with Karel for a first reconnaissance, we went down to walk on the Cobb. We climbed up on to the Upper Walk, I was beside Harold. After four or five steps he cast an apprehensive look down at the sea, all fifteen feet below, and raised a distinctly Romantic hand towards his brow: 'John, I'm terribly sorry, but I just can't stand this.' I thought for a moment he meant trailing around after Karel and Freddie while they discussed angles and lighting. But no, he turned and went back to the Lower Walk and strolled beside us down there. It was the height. When we went to the Undercliff, he walked a little way down to my location for the meeting; but then turned back, the rough going was too much. (But not for Karel, they did eventually spend a huge amount of production money to build a staircase and cable-slings for the brutes and the camera down to the ilex grove.)

Harold is at heart a dandy, I think; whence his acute sense of linguistic style and, less obviously, his truly bizarre social mask. He and Antonia stayed, when they were here, with some titled couple who have a house near Broadwindsor. In all small things he behaves like an Old Etonian: the voice, the mannerisms, everything else. Only his indifference to things rural and natural in general is London-Jewish still; and perhaps his obsessive neatness sartorially. There's a tiny echo of Mr Jorrocks about him: of a fish eternally out of water.

And a much stronger one of Byron and Chateaubriand, of someone imposing a lifestyle on all around him—a despairing world view from the middle of an agreeable, upper-class, active, 'famous' life. Of course he lacks the society-flouting panache and physical courage of the two great Romantics, the satanic touch; but perhaps his running off with Antonia is a sign that it is there. I suspect the role he acts is designed to quell it, also; and the neuroses, the drinking, to demonstrate the black heart beneath the bland exterior.

The one thing he failed to bring off in the first draft was the final scene, when Charles and Sarah meet again (in Victorian terms); I think because he couldn't face the need for emotion. He didn't argue at all when I rewrote the scene to put some of that back and read it to Karel and him in a session we had—all this side of things was done without any trouble or bad feeling, in a spirit of friendship and cooperation that must be rare in the cinema. There were one or two squabbles in the production office, but (thanks to Karel) this good spirit went all through the crew.

Lyme also was on the whole good; half the town got parts in the end as extras (luckily we lie outside the area where London professional extras have to be hired). There was some bad blood among the shopkeepers when the money was shared out for 'disturbance of business' and the rest, but that was not the unit's fault, just immemorial Lyme. One gentleman tried to get compensation for not having his shop on camera.

Both Karel and Meryl were nervous as cats about my seeing anything, and we saw very few rushes, so I cannot tell about the end result. I suspect it will be a brave effort; and not quite hang together. We shall see.

October 28 We drive down to Torquay for the night, to see the last few days' shooting at Kingswear. They have dressed the little station there to be Victorian Exeter and turned a nearby pub into Endicott's Family Hotel. White billows of vapour from the hired steam train, rain, dusk, crowds, the lights of Dartmouth across the river; and it is salving to see the now familiar faces again. Assheton, the art director, worried and self-depreciating as always; Ann Mollo, the set-dresser, Leon Clore [the producer] gloomy and grumpy (his mask; Eliz and I have decided that his 'bad temper' hides someone much more genial), Karel and Freddie. The sets look good. Meryl was there, flown in by Concorde for just this one day's shooting.

We all went on the ferry across the river to the Carved Angel at Dartmouth and had a farewell dinner for her; very relaxed, jolly, everyone relieved that the shooting is nearly over. This side of the film business is the nicest: the work done, the closeness built, the joshing. We crossed the river back near midnight, the tide running silently, very mild, a moon gleaming on the water. Jeremy and Meryl embrace—affection, there was nothing off-screen between them. In fact poor Jeremy's marriage with Sinéad Cusack temporarily broke up during the shooting. Karel told me he congratulated him one day after a good take on the scene where he has to tell Grogan his life is in a mess. Jeremy said, 'My God, I don't have to act that line.' Then embraces all round, and she gets into her car and goes back through the night to Heathrow for the morning Concorde back to New York.

October 29 We walked around Torquay front and harbour in brilliant sunshine. It truly did feel like the Riviera, some interesting plants grow in the cliff-gardens. An arbutus brilliant with fruit—as mine never are here, because of the birds.

Over to Kingswear for lunch, where I do a couple of interviews. Then the long set-ups for the station scene; we went off to look at some retired general's house by the river, a very beautiful setting, and poked round a strange old house, through the archway at the foot of the road to the ferry, with some mimosas and a huge fig tree in its garden, a warren of empty, haunted rooms.

Our own farewells, then home that evening.

November 4 I stay up until 2.30, watching, out of some sort of masochism, the egregious Reagan being elected. There is no hope for the Western World, it lies self-betrayed by its own stupidity and greed. I feel closest these days to Benn's wing of the Labour Party (*faute de mieux*); but am convinced capitalist politics has lost all touch with reality (and need) at the given point in history. It is my class that are traitors, the eternal clerks again, above all Fleet Street and television, the accursed 'media'. I loathe them all, the mediators; lock, stock and barrel. Nine tenths or more of their ethics is based on self-perpetuation. Karel and Leon started union-bashing during our little dinner party at Dartmouth. I say nothing, friendship is more important than pointing out the idiocy of demanding that the British Leyland workers behave themselves like decent robots while we sit around the table of the most expensive restaurant in the West of England; 'on the budget' (which is running a million dollars or more over), of course.

March 7, 1981 We saw the final version of the film, at long last, with a nervous Karel, Betsy and Tom. If I was being very cruel and objective, and marking Oxbridge style, I would give it a beta plus; I think my main quarrel would be over the cutting, too sharp for my taste, not enough time to linger. There have been some losses; one scene Karel has excised is the rather important final one with Grogan; which has upset (in a mild, friendly way) Harold. But Karel insists it was below par, Jeremy gave one of his few bad performances—it was all his (Karel's) fault. Another is the scene with the prostitute—'it seemed superfluous'.

But even beta plus—and everyone else except Eliz and I wants to mark it much higher—is far better than the wretched gammas and deltas I have had to suffer before. Fine performances from Jeremy and Meryl, some of the Undercliff photography beautiful; and many, if not quite all, of the jumps out of past into present work well. I knew before we went that the reality must be a little of a shock, and in part a deception, in the French sense also—just like the final text of a book. But we have grown to like and admire Karel—and Betsy—very much over the long period of preparation and filming. We are in many ways closer to them in philosophy and lifestyle than we are, say, to Tom and Fay; I had no trouble in saying gratitude to Karel. I feel it. It is only the suspicious old peasant in me that doubts good news. And even he would concede that the whole making of the thing was, internally, within the unit, quite extraordinarily peaceful and unfraught; a model of how such things should be done, in a communal art.

October 26 This is not a happy year. For weeks and weeks now I have woken up depressed, then gradually daytime 'normality' rescues me a little. It is partly the film and all its attendant publicity, career like a millstone round my neck; partly the way Eliz and I drift apart, without hatred or rows, by some process the reverse of osmosis. Her withdrawal is (outwardly) a matter of her hate for this house, for Lyme, for my 'drugs' (local history, old books, nature, etc.)—all that I use to escape from my present. Mine is not only from her, but from most of my contemporaries—from all in them that welcomes things like the new 'centre' party, the SDP. But it's more biological than political, a deep feeling that it is the selfishness of middle-class liberals that will finally end the human race. For years I have hidden my feelings here from my friends, half out of laziness, a quarter from never being able to argue on such matters face to face, a last quarter out of friendship—not being able to value truth above that. I nearly burst out against Ronnie Payne [a journalist on the *Sunday Telegraph*] one day this summer; and against Karel only last month, at his supper table, when he said that at least Reagan kept the Russians in check (he has joined the SDP recently). Tom Maschler, also. Most of them seem to me biologically blind, there is no other word for it. Their lives, their views, their judgements, are all dictated by a deep longing to maintain the social and political status quo— that is, a world where 'we' and our friends still maintain our absurdly privileged status. Which is of course maintained and propagated 'down' from the elite, by all our media. All our 'serious' newspapers, the television channels, everything else (including the literary establishment) spread the same manure (you too can be a top person), or cultural hegemony. I sometimes feel I would welcome a Russian invasion tomorrow, if it could take place without too much destruction and bloodshed. To be poor again, and have to struggle, against something better than the insane pressures of a best-selling novelist, the poison of fan mail. When I came back here two days ago it took me three hours to go through all the letters.

The film has been almost universally praised by the yellow press (sometimes for absurdly chauvinistic reasons, as in the *Evening Standard* and the *Daily Mail*), and damned by the more egghead, on both sides of the Atlantic. We all went to the premiere at the Haymarket Odeon ten days ago, I sat between Karel and Meryl. A very silent audience, as if puzzled; most puzzled when it ended, a very odd silence. This is apparently quite common. I liked it a little better the second time round, though still feel it fails—and where it matters most, alas. It looks very good, but is somewhere empty at the heart, perhaps reflecting a fault in the book. The American critics, Sarris, Kael and the rest, have suggested this. Meanwhile it has done very well at the first-run box offices, beating *Star Wars* in Los Angeles for receipts, breaking the record at the Haymarket Odeon. The Turners here in Lyme told me a story about an old lady who came out (our cinema has got an early release) and said "'Tis lovely, I didn't understand a word of it. But 'tis lovely'. Others in Lyme are apparently less kind; and deeply offended that their faces, as extras, have been cut, or are seen so remotely and briefly.

December 22 *The FLW* film failed both the Oscar and English Academy awards. We went to the latter and sat with Harold and Antonia, and the Ironses; shouting 'cheat' and 'con' when *Chariots of Fire* won the best film title (as it did later in Hollywood). Awful gloom at our table from Jeremy and Harold, while the rest of us rather enjoyed the vulgarity of it all. Harold smiled only once during the endless comedy spiels between the awards, when old Arthur Lowe did an impeccably timed routine. He looked across at me with a grin and little nod of the head, clowning himself: that one passes, yes? The rest didn't, for him; and he just drank. □

THE BEST PICTURE
HE EVER SAW
Ian Jack

FARNWORTH

Hippodrome

SW Corner of Egerton St & Cawdor St.

No upstairs.

cross sections

large cove moulding

Screen

Stage

Steps

Seats   Aisle   Seats

? 4ᵈ entrance on Cawdor St.

Main Entrance
↓ on ~~Egerton~~ St.
Corner of
Streets

Large 6' dia ?
~~6~~ Disc of naked
light bulbs in C
of ceiling

Records played before show started.
ALWAYS Victor Silvester. (Aargh!)

Dimmed out before start
of show. Bulbs in centre
dimmed first.
This was watched for.
Then a cheer went up.
(Kids Saturday pm
matinee)

Common to many cinemas — but Hip. was always like this :—
Irritating habit :— GAUZY CURTAINS ~~curtains~~ kept closed until the
film actually started. Trying to read the ms handwriting
on the BBFC certificate through the wavy curtains. Is it
the big film? Or what?

Screen

Plan →   Seats   ?   Emergency exits

↓ Steps
up

Tickets

1. Going back

One afternoon in the autumn of 1933 the writer J. B. Priestley drove
north from Manchester towards Preston and Blackpool. Priestley was
then England's most successful young novelist. Not yet forty, with five
novels and the international success of *The Good Companions* behind
him, he had decided as many novelists do to take a break from his
desk and forsake fiction for a bit and become an enquiring traveller,
so that (in this case) he might describe the condition of England. The
book that he made from the experience is called *English Journey* and
in it he wrote of that particular afternoon's travels in Lancashire: 'We
went through Bolton. Between Manchester and Bolton the ugliness is
so complete that it is almost exhilarating. It challenges you to live there.'

What did he mean by 'ugliness'? The answer from my own
memory suggests that what Priestley saw was: two dark rivers, the
Irwell and its tributary the Croal, their surfaces crowded with little
icebergs of industrial foam; a railway line and an abandoned canal
along the valley; a power station and various bleach works, chemical
factories and sewage beds beside the rivers; a coal mine or two on
the valley's western edge; many cotton mills, some five storeys high,
with even taller chimneys; streets of small Victorian houses with
doors that opened straight on to the pavement; meat-pie, fish-and-
chip and tripe shops; a few people who still wore clogs; smoke.

My father moved from Scotland to the centre of this landscape
in 1930. He was a fitter, a mechanic, and he'd found a job in a
Farnworth textile factory that made canvas belting and hose pipes.
Unemployment was severe in Scotland at the time, though in
Lancashire it was hardly much better ('We were going through the
country of the dole,' Priestley wrote). He lived in digs for some
months, and then returned to Fife for his wedding—Christmas Day,
1930, when the minister came to the bride's house for the ceremony.
Husband and wife were back in Farnworth by the turn of the year.
Had Priestley gone by train rather than by car, he might have looked
out of the window at Farnworth and seen their first proper home,
139 Cemetery Road. The street ran over the railway and down the
hill towards an old brickworks, the black junction of the Croal and
the Irwell, the disused canal—and the cemetery. Their house was one
of the last in a terrace which came just before you reached the
cemetery's entrance lodge and the monumental home of the dead.

Later, when they moved away, my parents used to speak wryly of this location.

Unless it was a Saturday or a Sunday afternoon, Priestley would not have seen my father, who would be repairing looms or crankshafts inside the weaving sheds of George Banham and Co. But he might have seen my mother, as one of the thousands of things that cross the eye's threshold every day, most of them ignored and lost to mind and memory. The eye may be a lens, but the mind, with its random fixative, is not a film. A crowd, a face; he might have seen her from his car as it bumped across the tram lines on Market Street or Manchester Road, a twenty-six-year-old woman of fair Scottish complexion, out shopping for that night's tea. In the autumn of 1933, she would be 'getting over' the death that spring of her first son, George, aged ten months, and seized with the happiness that she was pregnant again (and with another son, though she was yet to know that).

All four of her and my father's sons were born there, in this complete, almost exhilarating ugliness. Two of us survive. Earlier this year, in March 2004, my elder brother Harry and I got off the train at Farnworth, a place we left in 1952. What did we look like? Like a man of fifty-nine and man of seventy, greying or grey, a little lost, walking up the slope from the empty platform and into empty streets, looking for things that were no longer there. We might as well have been the ghosts of old Trojans, coming back a thousand years later to walk on the soil that buried old Troy. Our childhoods had been here somewhere.

Harry, as usual, pulled out the maps. He loves maps, he used to draw them for a living, and he rarely travels without them. Here was Cemetery Road, now crossed by the Manchester to Bolton expressway. Here was Railway Street, where he remembered Sally O'Lalley the abortionist (truly, a back-street abortionist) had lived. We found the steps that had once led to Banham's factory and the house in Lime Street that was once home to Nurse Grant: Nurse Grant, the town's 'nitty nurse', who combed children's hair for lice, Scottish, from Grantown on Spey, a family friend, her friendship enshrined in my parents' gift of 'Grant' as my middle name. What do I remember of her? That she had long hairs above her upper lip and lived with another old woman, Mrs Haydock, plump and black-shawled and infirm, who never stirred from her chair beside the fire.

How small this world had been, and how convenient. The factory, the railway station, Nurse Grant, the pub, the market, Mum and Dad's house—all only a few minutes' walk from each other. Not much of this survived. The factory and the pub had gone, the station buildings had been demolished, many streets of straight terraces had been replaced by new houses and gardens built in less regular and more spacious layouts. It was no longer a dense Lowry townscape, but it was not country or a suburb either. Really, the only way to look at it was as an ex-town, a place shorn of its dynamic ugliness, but also of its newspaper (the *Farnworth Journal*), its school (Farnworth Grammar), its five cinemas (the Ritz, the Savoy, the Empire, the Hippodrome, the Palace). Cotton-spinning in more than thirty mills had made all this possible. Cotton was no longer spun here, or anywhere else in Lancashire. Farnworth had become a place of absences.

Harry looked at the map again. Where the devil was Peel Street? Where was our first cinema, the Ritz?

2. The Ritz

My father first visited the Ritz in 1930, my brother in 1938 or 1939 (to see the Three Stooges in *Back To The Woods!*), myself in the late 1940s. Had any of us of heard of Cesar Ritz and his grand hotels

Ian Jack

when we first went through its doors? No, of course not, and not for a long time after. Cinema names seemed independent of any history. They may have been intended to suggest luxury, romance, good birth and breeding, foreign parts, ancient history, and therefore to be fitting vehicles for the films shown inside them; escapist images within escapist architecture. But how many among their audiences could have connected the Hippodrome to horse racing in ancient Greece, or the Rialto to Venice, the Alhambra, Granada and Toledo to Spain, the Lido to Mediterranean bathing, the Colosseum to Rome, the Savoy to the Strand, the Odeon to Paris, the Regal to majestic behaviour? Not me, certainly. Before they were anything else, they were the names of cinemas. Cinemas were what they described.

When my father came to Farnworth, the Ritz had been known by that name for only three years. Before 1927, it was the Queen's Theatre, a Victorian palace of varieties which continued as a venue for live stage acts after its screen was installed, films one week and hoofers the next. It was in this way that my father encountered the Glen Louise Girls, who were appearing at the Ritz in a variety bill which also included a snake charmer and The Three Aberdonians ('Too Mean To Tell You What They Do!'). The troupe and my father stayed in the same lodgings at a Mrs Walker's in Church Road. He was a twenty-eight-year-old bachelor; the situation might have been fun—just as it is in *The Good Companions*, when the working-class hero of Priestley's novel falls in with a group of touring theatricals, the eponymous Good Companions, and his view of life is thrillingly challenged and expanded. That didn't seem to have happened to my father. Many years later he would sometimes entertain us with stories of late-night card playing, of the surprise of discovering sloughed snake skins inside sideboard drawers, of actors who turned up unexpectedly from late-night trains and were found the next morning bedded down in the bath. But at the time he must have wearied of it, because quite soon he moved on to less chaotic lodgings. He was, after all, a man who needed to rise early to get off to the factory and his chisels and files, unlike Glen and her girls and The Three Aberdonians, and their evening shifts at the Ritz.

Glen must have liked my father, though, because she gave him or sent him half a dozen postcards of herself and her girls, and he must

have liked her, because he kept them. She wrote on each of them—
'to our Scoty' or 'Choose your girl, Jack!' or 'Stand easy deary. To
Harry. From Glen.' (In the picture she is the one with the modern
legs on the right.)

'What do you reckon Mum made of those cards?' I said to Harry
as we turned into the bit of Peel Street that survived.

'We'll never know now,' Harry said. 'But she might have thought
it was a funny business.'

Glen Louise Girls

Of course, the Ritz wasn't there. At first we thought it must have
occupied a gap site next to the Farnworth Christian Spiritualist
Church, and then Harry looked at the map again and decided no,
it had been further down the street where there were some new
houses and a parking bay. He remembered the building had a glazed
red-brick exterior and a sign with the letters R I T Z arranged
vertically, one below the other. Later, at our hotel in Bolton, he took
out a notebook and did a quick little sketch of the Ritz's proscenium
arch, together with sketches of Farnworth's four other cinemas. (One
of them begins this piece.)

What did he see at the Ritz? *The Wizard of Oz, Bambi*, and *The
Four Feathers* twice in one week—or maybe more than three times
if you add on the bits we sat through again.' The cheap benefits of
the 'continuous programme' over the separate performance. What
had I seen here? *Captain Kidd* (Charles Laughton and Randolph

Scott, 1945), *Oh, Mr Porter!* (Will Hay, 1937), *Annie Get Your Gun* (Betty Hutton, Howard Keel, 1950). From each I remember one scene. From *Captain Kidd*, a sailing ship becalmed; from *Oh, Mr Porter!* some washing hung over a railway line and getting entangled with a train; from *Annie Get Your Gun*, either a silver gun or a piece of bright jewellery on a bed of dark velvet—and a song about there being 'no business like show business', whatever that was. Mum took me to see the last one in the afternoon. It was bright when we came out—sunshine bright, a different kind of brightness from the film.

3. The Savoy

A British audience saw a moving picture for the first time in 1896. Early shows were in fairgrounds, music halls, shops, railway arches, anywhere that a projector and a white sheet could be set up and chairs arranged. Fires were a problem; nitrate film was highly combustible. In 1909, Parliament passed the Cinematograph Act which imposed fire safety regulations on venues. That was the real beginning of the purpose-built cinema and the architecture of escape. By 1914, London alone had 400 cinemas. By 1927, twenty million cinema tickets were sold every week. By 1940, there were 4.2 million cinema seats. By 1946, nearly one out of every seven British adults went to the cinema twice a week or more. Then, between 1945 and 1960, cinema admissions fell by more than two thirds, and a third of the 1945 total of 4,700 cinemas closed. An article by Sue Harper and Vincent Porter in the *Journal of Popular British Cinema* (volume two, 1999) refines some of these statistics by gender and class. In 1946, sixty-two per cent of the adult audience had been women. By 1960, they were only forty-seven per cent. The number of sixteen to twenty-four year olds in the audience doubled between 1946 and 1950. In 1939, the skilled working class and the classes below comprised sixty-nine per cent of the audience. By 1954, that proportion had risen to eighty-two per cent. That was a peak year for the cinema as a British working-class entertainment. Television culled audiences thereafter, though our family didn't get one until 1961 and so 'the pictures' remained a big part of our lives for longer.

We were, in any case, cinephiles. Dad was born in a small Scottish town in 1902, seven years after the Lumière brothers showed their first film in Paris and six years after they brought their box of tricks to Britain. He watched his first moving pictures, one reelers, on screens set up in public halls before the First World War. He loved Chaplin—had anyone ever been so funny?—and Douglas Fairbanks (Snr) and Pearl White. Later, during my childhood, historical pictures were his thing: *Ben-Hur*, *Spartacus*, *The Robe*, *Alexander the Great*, *Cleopatra*, *The Vikings*. Not musicals—perhaps this was why Mum snuck me into *Annie Get Your Gun* on her own. Not comedies, unless by visual comedians who had perfected their acts on stage (Chaplin, the Marx Brothers and, for a brief time, Norman Wisdom). As a late child, I had missed his middle period. Harry said: 'I think Dad's taste in films remained in the silent era. The first talkies he saw were just all static-camera yak-yak-yak. I think that must have been an awful let-down after some of those well-made, so-called artistic silents. He had his favourite performers though—Paul Muni, Claude Rains, Will Rogers, Wallace Beery, Charles Laughton, Will Hay, Will Fyffe.' All men and too many Wills, though I remembered a coloured print of Greta Garbo he'd carefully preserved in his keepsake book, whereas the Glen Louise Girls seemed less well regarded and were kept in a shoebox.

Harry and I had turned out of Peel Street and were now walking down Market Street, which becomes Manchester Road. He was remembering things. He has a beautiful memory—photographic is the only word. Here was where the trams turned, here was the ice cream shop, here the site of the hoarding that used to say BRITAIN'S BREAD HANGS BY LANCASHIRE'S THREAD and FOR A SECURE FUTURE, JOIN THE PALESTINE POLICE.

I thought about how much I owed him in terms of films and books when I was in my early teens and he in his twenties and we were living back again in Scotland, when Lancashire (in my case, though not in his) was no more than a smudge on the horizon behind me. Teaching himself about the cinema, he bought little blue Pelican paperbacks—Roger Manvell's *Film*, Paul Rotha's *The Film Till Now*—and I would look at their black-and-white stills from *Intolerance*, *Battleship Potemkin*, *Drifters*, *The Cabinet of Dr Caligari*. We shared a small bedroom. Lying late in bed on a Saturday or a Sunday morning, he'd tell me the stories of the films he'd seen at screenings by the local film society or in stop-gap bills at remote suburban cinemas or on trips to London. If you lived in

Ian Jack

Fife in 1958, to see Eisenstein or Renoir or *All Quiet on the Western Front* took character and strength of will.

'And then [my brother might say] you see the meat that the crew have to eat and it's crawling with maggots... And then the Cossack brings his sabre down and this old woman's glasses are smashed and there's blood in her eyes... And then he reaches out to catch this butterfly and you hear a shot and he's dead... And then Mister Hulot tries to play tennis like he thinks he was taught in the shop.' And then, and then.

Now we were in a street called Long Causeway and facing the Savoy, once the Ritz's rival as Farnworth's most superior picture house and now a 'Nine Ball Pool and Snooker Centre' with a Stars and Stripes painted on its sign. It looked like a 1920s building; high on its red-brick facade was a series of porthole windows. What did I see here? I think *Oliver Twist* (Alec Guinness controversially as Fagin, 1948). What do I remember of it? Only the first scene, as Oliver's mother struggles to the workhouse, and then not for her but for the storm and the bending trees, which were frightening. In fact I remember more of the cinema itself than any film I saw there: the orange light behind its translucent curtains, fading before the curtains drew apart; and the art deco rising sun above the screen. Whenever I see or hear the word Savoy, I think of the colour orange, and not of the hotel or the province in France.

My brother saw many, many films at the Savoy. One in particular was the *Arabian Nights* (Jon Hall, Sabu, Maria Montez, 1942). He saw it on the night of Monday, August 2, 1943, with Mum and Dad and our brother Gordon, two years before I was born. Gordon was seven and Harry nine. The war was on, but the family seemed settled. Mum, Dad, two little boys, a decent house with a bathroom and three bedrooms, a big garden with an air-raid shelter, a tandem equipped with sidecar so that all four of them could cycle off to the country on a Sunday, down quiet roads emptied of cars by petrol-rationing. Little George's death had, as it were, been conquered.

After the performance that night, Gordon said that the *Arabian Nights* was the best picture he'd ever seen.

Now, outside the Savoy, this was too sad to talk about.

Harry pointed out the Sundeck Tanning Studio and said it used to be a shop that sold foreign stamps to schoolboy collectors, and jokes—joke dog turds, for instance, which could be put on a salad plate and cause domestic consternation, though only once ('Oh not that thing again, Harry, please!'). Then we turned right and began to walk down Albert Road. It was dusk. Occasionally the great square bulk of an abandoned mill stuck up above the houses and stood in silhouette against the sky. Down Kildare Street we saw one that still had its chimney attached. 'The Century Mill,' Harry said. 'Ring-spinning, whatever that was'—not needing to add that Dad would have known. That everybody in Farnworth would have known, once.

4. The Empire

It was difficult to find the exact site of the Empire, a cinema which had been cheaply converted from a tram depot. The story was that the tram rails still existed under the carpet in the front of the stalls. According to the *Kinematograph Year Book* for 1940, it was the cheapest cinema in Farnworth with a top price of ninepence. 'Cowboy films and a bit of a bug-house,' Harry said. I remembered the story of the last words of George V, or possibly Edward VII, and the debate over whether he said 'How goes the Empire?' or 'What's on at the Empire?' We walked on past the municipal park and thought of having a drink in a pub we both remembered called the Shakespeare, but it was shut.

5. The Hippodrome

At last, the Hippodrome. At the corner of Egerton and Cawdor streets we discovered a level rectangle of concrete where the Hippodrome had once been—perfectly level, perfectly matching the cinema's boundaries, as though it were a kind of minimalist monument to the cinema-going habit, the tomb of the unknown audience. We went inside—that is, we left the pavement and walked over the concrete—and Harry began to describe what had been here. 'We're going down the aisle now,' he said. 'Up there on the ceiling'—he pointed at the sky—'there was a big disc of naked light bulbs, which dimmed before the start of the show. The ones at the centre of the disc dimmed first, and we looked out for that, and when it happened a big cheer would go up.' He was remembering himself as a child among an audience of children. 'Some kids would ask the manager, "Is the Three Stooges on, Mister?" and the manager would say, "Wait and see, wait and see."'

We paced around the square of concrete for another few minutes. The Hippodrome had been our local. Towards the end of 1933 our parents had moved across town, exchanging Cemetery Road for a council house on a new estate where all the streets were named after flowers: Lupin, Begonia, Pansy, Daffodil, and in our case Iris and then Lily avenues. The Hippodrome had matinees, and queues for matinees, and this is where both of us had seen Curly, Larry and Moe do cruel things to each other and never come to harm. On a Saturday morning we would sometimes walk to it, my hand in his, I imagine, across the playing fields and then between the twin smoking chimneys of Bolton Textile Mills, Numbers One and Two.

By now it was dark. Harry said: 'Farnworth never amounted to very much and now it amounts to nothing at all.' We found a mini-cab and asked the driver to take us to Bolton. 'You gents have been on a sort of sentimental journey then?' the driver said.

6. Arabian Nights

Why, among so many inexact memories, am I so certain that the family of which I was not yet then a part saw the *Arabian Nights* on Monday, August 2, 1943? My father wrote the date down, not in a diary and not at the time, but in October that year and in his keepsake book. Looking at his writing now, in the purple ink of a fountain pen, I understand what he was trying to do. To record, obviously, but also to restore and bring to life, as a writer might doodle the name of some absent lover, as the next best thing to the lover's presence in the room.

> Monday 2nd August 1943. Went to 'Savoy' and saw 'Arabian Nights'. Gordon told his Mummy it was the 'Best' picture he'd ever seen. I took his hand up Kildare Street on the way home. He was exceptionally cheerful and lively.

> Tuesday 3rd August. Both complained of being ill. Gordon slipped back upstairs to bed but Harry went to school. He came home at dinner [lunch] time and went to bed. Gordon was very hot at night.

And then, and then. Events move quickly. On August 4, his glands begin to swell. On August 5, Dr Tinto comes and suspects diphtheria and an ambulance takes both boys to hospital. On August 7, Gordon looks worse. On August 14, Gordon says he feels better. On August 15, he is very low. On August 16, at 12.15 a.m. in Hulton Lane Hospital, Bolton, he dies.

On October 11, my father writes: 'Life is very hard.' On October 27, he writes: 'For the loving worm within its clod/Were diviner than a loveless God.' On Christmas Eve, he writes: 'My Dear Wee Gordon. How we miss him.'

When I asked Harry about the *Arabian Nights* on our trip to Farnworth, he said he hadn't thought it was up to much, hadn't been as taken with it as Gordon had. I have never seen it. No video or DVD version exists in Britain, though a video is available in the USA. *The Radio Times Guide to Films* (2004 edition) says of it: 'This piece of Hollywood exotica, made to cash in on the success of *The Thief of Baghdad*, stars Jon Hall as the Caliph, Sabu as his best buddy and Maria Montez as his suitor. The actors have their tongues firmly in their cheeks and the whole show is on the brink of send-up, which is exactly where it should be. Producer Walter Wanger was one of Tinseltown's more enterprising independents, though he was later brought to his knees by the crippling costs of *Cleopatra*.' The script is from stories by the Victorian orientalist, Sir Richard Burton. The film is in colour and lasts eighty-six minutes.

Ian Jack

I wondered if the British Film Institute's National Film and Television Archive had a copy, and at first they thought they had and then they said they hadn't. But I decided to take up the invitation to see the archive anyway—it is probably the largest and most comprehensive of its kind in the world. I took the train from London to Berkhamsted in Hertfordshire, and then a taxi up a hill to a cluster of farm buildings which are the archive's offices. Andrea Kalas, the senior preservation manager, showed me around.

The archive contains books, documents, letters, posters, stills, but its chief holding is its collection of about 475,000 separate cinema and television film titles—about a billion feet of film. We went to the various air-conditioned and dehumidified stores. The flammable nitrate stock was kept in small cells with heavy steel doors and water tanks above—much more of it is stored separately in Warwickshire. The newer and more fireproof acetate and polyester films rose shelf by shelf to the ceilings of large warehouses, called vaults. Men and women in white coats worked in rooms that looked like laboratories. Here I began to see films in a different way. Projected, they were interesting images. In a can, they were only chemicals with a chemical history. Films were cellulose coated with emulsion. At first and until about 1960, nitrate had collected the silver in the emulsion—silver refracted light. Then there was a switch to acetate. Since the 1980s, polyester has been the chosen substance. Nobody knows how durable this will be. All film, Andrea Kalas said, is inherently unstable. It decomposes.

The most valuable work of the archive is to restore deteriorating film and transfer the images to newer stock—film-to-film reproduction. In one room, a woman in a white coat demonstrated what happened to old films—I think the example may have been Shackleton's *South*.

She opened a can and the contents looked like brown sugar crystals. Another can; yellow ochre dust. A third can: acetate film that had bonded and yellowed like a large reel of flypaper and gave off a sharp smell. Andrea Kalas said that was known as 'vinegar syndrome'.

I had come here with thoughts of injustice, of how I could never see Gordon and yet—somewhere—the best and last film he ever saw would be as lifelike as ever, filled with people talking and moving. But now I saw it differently. The truth is that every principal in the film is now dead, poor Sabu at the age of thirty-nine. As for their lively images, if they have an infinite future it will be thanks to technicians in white coats, tending the chemicals that contain them.

Always and everywhere, this unequal struggle to preserve and remember. □

THE COMPREHENSIVE
FULLY RESTORED MASTERPIECE SERIES ON DVD

'The forthcoming DVD collection of Merchant Ivory
classics is essential if you love movies'

Baz Bamigboye - The Daily Mail

'A unique contribution to cinema...they have at their
fingertips a profound understanding of the mood,
language and landscape of great cinema'

Simon Jenkins - The Times

The Merchant Ivory Collection is a superb series of some of the
best films of the modern era. Digitally restored and remastered,
they are now available to own on DVD.

THE ENEMY
Tessa Hadley

The Enemy

When Keith had finished up the second bottle of wine he began to yawn, the conversation faltered companionably as it can between old friends, and then he took himself off to bed in Caro's spare room, where she knew he fell asleep at once between her clean white sheets because she heard him snort or snuffle once or twice as she was carrying dishes past the door. She relished the thought of his rather ravaged fifty-five-year-old and oh-so-male head against her broderie anglaise pillowcases. Caro herself felt awake, wide awake, the kind of awakeness that seizes you in the early hours and brings such ultimate penetration and clarity that you cannot imagine you will ever sleep again. She cleared the table in the living room where they had eaten together, stacked the dishes in the dishwasher ready to turn on in the morning, washed up a few delicate bowls and glasses she didn't trust in the machine, tidied the kitchen. In her bare feet she prowled around the flat, not able to make up her mind to undress and go to bed. Tomorrow was Sunday, at least she didn't have to get up for work.

What was it about Keith, after all this time, that could still make her restless like this; could make her feel this need to be vigilant while he snored? When they sat eating and drinking together she hadn't felt it; she had felt fond of him, and that his old power to stir and upset her was diminished. He was nicer than he used to be, no doubt about that. They had talked a lot about his children; the ones he had had with Penny, Caro's sister, who were in their twenties now, and then the younger ones he had with his second wife Lynne. She had been amused that he—who had once been going to 'smash capitalism'—took a serious and knowledgeable interest in the wine he had brought with him for them to drink (he had come to her straight from France; he and Lynne seemed to spend most of the year at their farmhouse in the Dordogne).

Nonetheless, the thought came involuntarily into her head as she prowled, that tonight she had her enemy sleeping under her roof. Of all things: as if instead of a respectable middle-aged PA living in suburban Cardiff she was some kind of Anglo-Saxon thane, sharpening her sword and thinking of blood. Just as the thane might have, she felt divided between an anxious hostility towards her guest and an absolute requirement to protect him and watch over his head.

Tessa Hadley

In May 1968, Caro had turned up for a meeting of the Revolutionary Socialist Student Federation at her university wearing a new trouser suit: green corduroy bell-bottoms with a flower-patterned jacket lining and Sergeant-Pepper-style miltary buttons. The meeting was to organize participation in a Revolutionary Festival in London the following month, generating support for the Vietnamese struggle for national liberation. The festival was already provoking all kinds of ideological dissent: the Trotskyists thought the whole project was 'reformist', and the Communist Party were nervous at the use of the word 'revolutionary'. The Young Communists were going to appear riding a fleet of white bicycles which they had collected and were donating to the Vietnamese.

Caro had bought the trouser suit because her godmother (whom she had adored as a little girl but had stopped visiting recently because of her views on trade unions and immigration) had sent her twenty-one pounds for her twenty-first birthday. She could have put it aside to help eke out the end of her grant, but instead on impulse she had gone shopping and spent it in a trendy boutique in town that she had never dared to go inside before. It was months since she had had any new clothes; and she had never possessed anything quite so joyous, so up-to-the minute and striking, as this trouser suit. She knew that it expressed perfectly on the outside the person she wanted to be from within. With her long hair and tall lean figure it made her look sexy, defiant, capable (in skirts she often only looked gawky and mannish).

The meeting was in a basement room in the History Department as usual. As usual, it was mostly men, though there were three or four girls, bright history and politics students, friends of Caro's, who came regularly. (The girls really did get asked to make the tea: and really did make it.) They sat at desks arranged in a square under a bleak electric bulb with an institutional-type glass shade, surrounded by maps on the walls that were of course nothing to do with them—Europe after the Congress of Vienna, The Austro-Hungarian Empire in 1914—but none the less gave the place an air they all rather enjoyed of being a command centre in some essential world-changing operation. By the time Caro arrived the usual thick fug of cigarette smoke was already building up (she smoked too, in those days). She was greeted, because of the trouser suit, with a couple of wolf whistles, and everyone looked up. It was complicated to remember truthfully now just how one had felt about that whistling. A decade later it became obligatory for women to be indignant at it and find it degrading; at the time however she would probably have felt without it that her trouser suit had failed of its effect. You met the whistle without making eye contact but with a little warm curl of an acknowledging smile, a gleam of response.

Two men had come from Agit Prop, to talk to the meeting about the Festival (Agit Prop was a loose association of activists and artists named after Trotsky's propaganda train and dedicated to promoting revolutionary messages through aesthetic means). That was how Caro met Keith Reid for the first time: when she arrived he had already taken his place in a chair at the centre of things, commanding the whole room. Keith was a very attractive man—it was the first thing you needed to know about him, to get any idea of who he was, then. Not handsome, exactly: off-centre quirky features held together by a fierce fluid energy, fragile hooked nose, hollow cheeks, a lean loose strong body, a shoulder-length mess of slightly greasy dark curls. He had a Welsh accent: it was a Valleys accent in fact—he was from Cwmbach near Aberdare—but in those days Caro had never been to Wales and couldn't tell one accent from another. At a time when Left politics was saturated in the romance of the workers, this accent was in itself enough to melt most of the women (and the men).

He looked at Caro in her trouser suit.

—Don't you find, he said, —that dressing up like that puts off the working classes?

She thought about this now with stupefaction. Had she really once inhabited a world where such absurdities were a real currency? She should have laughed in his face. She should have turned round and walked out of the meeting and never gone back.

—No, she said, calmly taking a place directly in Keith's line of sight, so that he could get his eyeful of the offending item. —I find it gives them something good to look at.

Of course she wasn't really calm. She was raging, and humiliated, and struggling with a muddled and not yet confident sense of something fundamentally flawed and unfair to do with men and women in what he had said and all that lay behind it: everything that was going to overflow into the flood of feminism in the next couple of decades. And no doubt at the same time she was scalding with shame at her bourgeois depraved frivolity in the face of decent suffering working-class sobriety, just as Keith meant her to be. And she was thinking how she would make him pay for that.

They had such energy, then, for all the battles.

After the meeting the visitors from Agit Prop had needed a floor to stay on and Caro had taken them back to the disintegrating old mock-Tudor house, its garden overgrown as a jungle, which she shared with a motley collection of students and friends and politicos. (Later she had had trouble with that house; it was rented in her name, and some of the people using it refused to pay their share. She had to hassle them for it, and came home once to find RACHMAN BITCH scrawled in red paint on her bedroom wall.) They sat up until late smoking pot and sparring; Caro and Keith arguing not about the trouser suit, which wasn't mentioned again, but about the dockers' support for Enoch Powell and its implications for the alliance between left alternative politics and the working-class movement. Caro had been on the anti-racist march to Transport House: Keith thought she was overstating the problem in a way that was typical of bourgeois squeamishness in the face of the realities of working class culture.

The way Keith dominated a room and laid down the law and didn't seriously countenance anybody else's opinions should have made him obnoxious; but his ironic delivery in that accent of his made it seem as though there was something teasing in his most exaggerated assertions. Everyone was willing to listen to him because he was older and his pedigree was impeccable: a miner's son, kicked out from Hornsey Art College for his political activities, he had been working on building sites ever since. In any case, that sheer imperturbable male certainty was intriguing to women in those days. They felt in the face of it a complex mix of thrilled abjection with a desire to batter at it with their fists; also, probably strongest, they believed that given the chance they would be able to find out through their feminine sexuality the weaknesses and vulnerable places behind the imperturbable male front. (This last intuition was all too often accurate.)

Eventually Caro found sleeping bags for everybody and they distributed themselves around mattresses and sofas and floors in the high-ceilinged damp-smelling rooms of the house. And then at some point in the night Keith must have got up again and wandered about until he found, not Caro, who had half expected him, but her sister Penny, who happened to be staying with her for a few days. Penny was a year older than Caro but didn't look it: most people took her to be the younger sister. She was smaller, softer-seeming, prettier. Caro found them in the morning twined around one another in their zipped-together sleeping bags. All she could make out at first was the mess of Keith's dark curls and his naked young shoulders, tanned and muscular from the work he did; and then she saw how down inside the bag Penny's head with its swirl of auburn hair like a fox's brush was wrapped in his brown arms against his chest.

She remembered that she had felt a stinging shock. Not heartbreak or any kind of serious sorrow: she hadn't had time to do anything like fall in love with Keith, and anyway, love didn't seem to be quite what it was that could have happened, if things had gone differently, between them. It was more as if she felt that, if you put the two of them alongside Keith Reid, it was in some obvious way she and not Penny who was his match, his mate. Penny all through the loud debate of the night before had sat quietly while Caro met him, point for point, and smoked joint for joint with him. Also, there was unfinished business between her and him: some contest he had begun and had now abruptly—it made him seem almost cowardly—broken off. Even as Caro recoiled, just for that first moment, in the shock of finding them, she knew she was learning from it something essential she needed to know for her survival, something about the way that men chose women.

Penny had given up after one year at art college and was living at home again with their parents in Banbury. She was thinking about going to do teacher training. Instead, she embarked on the relationship with Keith: it did almost seem, in retrospect, like a career choice. That whole long middle section of Penny's life, twenty years, was taken up in the struggle with him: pursued by him; dedicating herself to him; counselling him through his creative agonies when he was writing; bearing his children; supporting his infidelities, his drinking, his disappearances, his contempts; making every effort to tame him, to turn him into a decent acceptable partner and father.

Tessa Hadley

Then when Penny had finished with him once and for all, he slipped
without a protest into cosy domesticity with his second wife, as if
there hadn't ever been a problem. —I was just the warm-up act,
Penny joked about it now. —Softening him up ready for the show
with Lynne.

Through all of it, Caro had supported her sister: sometimes
literally, with money, mostly just with listening and company and
sympathy. When Keith went back to live in Wales and got Welsh
Arts Council funding to make the first film, Penny had two small
babies. Instead of finding a house in Cardiff, even in Pontypridd,
Keith had insisted—on principle—on taking her to live in a council
house on the edge of a huge bleak estate on the side of a mountain
in Merthyr Tydfil where she didn't know anyone, and no one liked
her because she was posh and English. It was half an hour's walk
with the pushchair down to the nearest shops. When a job came up
in Cardiff, Caro moved down there partly to be near enough to help
(she was also escaping the fag end of a tormenting love affair): most
weekends after work she drove up to Merthyr to give a hand with
the kids, take Penny to the nearest supermarket, and try to persuade
her to pack up her things and leave. Penny had made the house inside
gorgeous on next to nothing, with rush mats and big embroidered
cushions and mobiles and chimes pinned to the ceiling; she painted
the lids of instant coffee jars in rainbow colours and kept brown rice
and lentils and dried kidney beans in them. But the wind seemed
never to stop whistling around the corners of the house and in
through the ill-fitting window frames, setting the mobiles swinging.

Keith usually wasn't there and if he was he and Caro hardly
spoke. One strange Saturday evening he had had a gun for some
reason: perhaps it was to do with the film, she couldn't remember,
although that wouldn't have explained why he also had live
ammunition. He had claimed that he knew how to dismantle it, had
taken bits off it and spread them out on the tablecloth in the corner
of the room where the children were watching television: he was
drinking whisky, and erupted with raucous contempt when Penny
said she didn't want that horrible thing in her home. He picked the
gun up and held it to Penny's head while she struggled away from
him and told him not to be so silly.

—Don't be such a bloody idiot, Keith, Caro said.

—Shut it, sister-bitch, he said in a fake Cockney accent, swinging round, squinting his eyes, pretending to take aim at her across the room. Presumably without its bits the gun wasn't dangerous, but they couldn't be sure. They hurried the protesting children upstairs improbably early, bathed them with shaking hands, singing and playing games so as not to frighten them, staring at one another in mute communication of their predicament.

—Put the kids in the car and drive to my place, Caro said, wrapping a towel around her wriggling wet niece, kissing the dark curls which were just like Keith's.

—Wait and see, said Penny, —if it gets any worse.

In the end Keith had not been able to put the gun back together, and had fallen asleep in front of the television: Penny hid the ammunition in her Tampax box before she went to bed. She had been right not to overreact: Keith wasn't really the kind of man who fired guns and shot people, he was the kind who liked the glamour of the idea of doing it.

Caro could remember going to see Keith's film at the Arts Centre in Cardiff—not at the premièrc, she hadn't wanted to see him fêted and basking in it, and had made her excuses, but in the week after— and it had made her so angry that she wanted to stand up in the cinema and explain to all those admiring people in the audience how unforgivably he used real things that mattered and milked them to make them touching, and how in truth whenever he was home on the estate that he made so much of in the film he was bored and longing to get away to talk with his film-making friends. Actually the audience probably weren't really all that admiring, the film had got mixed reviews. She had seen it again recently when the Arts Centre did a Welsh film season, and had thought about it differently: only twenty years on it seemed innocent and archaic, and its stern establishing shots of pithead and winding gear were a nostalgic evocation of a lost landscape. The one he did afterwards about the miners' strike was his best, she thought: it was the bleakest most unsentimental account she ever saw of the whole business, capturing its honour and its errors both together; the ensemble work was very funny and complex (apart from the leads he had used non-professional actors, mostly ex-miners and their wives). His career had neither failed nor taken off since then: there always seemed to be work, but it was always precarious (it was a good job Lynne made money with her photography).

In the end Penny made friends with some of the women from the estate she met in the school playground, and got involved with the tenants' association, and had her third baby in Prince Charles Hospital in Merthyr, and probably looked back now on her time on the estate with some affection. She grew very close, too, to Keith's parents in Cwmbach: she saw more of his father in his last illness than Keith did, she really seemed to love the reticent, neat old man, who had been an electrician at the Phurnacite plant and in his retirement pottered about his DIY tasks in their immaculate big post-war council house, putting in a heated towel-rail in the bathroom, making a patio for the garden. She stayed good friends with his mother and his sister even after she and Keith were separated.

When Penny eventually decided that he and she should go their different ways (she moved out when he tried to move his latest girlfriend, an actress with a drug habit and a dog, into the house with them), she did the teacher training she had put off for so long, and met her present partner, a biologist working in conservation who was everything suitable and reasonable that Keith was not. They lived now in the country near Banbury, not far from where Penny and Caro had grown up. Meanwhile Keith met Lynne, and they shared their time between London and the Dordogne. So that in the end it was Caro who was left living in Wales, and if she thought sometimes that it was partly because of Keith Reid that she had ended up making her life there she didn't mind, she just thought that it was funny.

She turned out all the lights in the flat; she could see well enough in the light that came from the street lamp outside her front window to pour herself a whisky in hopes that it would help put her to sleep. She sat to drink it with her feet tucked under her on the end of the sofa where she had sat an hour or so before listening to Keith; she heard a soft pattering of rain and a police siren, too far off to think about. In the half dark, awareness of the familiar fond shapes of the furniture of her present life—tasteful and feminine and comfortable—was like a soft blanket settled around her shoulders. She should have felt safe and complete; it annoyed her that she was still gnawed by some unfinished business just because Keith Reid was asleep in her spare room. There were other men who had been much more important in her life, and yet when they came to stay (sometimes in the spare room bed and sometimes in hers), it didn't bother her this way.

Her heart had sunk when halfway down the second bottle Keith began to wax nostalgic and maudlin about the Sixties and the decay of the socialist dream. You heard this everywhere these days, in the newspapers and on television; usually of course from people who had been young then. The formula, surely inadequate to the complicated facts, was always the same: that what had been 'idealism' then had declined sadly into 'disillusion' now.

—But remember, she had insisted, —that in 1968 when we marched round Trafalgar Square we were chanting 'Ho Ho Ho Chi Minh'! I mean, for Chrissake! Ho Chi Minh! And at that Revolutionary Festival you could play skittles with French riot police helmets stuck on Coca-Cola bottles. And remember us getting up at the crack of dawn to go and try and sell *Socialist Worker* to workers in that clothing factory in Shacklewell Lane. Expecting them to spend their hard-earned money on that rag with its dreary doctrine and all its factional infighting. And I used to go back to bed afterwards, when I got home, because I hated getting up so early. Remember that we spoke with respect of Lenin, and Trotsky, and Chairman Mao, all those mass murderers. Remember that we had contempt for the Welfare State, as a piece of bourgeois revisionism.

—There were excesses, Keith conceded fondly. —But then, excess was in the air. Anything could have happened. That's what's missing now. Caro, you sound so New Labour. I'm still a revolutionary, aren't you? Don't you still want socialism?

She shrugged. —Oh, well, yes, socialism, I suppose…

That conversation had ended awkwardly, each embarrassed by what they thought of as the other's false position. Keith probably thought that Caro had 'sold out' (he might even have put it in those words, perhaps to Lynne). She worked as Personal Assistant to a Labour MP, a man she mostly liked and respected. (Before that she had worked for Panasonic.) On the second and fourth Mondays of every month she went to Amnesty International Meetings in a shabby upstairs room of the Friends' Meeting House and was currently involved in a campaign for the release of a postgraduate student imprisoned in China for his researches into ethnic Uighur history. This compromising pragmatic liberalism might in time turn out to be as absolutely beside the point as the articles she had once written for *Black Dwarf*: who could tell? Your ethical life was a shallow bowl brimming impossibly; however dedicatedly you carried it about with you there were bound to be spills, or you found out that the dedication you brought wasn't needed, or that you had brought it to the wrong place.

While Caro was tidying up she had had to go into the spare room to put away her grandmother's nineteen-twenties water jug, painted with blue irises, in its place on the lace mat on top of the bureau. This could have waited until the morning when Keith was gone; perhaps she had just made it an excuse to go in and take the measure of him uninhibitedly, free of the wakeful obligation to smile and reassure. She swung the door quietly behind her to admit just a narrow ribbon of light, then stood waiting for her eyes to adjust, breathing in the slight not unpleasant fug of his smell: good French soap and cologne and a tang of his sweat and of gas flavoured with the garlic she had put in her cooking. He slept on his side with his face pressed in the pillow, frowning; his chest with its plume of grey-black hair down the breastbone was bare, the duvet lay decorously across his waist, under it he seemed to have his hands squeezed between his jackknifed knees, his mouth was open, he made noises sucking in air. She wondered all the time she stood there whether he wasn't actually aware of her presence and faking sleep.

He didn't look too bad. He took good care of himself (or Lynne took care of him): he hadn't put on much weight, although where he had been lean and hard he was nowadays rangy and slack, with jutting bowed shoulders under his T-shirt and a small soft pouch of belly above his belt. He probably still had the power of his sexual attraction; whereas Caro who was a couple of years younger knew she could no longer count on hers, even though she also took care of herself, and was slim, and had her grey hair done at Vidal Sassoon (she thought now that this old gender inequity probably had less to do with patriarchal systems than with desires hard-wired into human evolutionary biology). Keith had opted to deal with his advancing baldness by cutting very short even the rim of hair he had left growing behind his ears and at the back; this was a good move, she thought, pre-empting pretence and turning what might have looked like a vulnerability into an assertion of style. However, it made the starkness of his craggy head shocking. All the years of his age, all the drinking, all the history and difficulty of the man, was concentrated in the face laid bare: its eaten-out hollows, the high exposed bony bridge of his nose that rode him like the prow of a ship, the deep closed folds of flesh, the huge dropped purple eyelids flickering with sensitivity.

She sat thinking now about the time when Keith was the most attractive man in the room, the man you couldn't afford to turn your eyes away from, careless and dangerous with his young strength. It hadn't been a good or tender thing exactly; it hadn't had much joy in it for Caro. Nonetheless she quaked at the power of this enemy, stronger than either of them, who had slipped in under her roof and was stealing everything away.

When Keith had telephoned from France to say that he had to come over for a couple of days to talk to some people in Cardiff about a new film project, Caro had planned and shopped for an elaborate meal. She didn't make anything heavy or indigestible, but unusual things that took careful preparation, little Russian cheese pastries for starters, then fillet of lamb with dried maraschino cherries and spinach, and for dessert gooseberry sorbet with home-made almond tuiles. Because she lived alone, she loved to cook when she was entertaining friends.

She had spent all day getting ready what they had eaten in an hour or so. And of course the food had taken second place to their talk, with so much to catch up on; although Keith had helped himself hungrily and appreciatively. In her thirties she had resented furiously this disproportion between the time spent cooking and eating; it had seemed to her characteristic of women's work, exploitative and invisible and without lasting results. She had even given up cooking for a while. These days she felt about it differently. The disproportion seemed part of the right rhythm of all pleasure: a long, difficult, and testing preparation for a few moments' consummation.

Now she used her mother's rolling pin to roll out her pastry; she kept Keith's mother's recipes for Welsh cakes and bara brith. In her tasks around the flat—polishing furniture, bleaching dishcloths, vacuuming, taking cuttings from her geraniums, ironing towels and putting them away in the airing cupboard—she was aware that her mother and grandmother had done these same things before her, working alone in quiet rooms, or with the radio for company. In truth she had had a stormy relationship with her parents, and used to think of her mother's domesticated life as thwarted and wasted. But she had learned to love the invisible work, the life that fell away and left no traces. This was how change happened, always obliquely to the plans you laid for it, leaving behind as dead husks all the preparations that you nonetheless had to make in order to bring it about.   □

RATS
Maarten 't Hart

TRANSLATED FROM THE DUTCH BY

MICHIEL HORN

Isabelle Adjani with imports from the eastern bloc

O nly as I watched the little tugboat disappear towards IJmuiden, just west of Amsterdam, did I begin to have doubts about what had been proposed to me. Walter Saxer had said I needed to be present during a few takes in which '*zwanzig Ratten*', twenty rats, had to perform in Werner Herzog's remake of *Nosferatu*. Walter was the executive producer. I had managed to get the number of rats down from twenty to ten, but otherwise made no objection. But I had reached my agreement with Walter two weeks ago; when I made it I could never have imagined what would happen over the next two weeks.

Perhaps the tugboat, already no more than a speck on the horizon topped by a wisp of smoke, would come back for us after the shoot. But in that case, why was the sailing ship on which I found myself heading in the opposite direction? Seen from the tug, it had seemed like a large, even impressive, sailing ship with its wind-filled brown sails. There was no wheelhouse; the compass was right out in the open, as was the wheel behind which a young man with a moustache stood calmly peering into the distance. I walked over to him and asked: 'So what's the plan? What are we going to do?'

'Hey,' he said, 'it's you. I didn't know you dealt with rats—aren't you always writing about women?'

'Is the difference between women and rats all that great?'

'I would have thought so.'

'Not so, a tame rat is the sweetest creature on earth, a wild one is unmanageable. It's the same with women.'

'You seem to know all about it! You're not going to release them on the ship, are you?'

'I don't know what Herzog has in mind.'

'Just as long as you don't release them.'

'Are we going to keep cruising around here off IJmuiden?'

'No, why do you ask?'

'Don't I get to go back once they've finished filming?'

'Back? We're not going back.'

'Then where are we going?'

'Where you guys are going I don't know. The ship's been rented for a voyage from IJmuiden to Hellevoetsluis, which we hope to reach by eight this evening. With this breeze we should be able to do it, too.'

'But this is crazy! Do I have to come along to Hellevoetsluis? I've got to see a student at three-thirty.'

'I really haven't got a clue what's going to happen. John and I are taking this ship to Hellevoetsluis, and perhaps you guys are coming along, or perhaps they'll let you off somewhere along the way. Ask those Germans, they know exactly what's going on.'

Turning to a dark, stocky man at the railing, I asked him in German what was going to happen. But it turned out he spoke only French, and when I repeated my question in French he said, 'I don't know.'

I walked along the railing towards two young women. I had met one of them twice already, but still didn't know her name, so in my thoughts I called her The Girl with the Sad Face. I didn't recognize the other girl. She might have been quite attractive, but she camouflaged this with her clothes: threadbare jeans, a brown vest with lots of holes, and a blouse from which buttons were missing so that it hung open. Her long hair, which looked as if she hadn't washed it for a month, was tied back with a grubby, reddish-coloured ribbon. She wore neither shoes nor stockings and her feet were dirty.

'Are the rats dangerous?' she asked in German as I came closer.

'Absolutely not.'

She smiled, the other girl did not.

'What's going to happen now?' I asked.

'We'll find out,' the sad-faced girl said.

'Do we have to come along to Hellevoetsluis?'

'Was ist das, Hellevoetsluis?'

I stopped asking questions, not only because I was struggling to find the German words for what I wanted to ask: what takes have been planned, how long will they last, where will I be able to disembark? but also because gliding calmly over the sea, with those swelling yet virtually silent sails overhead, created in me a kind of carefree and peaceful surrender to whatever awaited me. High above the brown sails stretched the vault of the slightly misty blue sky, and there was no sound except the babbling of the water as the ship glided along.

My two cages, five rats in each, stood next to a box of baguettes and fruit. The rats were huddled together on the sawdust. One stretched, yawned and lay there sunbathing. Why shouldn't I do the same? There was no sign that filming would begin soon.

Werner Herzog was standing at the railing and four men were sitting on the hatches, snoozing in the sun. I sat on the hatches too, with my legs stretched out, rolled up my shirt sleeves, and rested my head on a rolled-up sail. Far overhead, the sun shone down on me between the sails. I closed my eyes, felt the warm sun on my eyelids and thought: this actually feels like happiness.

Two weeks before I had received a phone call from Walter Saxer. 'You specialize in rats, don't you?' he asked.

'More or less,' I said.

By 1978, I had published several novels and short story collections but I was still working at the Zoological Laboratory at the University of Leiden. My area of expertise was the physiology and behaviour of rats; I had written a book on the subject five years before.

'We're having a problem here in Delft. Could you perhaps come to our office to discuss it? It's hard to explain over the phone.'

When I pushed open the door of Walter Saxer's office in Delft, two days later, I was startled to see several dozen coffins standing in a long corridor. I walked past the coffins, and into a small room where I came across a young woman. She was so beautiful that I could only ask her in confusion, 'Where can I find Walter Saxer?'

'Don't know,' she said brusquely in a deep alto voice. I reached a corridor with glass walls through which more rooms were visible. In one of the rooms there was a girl with a very sad face, a slight man and a caged animal that I was completely unable to identify.

'I'm looking for Walter Saxer,' I said.

The girl nodded at the animal in the cage. It resembled a bat more than anything else, and like a bat it was hanging upside down. It looked at me with small, shrewd eyes. Two young men entered after me, and at once one of them shouted, 'The rat king!'

'*Ach so,*' said the slight man standing by the cage. He introduced himself as Walter Saxer, offered me a chair and began to tell me in beautiful German about the problems he was having with the municipality of Delft. It was unwilling to grant permission for the release of 10,000 tame rats imported from Hungary, in an alley that would be completely blocked off with high fences. At the end they would all be recaptured. Surely I agreed that couldn't do any harm but how could this be made clear to the Delft municipal authorities? Could I think of ways of persuading them at this late stage that they were mistaken?

'What grounds have they given for their refusal?'

'The officer of public health was asked for advice and gave a negative recommendation, and they're also saying it's ill-considered from the point of view of animal welfare.'

'Of course they're afraid that a few of the ten thousand will escape.'

'We'll make sure that can't happen.'

'Even with that many?'

'Sure, sure, we've got enough people.'

While ever more people crowded around the table and explained to me in various languages how important it was to be able to use the 10,000 rats in the film and how everything would be done to prevent escapes—and, besides, the rats had been sterilized—I kept looking at that uncommonly large bat (or perhaps it was a flying dog?) and at the girl with the sad, sad face.

I soon realized that they mistakenly believed that 'sterilized' meant the rats could not procreate, whereas it meant only that they were bacteria-free. I left them undisturbed in their delusion because it didn't make a bit of difference whether the rats were sterile or not. If they were let loose in that alley only one thing would happen: all 10,000 of them would huddle together in one great big pile because tame rats are the most easily frightened creatures on earth. They are as scared of catching cold as little old ladies, so they look for a warm spot as quickly as possible, and what could be warmer than being packed together with others of their own kind? No, even a hundred famished cats couldn't get that pile to move. I expressed my doubts about the success of the proposed shoot.

Everybody stopped talking. Along the corridor came a man who, though no taller than I am, had an air about him of being, as the Bible says of King Saul, 'higher than any of the people from his shoulders and upward'; a man with that unmistakable hint of Christ in his face, even though no one knows what Christ looked like. It was Werner Herzog. He began to tell me at once that the rats were *ausserordentlich wichtig*', extraordinarily important to him, and something dramatic entered his voice, something that convinced me that I had to help him because it was almost a matter of life and death for him.

A little later we went for a walk along the canals of Delft. Herzog wanted to show me the alley where the rats would be filmed. He pointed at the trees whose branches were being rejuvenated by the first signs of green: 'For technical reasons, the scenes I am filming now will appear at the end of the film, but the problem is that by the time I shoot the earlier scenes the trees will be completely green: it will look as if the seasons are occurring in the wrong order.'

'I understand,' I said. I wanted to add something about how I always find it hard to watch films because the oddest things happen in them. You see a man on a country road, you notice the plants at the side of the road. There is pilewort and coltsfoot, the cow parsley is still close to the ground—in short, it's the beginning of spring. You see a close-up of the man's face for a moment, and then he is walking along that country road again and all of a sudden the cow parsley is flowering and you see comfrey and common speedwell, although you gather from the story that the man is supposed to be walking along the road at the same time as before the close-up. Or you see— in a Woody Allen film—a girl with long blonde hair that looks like it hasn't been washed for three days. Less than a second later, while the girl is still sitting next to Allen, her hair has suddenly been washed. Such things happen so often in films that I'm quite unable to watch them without feeling irritated.

I couldn't tell Herzog all this because my German wasn't up to it, but the fact that he would take something like this into account made him seem even more sympathetic. Through the alley where he wanted to film the rats, we walked in the direction of the setting sun which was turning the alley golden. Herzog explained how he pictured the way the rats would have to run.

'But that's very difficult,' I said.

'Can't you come and give us a hand?' he appealed.

'I'm willing to come, but quite honestly, I can't get ten thousand unknown rats to start moving. If they were my own rats it would be a different matter. Only, I'd never be able to get hold of ten thousand.'

'But you know so much about them, I'm sure you would be able to give us good advice.'

'What kind of rats are we talking about?'

'Tame, white lab rats. We'll dye them black before we start filming.'

'How?'

'That I don't know, but Walter does; there are good dyes that are completely safe. You've never heard of them?'

'No, and it strikes me as unnecessary, tame dark rats exist as well. I have dark chocolate-coloured and ordinary brown-coloured rats myself.'

'Perhaps we could use them during the sea voyage?'

'Fine by me.'

Why didn't I protest against the dyeing? Why did I consent to the proposal of dyeing 10,000 white rats black? But the sun shone so beautifully that spring evening and the first green leaves glowed so brightly on the trees, and in Herzog's voice I could hear, as well as overconfidence, such a melancholy undertone that I simply had to take his side. I also promised to write a newspaper article about the rat problem.

Three days later Walter's office phoned to ask me to talk about the rat problem on television, preferably with a rat on my shoulder to prove how cute they were, because the municipality of Delft were refusing to relent. So I travelled to Delft once more, this time with a couple of my own rats, and was taken to a square near the Grote Kerk where they were filming. Herzog greeted me with the words: '*Sie sind das einzige Plechtanker das ich noch habe*'— you are the only sheet anchor left to me.

The square was filled with hundreds of pall-bearers who were carrying the rough-finished pine coffins I had earlier seen in the corridor. It looked eerily unreal. Moreover, the collared turtle doves in the square cooed so loudly that there was going to be at least one anachronistic sound in the film: collared turtle doves didn't reach Europe until the beginning of the twentieth century and *Nosferatu* was set in the Middle Ages.

Then I suddenly saw the carriage standing next to the church entrance and the luggage that had fallen off it and a horse lying in front of it. I have never seen horses as ordinary animals: they are more like human beings who are larger, more noble and prouder than us. Would it have lain down there of its own volition? I couldn't imagine that was true. It had probably been anaesthetized, would soon come to and was only lying there for a bit while they were filming. That wasn't so terrible, was it? At a signal from Herzog, the huge funeral procession began to move.

Herzog shouted, 'Isabelle,' and from behind a transept emerged a deathly-pale young woman who roamed among the coffins and cried: 'I know the reason for all this evil!' Then, as if by magic, everything stood still, and after a minute or so the pall-bearers returned to the square with their coffins. After an embrace from Herzog, Isabelle Adjani returned to the transept, and again the pall-bearers walked to the church, and the shout resounded: 'Isabelle,' and everything was repeated up to and including 'I know the reason for all this evil.' The repetition made it more oppressive even though nothing had been changed from the first time. But Herzog was still dissatisfied, and everyone took up their positions once more. The Girl with the Sad Face held a small black clapperboard before the camera and snapped it shut once again.

It was just as if the horse had waited for that signal to come to. It suddenly kicked its legs, lifted up its head, and snorted. Three young men ran up to it. One of them sat down on its head with a thud, as if it were a bar stool, the second fell on its body, and the third rammed a syringe into its rump. A gaunt man emerged from the crowd of spectators, walked up to me and said, 'If they treat a horse this way, how will they treat ten thousand rats?' He vanished, like a prophet in a biblical story, and the horse once again lay there as if dead. The turtle doves almost drowned out Isabelle's line, 'I know the reason for all this evil.' The pall-bearers carried the coffins in such a way that you knew for certain they were empty and that diminished my respect for Herzog. Everybody was acting, except for the horse and the turtle doves. And yet it should be possible to teach a horse to lie motionless in a square without resorting to injections.

The horse regained consciousness for a second time and once more the three lads ran up to it and everything happened as though this, too, had to be filmed again. Only after six reruns of the coffins (which should have contained a few rocks at the very least) being lugged around and Isabelle roaming among the coffins was the horse permitted to come to. When it finally left the square on unsteady legs there was no one to stroke it or pat it on the rump or speak to it encouragingly. It was led away by a farmer who, in exchange for some cash, had rented out his horse for something he would never have submitted to himself.

Then I stood before the camera myself, with a rat on my shoulder, and told my interviewer that releasing the rats wouldn't be a problem. 'They won't escape and they won't spread any diseases, only they won't run, and it's a bit odd to be using dyed white rats because the film is about the bubonic plague and the plague is spread by black rats.' But the next day they didn't broadcast that last bit and I was seen only in my role as apologist for Herzog's plans.

'Would you please come over for a while, we'll send a car for you,' a young woman's voice said over the telephone.

'What's the matter?'

'The rats have arrived and we really don't know how to deal with the situation. Could you please come and help us?'

'How?'

'With cages, with food, with water bottles.'

'Yes, but surely you don't think I've got cages, food and water for ten thousand rats?'

'Please come all the same, in any case you can offer advice, because this can't go on, really it can't.'

The white rats from Hungary were in a barn in 't Woud, a village near Delft. As soon as I entered the barn I saw scores of large cages stacked up in pyramid formation, and in the cages an unimaginably large number of rats. It's not that bad, I thought: the 10,000 seemed fewer than I had expected, but before I could get closer to the cages, the young man who had driven me there from Leiden said: 'The rest of them are here.' Behind an opaque plastic curtain there turned out to be a much larger area of the barn and there, too, cages were stacked up in pyramids as far as the eye could see. I stared at the rats in amazement. It was an unforgettable sight. There was a tremendous unrest in all the cages. I knew at once what the unrest meant but didn't want to admit it to myself so I said, 'They need food and water.'

'Yes, but on the way over here practically all the bottles broke.'

'And they haven't been fed either?'

'No, I don't think so.'

'How were they transported?'

'On a truck, under canvas, for three days.'

'Is there a hose available?' I asked.

'What for?' asked the farmer whose barn it was.

'To hose them down,' I said. 'They're crazed with thirst, completely, totally insane. They've got to have water immediately and there are hardly any bottles, so we'll just have to hose them down so they can lick each other's fur.'

Apart from the farmer and his wife, there was also a bunch of children in the barn, small boys who began to aim a garden hose at the immense sea of rats. When the first jet of water reached a cage, you saw a huge difference in the squirming mass at once. The rats began to lick each other but it didn't really help much because as soon as you aimed the hose at another cage, the squirming resumed in the cage where the spray had just been.

'There's thirteen thousand of them here,' the farmer said, 'that's what they told the truck driver, and the agreement was for ten thousand and that I'd get fifty cents per rat to put them up. I have to get six and half thousand or out they go before the day is done.'

'In an hour a hundred will be gone,' I said, 'and by tomorrow morning a thousand for sure.' I was taken aback by the flatness of my voice.

'I don't give a damn about that.' said the farmer. 'There's thirteen thousand of them—that's what I'm interested in. I have to get six and a half thousand, not five.'

I heard what he said but couldn't take it in. I could only think: this can't be happening; could only look with astonishment and dismay at all those cages in which still-healthy rats, working with that almost merciful-seeming haste which is evident only when they are eating each other, were busily pulling intestines out of the holes they had bitten in the flanks of fellow rats who were mostly still alive. I had never seen cannibalism on such a large scale.

In every cage you could see a great devouring, perhaps ten dead or partly eaten rats and a hundred or more of their companions who were gorging themselves, starting with the contents of the belly and moving on to the muscle mass, leaving in the end nothing but the tips of tails and a few stray incisors. Without an adequate supply of water there was nothing I could do even though I heard myself say, 'We must get hold of water bottles immediately, the rats must be split up into many more cages, twenty rats per cage at most, and they must have food.'

'They've got to leave,' whispered the young man who had picked me up. 'They're not supposed to be here. When they arrived the police showed up. And there's at least ten kids watching: by this evening

everybody around here will know that the rats have arrived anyway.
That's why they've got to leave. We'll load them into a cattle truck,
we'll pretend like we're driving back to Germany and then we'll take
them somewhere else. Walter has already rented another barn.'

'But first they've got to have water and food,' I protested.

'First they've got to leave. We're going to get into a lot of trouble
with the municipality of Delft when they hear the rats have arrived
anyway.'

'You'll get into even more trouble with the Humane Society when
they hear about these parched cannibals.'

'All the more reason to get them out of here.'

While we stood there whispering, I saw that everywhere there
were small holes in the sides of the cages through which young rats
were squirming out. They were already walking along the beams
high above us and shuffling fearfully across the floor, where a good-
natured, sleepy tomcat stared at the moving white spots in wonder
without advancing towards them.

The rats' escape underlined my powerlessness. What could I
accomplish here? I know the reason for all this evil, I thought: it's
a film. A film about the Black Death in Europe, set in a time when
no one had a clue that black rats were responsible for spreading the
bubonic plague. And for the sake of this film 13,000 *white* rats were
gathered here in two groups: those who were eating and those who
were being eaten.

When I was outside again and looked up at the calm, white clouds
and inhaled the spring fragrance which spread a false sense that all
was well, it was just as if the scene inside the barn wasn't real, as if
I really had been dreaming. Nevertheless, I felt so dejected and so
incapable of doing anything myself that I gave the young man the
addresses of two of my students who had worked with rats. 'Perhaps
they'll agree to come and help you,' I said. Before me, a small white
rat scurried into the safety of a growth of cow parsley.

My students sacrificed their Whitsuntide holidays to put an end
to the cannibalism with water bottles and cages they bought in
Zevenaar. Money was one thing Herzog did not lack, and it opened
many doors that otherwise would have stayed tightly shut, certainly
during the holiday weekend (the rats had arrived on the Friday
before Whit Sunday). I was amazed that the decision to buy 500

cages and 1,000 bottles was made so easily. But Herzog had already paid four and a half Deutschmarks for each of his bargain-basement eastern-bloc rats (at twenty guilders, a tame, bacteria-free Dutch rat would have cost him nearly five times as much) and 5,000 guilders to put them up in a rented barn for a day and a night, and the same amount for the rental of a second barn to which they were moved in the deepest secrecy.

I learned all of this from Marga and Yolanda, the two students I had recommended because they were fond of rats and because they were tough and persistent in unfavourable conditions. For fifteen guilders per hour, a princely wage in their view, they tried to save as many animals as they could. As a result, at the end of the weekend rather more than 8,000 rats survived of the 13,000 that had been hauled along Hungarian, Austrian, German and Dutch roads on a flatbed truck, covered only with canvas.

In spite of everything that had happened, I now lay sunbathing on a sailing ship. I had allowed myself to be persuaded to help with some takes involving my own rats. Why? Was it because I had made a promise to Walter? It's true that a commitment to keeping one's word does weigh heavily with me. Was it because of The Girl with the Sad Face? Or was it because I had walked with Herzog by canals and along that alley bathed in golden light and had realized in listening to the melancholy, emphatic sound of his voice, that the difficulties of writing are magnified in the film-making process into obstacles that can barely be overcome? Could the sound of that voice make me forget the horse? Or was it because of the Dutch word he used—*Plechtanker*, sheet anchor? I lay there in the sun, the sea breeze rustled through my hair like a woman's hand. The full sails looked browner than the rats, who had been dyed by now. Yolanda had told me all about it and the story should have been enough to end my involvement.

The first hundred rats were put in a wire cage and dipped into the boiling water in which the dye had first been dissolved. The rats were immersed only briefly; nevertheless, when they were taken out of the dye bath they were all dead. The water was cooled down and the rats were immersed for ever shorter periods of time, and the result was that the fur of those who survived the immersion turned a light grey. Herzog's crew dried these rats with a hairdryer—even though rats have a deep aversion to the slightest breeze. And what was the end result of all this effort? The rats immediately began to wash and brush themselves intensively, so that after only a day little or nothing remained of the dye. But this time, I told myself, I was present. This time I would be able to make sure that they would treat my naturally brown rats more humanely.

But as I lay there in the sun, it was as though none of it had happened, as though I found myself more or less by accident on a sailing boat that was making a pleasure cruise along a no-longer visible coast. Through my eyelashes I looked at The Girl with the Sad Face; the sun wasn't able to make her smile but it brought out freckles that made her seem younger. Even the sun couldn't do anything for the slovenly girl. A handsome young man approached my rats hesitantly. It was Bruno Ganz, who was playing the role of Jonathan Harker. He motioned to me to join him. 'Are they dangerous?' he asked in German.

'No, no,' I said.

'I have to pick up two of them in the film. Do they bite?'

'Never.'

I opened a cage, took out a male rat and showed him how easy it is to hold and pet them, and with some reluctance he took the animal from me. When it became evident that it would not bite him either, his rather gruff expression softened and he lifted the rat up high and showed it to the swarthy men standing at the railing. Who were they? Who were the others standing idly in the gangway? Altogether I counted fourteen people, the two girls and myself included. The ship had a two-man crew. But who were all the others? Cameramen? Actors?

I retrieved the rat and returned it to its cage. I had been on board for an hour and as yet no one had told me what was going to happen and how I would get back to shore on time for my appointment in the afternoon. Ganz remained standing by the two cages and in an obvious effort to allay his lingering fear was talking softly to the sunbathing rats. Nothing else was happening at all; even the seagulls who had accompanied the ship from IJmuiden had disappeared. How long would it be? I still refused to believe that I would have to go all the way to Hellevoetsluis—surely Walter would have told me?

Suddenly I heard someone say something in French about a speedboat. A speedboat from Hoek of Holland with Walter on board would show up at six this evening? Six o'clock! It was now ten. Would I have to stay on board for eight hours? And what about my appointment? What would they say in the lab if I didn't show my face all day? Hell, what a mess! I got up, shook myself, and suddenly felt hungry, a clear sign that my mood was deteriorating. I headed over to the box containing baguettes and fruit, and filled myself up with two bananas, an apple and a chunk of bread. My mood improved at once, not least because I deduced from the contents of the box that the voyage would not be long. There was just enough there for my lunch—you couldn't possibly feed fourteen people with it for an entire day. So everything would be finished by lunch time. Well, I should be able to last another two hours.

I returned to my sunny spot on the rolled-up sail, closed my eyes once more, and heard the voice of my conscience. To silence it I tried my usual method against boredom. Long ago, influenced by *Spanish Testament*, Koestler's book about his imprisonment during the Spanish Civil War, I had started to commit poems to memory. I would be able to recite these to myself if I were ever in a cell and bored or if I were ever a hostage. Well, I wasn't in a cell, but I was a prisoner of a kind and a hostage to my conscience, and so I began to recite everything I could remember. It turned out to be a supply that would last me through barely two and a half hours as a prisoner or hostage.

I ambled over to the small store of food and ate a little—I wanted to leave something for the others—walked to the afterhold and looked in. A small old man was sunk in prayer next to a stove that was of course unlit. I stared in amazement at his folded hands and listened as he murmured in heavily accented German: 'O God, have mercy on his soul as we commit his body to the deep, hoping in the resurrection of the body on the Day of Judgement, when Thou shalt appear in the clouds of heaven and Thou shalt be all in all.'

After he had said the prayer he opened his eyes for a moment but did not see me and started again: 'O God, have mercy...' My amazement, which had made me stop and stare, gave way to an awareness that I was intruding and I walked on, making as little noise as possible. What was the purpose of the prayer? What was the point of repeating it? Was the man trying to learn a prayer by heart? Was he an actor? But if he was learning it by heart, why was he doing so with folded hands and closed eyes? It was suddenly a bit upsetting and I had to take an apple from the box of food supplies, by now greatly depleted, to combat the distress I felt. The actor was probably unaccustomed to saying those words and so he needed to rehearse them, and perhaps praying really was such a strange action to him that he needed to practise it. I felt a sharp sadness about the difference between the actor, who evidently knew neither the words nor the motions, and myself, who knew them very well but never said or performed them any more.

I suddenly recalled a poem I had failed to recite to myself earlier. I had got to know it through a girl. When the results of the final exams for my class had been announced, this girl had been the first to congratulate me. I'd seen her walking along the halls of my school for years but had never exchanged a word with her, and all of a sudden she had stood there, shaken my hand and said, 'You know so much about English literature: I really envy you for that. Do you know that poem by W. H. Auden, "Musée des Beaux Arts"?'

'No, I don't,' I replied.

'Too bad,' she said, 'I really wanted to know what you think of it.'

'I'll read it,' I promised, 'and when you write your final exams next month I'll congratulate you and give you my opinion of it.' But before she could take her final exams, one morning as she was cycling to school, she slipped and fell at the very moment that a truck was passing. It consoled no one that she had died instantly, and after the event I kept thinking: could she have had a premonition of her death? Why else had she mentioned that poem to me?

> About suffering they were never wrong,
> The Old Masters: how well they understood
> Its human position; how it takes place
> While someone else is eating or opening a window or just walking
> dully along; ...

> In Brueghel's *Icarus*, for instance: how everything turns away
> Quite leisurely from the disaster; the ploughman may
> Have heard the splash, the forsaken cry,

But for him it was not an important failure; the sun shone
As it had to on the white legs disappearing into the green
Water; and the expensive delicate ship that must have seen
Something amazing, a boy falling out of the sky,
Had somewhere to get to and sailed calmly on.

'How everything turns quite leisurely away from the disaster.' Was
that all there was to it? Was this film-in-progress, for which 6,000
rats had already died, in some way a disaster? I didn't know, I was
not against these film people—I admired Herzog. But go to the wall
for him, that was out of the question. It was almost as if he realized
that I was becoming more and more dubious about his film, because
he suddenly appeared at my side and said, 'Marvellous that you were
able to join us, we're going to do the following. First we're going to
film the opening of a coffin with an axe, and at the same time rats
have to be sitting on a few of the other coffins. Will that be possible?'
'Sure,' I said, 'no problem. They'll stay right where they are.'
'Then we'll film Jonathan jumping overboard and it would be
good if the rats could walk on the railing at that time. Is that possible
or will they fall into the water?'
'No, they'll keep on walking nervously and carefully, unless the
ship makes an odd and very sudden movement.'
'*Schön*, beautiful! And then if at all possible they should come
crawling out of the compass.'
'That'll probably be fine too,' I said.
I followed him into the hold. For two hours we were busy with
the scene in which Jonathan Harker enters the hold with an axe,
moves to a coffin, picks up two rats and nonchalantly tosses them
into an open coffin (which was not to be visible in the film). I
understood then why the actor had spoken to the rats for such a long
time and had fed them a banana, because he had to steel himself each
time before he was bold enough to pick them up.
Nothing is as nerve-racking and oppressive as the apparently
essential repetition of filming, and I was exhausted when I got back
on deck at 3.30. The sun still shone pleasantly and the coastline was
visible through the haze. I lay back on the rolled-up sail again but
did not close my eyes this time because they were filming Jonathan's
leap overboard. When he opens the coffin the contents frighten him

so much that he runs outside and jumps over the railing without the slightest hesitation, or so the script had it.

As soon as Bruno Ganz was in the water, filming stopped and Herzog jumped overboard as well, carrying two life jackets. Very soon we saw them as two minuscule red dots floating far off in the water. They were in the water for twenty minutes exactly—the French sound engineer was using a stopwatch—and Ganz was ashen-faced when he scrambled back on board, in complete contrast to Herzog who jauntily crossed the deck in his dripping clothes and lay in the sun to get dry, while the actor went to change in the afterhold.

When he reappeared on deck, he immediately came up to me and told me, not just once but ten, eleven times in a row, that the ship had disappeared so quickly that he had suddenly thought: I'm drowning, I'm going to die, even when Herzog jumped in after him with the life jackets. 'It was so cold,' he said, 'it was just like I was going to die of the cold if I didn't drown first.' In an evident wish for objective confirmation of how cold he had felt, he wanted us to measure the temperature of the sea. Together we lowered a small pail overboard, filled it with water, looked for a thermometer, and determined that the water was seven degrees Celsius, warmer than he wanted it to be; but the mere thought of it chilled me, even though the sun was blazing down on my face.

As Ganz kept on talking, angrily and bitterly, in a voice that was at the same time sonorous and shocked, he kept trying to capture the moment when he had thought he was done for. The others had all moved away, they had returned from the hold, were lying on the deck, and within a few minutes you could hear the calm breathing of sleeping people everywhere. Herzog lay very close to me, and I had a good view of his face; he snored lightly. Elias Canetti says that the observance of sleep arouses affection: 'Those you have seen asleep you will never be able to hate.'

It was past six o'clock now, and suddenly I remembered that I had missed my appointment. I looked out over the water, saw the Maasvlakte industrial area looming up in the distance, but there was no speedboat approaching. I wanted to get off, I wanted dinner, I wanted to go home: there was a meeting of my record club that evening, and I didn't want to miss that for anything.

We had met faithfully every three weeks for the past decade. One of us would put on a record and the others would have to say what piece was being played. Whoever failed to identify it was mocked mercilessly as a hearing-impaired dimwit or worse, and as I happened to write an occasional newspaper column about music, I was forever hearing how scandalous it was that a completely ignorant scribbler like me couldn't at least guess that the composition lying on the turntable was a symphony by Edmund Rubbra, a work by Mrs Beach, or a piece for piano by Charles-Valentin Alkan.

If only we could start filming again before the speedboat arrived: a few rats on the railing and on the compass—those scenes needn't take long. But Herzog was asleep and so was the cameraman. The two girls were also sleeping, although in my view the slovenly girl hadn't earned the right to sleep because she hadn't done anything yet. Only Ganz was awake, and he sat there looking upset and anxious. The elderly actor passed behind the wheel and was gone. The box of baguettes and fruit was quite empty, the sea was calm, the sun shone on the round, white oil tanks at Maasvlakte, and although it was busy on the water there was still no sign of a speedboat.

Then I saw, in the far distance, a large, motionless four-master, its sails reefed. Without stopping to think, I gave Herzog a push. He woke with a start. I pointed to the sailing ship, and at once he understood, without my having to say a single word, that he could provide his film with something extra, completely free of charge. In no time at all everybody was on the move and the camera was fixed on its tripod. Two men dragged a large parcel, wrapped in sailcloth and held together with rope, and balanced it on the railing. Herzog told two actors how to throw that parcel overboard after they had said a prayer. I realized that the parcel was meant to contain a corpse: it narrowed towards one end and the outline of a head could be seen at the other. Everything was rehearsed twelve times, except for the throwing, while we kept on circling the motionless four-master.

During all that praying and throwing, my rats had to scurry along the railing and this, too, had to be rehearsed; my poor animals shuffling along the wide, wooden railing, defecating busily. Then Herzog finally filmed the scene with the camera mounted in such a way that the four-master was visible diagonally behind the praying men and the corpse on the railing.

The elderly actor mumbled the prayer so inaudibly that he might just as well not have memorized it. As he whispered the words with meek sincerity I was taken back sixteen years to the time when I lived with my uncle and aunt. For the first time in their lives they had seen a film and in the film someone said a prayer. They were both deeply shocked: a prayer acted before the camera, that was the worst form of blasphemy. Closing one's eyes and calling on God but not meaning it, just acting, pretending. Now that I saw it with my own two eyes I found myself in complete agreement with my uncle and aunt. But at the same time it seemed to me that, if you consider praying in a film as blasphemy, you should condemn all acting.

The four-master had disappeared from sight some time ago, the sea was getting rougher, and I noticed a sensation in the area of my stomach that I didn't care for at all. It was now eight-thirty, the filming had stopped, there was no land in sight, and no sign that we were about to moor in Hellevoetsluis. John and the moustached ship's mate were constantly trying to determine their position, and every few minutes Herzog shouted into the speaker of some kind of radiophone: '*Walter, melden Sie sich bitte,*'—Walter, please call in. This was invariably followed by the sound of heavy static.

John and the helmsman were drawing circles on marine maps, pointing with a sharp pencil at the locations where they guessed we could be. They might just as well have outlined the North Sea and said: we're sailing somewhere within this circle. In my mind I heard the Second Symphony of Vasily Kalinnikov, which I had intended to put on the turntable, but the gentlemen of the club seemed very far away and it was getting dark. The wind was picking up and the ship was now rolling unpredictably.

John reefed the sails and the 210 horse power Rolls-Royce engine rumbled obediently but seemed hardly to move us forward in the direction of land—if that was where we were heading. I asked the helmsman how fast we were moving.

'Three, maybe four knots.'

'Where are we?'

'We're lost. Don't have the faintest idea where we are.'

'And we're not moving ahead all that quickly.'

'No, the wind is offshore. Oh well, we can always send out an SOS.'

'In that case you must know where we are.'

'Somewhere on the North Sea off the Zeeland coast.'

'I thought we were supposed to be in Hellevoetsluis by eight.'

'That was the plan all right.'

'So how did we get lost?'

'I just don't get it; we suddenly lost sight of land and began to drift.'

'If we set course directly for the coast we should see it soon, right?'

'I hope so.'

I walked along the gangway to the middle of the ship, took a position at the railing and looked out over the water. Intently I tracked the movement of the waves with my eyes, trying to anticipate whether the next moment we would go up or down, and mostly I succeeded; but when, from time to time, I failed, my stomach lurched with a very unpleasant hollow sensation.

The Girl with the Sad Face and three members of the French camera crew were hanging over the railing, and I saw that one of my rats was throwing up, too. I suddenly felt guilty and at the same time I shivered. It was freezing. I was wearing only a thin windbreaker over a T-shirt. The others had apparently anticipated cold weather because they had put on thick sweaters and duffel coats in the course of the evening, and even the slovenly girl was now wearing a fur coat over her sweater.

In the hold, several members of the camera crew lay on straw mattresses between the coffins, and I located a spot between two coffins as well. But I hadn't been there for five minutes when my stomach protested so emphatically against the stuffy atmosphere in the forecastle, where it was impossible to anticipate the motion of the waves, that I ran outside again. I managed to hold off being sick but the cold pierced me to the skin. I could stay on deck for about ten minutes, then I had to warm up in the forecastle, from which I was driven back once again by rapidly growing nausea. For a while I shuttled back and forth that way, then tried to stay on the stairs, my head above the hatch so I could see the waves, my body somewhat sheltered from the rising wind.

Suddenly I heard Herzog's voice and saw activity near the wheel— were they about to start filming again? I stared in bewilderment at the French sound engineer who was carrying his equipment to the open wheelhouse. He paused briefly along the way to make an offering to the sea. The cameraman also looked like death warmed up, and his assistant seemed to have become one with the railing. Nevertheless everything was set up again and, sick as the crew was, they resumed filming: the elderly actor behind the steering wheel, the rough sea, the progress of the ship. No one needed to act any longer, the script had become reality. We were lost at sea, we were seasick and miserable, and that was exactly what Herzog needed for his film.

He motioned to me. The rats had to go into the compass. It went well. One rat climbed down a tube and got stuck. Its tail remained visible, extending from the end of the tube and pointing at the heavens like an awl. For some reason or other this looked creepy, and only then did I realize that I, who had so often championed an image of the rat that differed from the customary one, was involved in the making of a film that not only confirmed the common view of rats but even exploited it. Thanks in part to my rats, *Nosferatu* would be a horror film. Of course I had known that from the outset—it was, after all, a film about a vampire, but I had thought: it's only imaginary. I couldn't sustain that line of thought any longer because the film and what I was experiencing had become one and the same. That extended tail effectively turned my help with the film into a problem different from the one created by the death and the dyeing of the rats from Hungary. These shipboard rats, these were my rats, rats I had handled until they were so tame that you could do almost anything with them. And the only thing all that careful handling had turned out to be good for was to serve the purposes of people who wanted to use them as scary beasts in a film.

When Herzog filmed a badly frightened rat that was walking along a ledge behind the steering wheel, I would have blushed with shame if the blood had been able to rise to my pale cheeks. This was how everything always went wrong, this was how you unsuspectingly allowed yourself to be misused, this was how you were exploited. Six thousand rats had already died and more than 200 were still dying every day. The elderly actor stood at the wheel; being genuinely afraid, he didn't have to act and in that way Herzog created the unforgettable image of a lonely old man who, without knowing exactly where he was, was steering a ship on the off-chance of reaching land. The elderly actor's ripped white shirt was flapping in the wind; he must have been suffering from the cold even more than me, but he didn't shiver, nor did his teeth chatter. He just stood there, his glassy eyes fixed on the compass, from which one of my rats poked its head every now and then.

Apart from the sad-faced girl who should have been holding the clapperboard in front of the camera but instead was hanging over the railing and the slovenly girl who was consoling her (perhaps that was why she had come along?) everybody was working. The two crew members were trying to reef the large sail on the mainmast because it caught so much offshore wind that we were making scarcely any headway; the others were filming, except for Ganz. Where was he? When they had finished shooting the scene with the compass and were going on to film another—all they needed to do to record as much fear and misery and vomit as they wanted was simply start the camera—I decided to look for him.

I found him on the straw in the hold, and he said in a scared voice, 'We're taking on water, everything here is under water.' It was true: every time the ship moved down into a wave, water gushed in through a crack that was normally above the waterline. The coffins weren't floating around just yet, but it was only a matter of time before they did. I looked into the actor's frightened eyes. I only half-listened to his cursing and complaining, not because I was afraid of the water we were taking on (he was afraid, so I didn't need to be) but because I suddenly thought: perhaps Herzog deliberately arranged for us to lose our way for the sake of his film?

I climbed the narrow stairway to calm my stomach, but it was bitterly cold on deck. Yet I was able to stand up to the cold long enough to ask the helmsman, who was still working on the sails, whether it was normal for the ship to be taking on water.

'Sure,' he said, 'that's not so awful. We can always pump it out.'

'Any idea yet where we are?'

'No, we've lost our course completely, we've got to get back to the coast as soon as possible because we're not equipped to sail in the dark, we don't have any navigation lights.'

The full significance of his words only sank in well after midnight. The sea was pitch dark, though now and then a crescent moon peered around the clouds to illuminate the waves. I couldn't stay inside, not only because my stomach wouldn't tolerate a sojourn in the dingy hold but also because I was afraid, really afraid, and wanted to look danger in the eye. Because we were not alone on the dark sea. The green and red navigation lights of other ships glowed around us. Either we were close to the coast or we were in a heavily travelled part of the North Sea. That would have been rather comforting had we not been so vulnerable; if a large ship were to approach us, we would have little chance of avoiding a collision. Added to my fear was coldness, the sort of coldness that makes you think: I'll be this way forever; even if I lie under woollen blankets or in a hot bath, I'll never be warm again. From time to time I tried to warm myself in the hold where the film crew were lying on the straw mattresses. But merely the smell of vomit that hung in the air was enough to cause an uprising in my stomach.

Yet Herzog was still talking, preaching almost, to Ganz in the semi-darkness, surrounded by people who were dozing on the mattresses and getting up occasionally to be sick. '…And only then you'll discover what you're worth. To go on to the end to find out whether you're brave enough, to determine your limits. That's what it was about, that was the point of our leap into the sea. It's not about the film, it's not about achievements, it's only about learning to be brave and to know who you are and what you're capable of.'

'Yes,' said Ganz, 'but it was too cold to find that out.'

'Mut muss' du haben und nicht feige sein,'—you must have courage and not be a coward—Herzog snarled suddenly.

The lamp swayed so that his shadow roamed spookily between the hammocks and coffins. I climbed back up, returned to my spot at the railing and gazed at the waves. It was as though I were standing on a tall tower, and I felt a strange, tingling sensation in my legs, a scary desire to jump. All I had to do was climb on the railing, take just one leap. What would you feel if the ship vanished quickly into the gloom and you were in the sea all by yourself? What would it be like to drown? 'To die is different from what anyone supposed, and luckier,' wrote Walt Whitman.

I resisted the urge to jump and joined the helmsman, the only other Netherlander on board. I wanted to talk with him for a bit, hear his good-natured voice for a while in order to allay that tingling sensation in my legs.

'Have you ever sailed at night before?'

'No, I've never had to cope with this.'

'It's bloody cold.'

'That's not the worst part, we haven't got any lights.'

'But what about those big lights we were using for the filming this afternoon?'

'Well, holy shit, you're on to something there, of course we've got those lights. They've got to be turned on, they've got to be turned on at once, wait, you hold the wheel for a moment, take good care the needle stays right on this spot here; why didn't we think of that before?'

And so I stood at the wheel, and it seemed as though the chattering of my teeth made the rudder shake, because our movement became less steady than before. Nevertheless, brief though it was, it was an unusual, splendid experience, something to draw strength from, to make me forget the tingling in my legs and the meanderings of my stomach. Then the helmsman was back, together with the light crew, who elicited a roar from the generator that must have been heard a long way off, and a few moments later we were sailing along like an enchanted fairy-tale pleasure yacht, the film lights aimed at the reefed sails, towards the point where clouds and water meet.

From time to time I looked at my watch, not to check what time it was but to see whether time was still passing. So firmly did I believe that nothing would ever change, that it would never be day again, that I was not the first to notice the wavering signal of a lighthouse. It made for great excitement on board. John and the helmsman started to pore over their maps, and the Frenchman with the stopwatch measured the time between flashes of light. On the basis of this information it was possible to identify the flashes as the Flushing lighthouse. To me it looked at times like that white spot Kierkegaard writes about, the white spot you can see when you're out on the sea and which tells you: this night your soul shall be required from you. It was a nonsensical thought but I couldn't rid myself of it, until the lighthouse disappeared from sight because we hadn't made the right adjustments, and the water was just as dark again as it had been earlier.

Suddenly I could see a small boat coming towards us. Its red and green lights seemed to be moving over the water by themselves, partly because the boat went so fast; and yet, although the boat came towards us unexpectedly, there was ample time to warn everybody in the hold. Suddenly we were all standing at the railing, and the boat came alongside. Out of the small pilot house emerged Walter Saxer and a completely bald man in a coat that flapped around him. It was Klaus Kinski in his Nosferatu costume. 'Our vampire, our vampire,' screamed the slovenly girl.

I regarded the figure on the boat with amazement. With his fake bald head he spoiled, for me at least, a sea voyage which had come increasingly to resemble a penance for collaborating on the film. The vampire reminded me how artificial, how affectedly ghastly and lugubrious Herzog intended the film to be. Fortunately the boat disappeared again after we had been told that it would lead us to Hellevoetsluis. Moments later we could only see its sidelights glide over the waves, like the moon but nearer the horizon. The wind dropped suddenly and the water evened out, allowing us to see farther, but the coast was not yet visible.

I went into the hold, tripped over a sleeping Frenchman (he did no more than give me a friendly smile on waking up), then landed on a straw mattress. I didn't even manage to find the most comfortable position because I fell asleep at once.

When I woke up on hearing shouts on deck I found myself lying right next to Werner Herzog. He woke up, too, and turned his face towards me. It was partly covered by the hood of his heavy-duty yellow rainjacket, so that one eye disappeared behind the hood and the other regarded me with suspicion as if I were a character in a horror film.

When I climbed up to the deck I saw that we were in some kind of harbour. Six men were pushing against a bollard next to which we seemed to have run aground, but before I was able to pitch in to help we were suddenly free again. It took twenty minutes to moor the vessel because we kept drifting off, and then we stood on the quay for an hour because the cars that had been ordered for us turned out to have lost their way too.

On the way back to Delft I kept murmuring to myself softly, 'You must have courage and not be a coward,' because I wanted to tell Walter that I no longer wished to help with the film. Tomorrow there would be filming in Hellevoetsluis: rats on the ship's gangway, rats in a coffin. A warm meal stood waiting for us in Delft and we all sat around the table, in the dead of night, and this all made it harder for me to tell Walter, who was seated well away from me, that I wanted to have no more to do with the film.

I asked if I could be taken to Leiden because I didn't want to leave my wife Hanneke in uncertainty. No one was willing to take me. Only Walter's prolonged persistence made someone agree to make the journey. And yet, in response to all this kindness, I told Walter, 'I can't help with the film any longer.' His expression hardened, and suddenly it seemed impossible to explain in German why—'*feige*', cowardly as ever—I was now walking away. It was only when, back at home, I entered the bedroom at the crack of dawn and heard my wife sob, 'I thought you had drowned, I thought you had drowned,' that I knew I had done the right thing; in so far as you can ever do the right thing if, like me, you are thoughtless and impulsive, and perhaps loyal, too, but above all else, cowardly.

My ten brown rats recovered from their experience at sea and returned to the Zoological Laboratory in Leiden to live long and comfortable lives. The Hungarian rats suffered a very different fate. I heard what happened from my students who couldn't bring themselves to abandon the animals. The municipality of Delft continued to refuse permission for the rats to be released in the city so Herzog moved to Schiedam where the authorities were more flexible. While he was filming there, the rats were allowed to move around freely on a quay. Afterwards, they were recaptured but around a thousand rats turned out to have escaped, whereupon Schiedam, too, put an end to filming. Herzog still needed a few more shots using the rats and finally completed filming in Hamburg. The rats were now redundant. Nobody cared for them. Three and a half thousand tame rats were left to wander the streets of Hamburg until they were eaten by cats or dogs or died from lack of food and water.

□

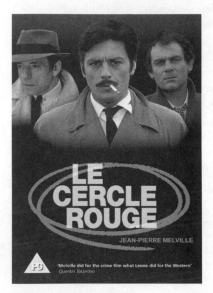

ART BY DIRECTORS
Karl French

PAINTINGS, DRAWINGS, PHOTOGRAPHS AND
STORYBOARDS BY EIGHT FILM DIRECTORS

Akira Kurosawa (1910–1998)

As a child, Kurosawa dreamed of becoming an artist. He was encouraged in this by his primary school teacher and, to a degree, by his father, who insisted he complement his artistic education with a course in calligraphy. On leaving school at eighteen, one of his paintings was accepted for the Nika exhibition, a prestigious annual art festival, but he failed to take his formal training any further.

In an interview towards the end of his life, Kurosawa was asked why he hadn't become a painter. He replied: 'Because I failed the exam.' Again at his father's insistence he had applied to a famous art school but had been rejected. After this he educated himself, visiting art galleries and studying individual painters. He persevered for a few more years, taking commissions from popular magazines. Then, at the age of twenty-five, having never contemplated a career in films, he answered an advertisement from Photo-Chemical Laboratories seeking trainee assistant directors. He was accepted and began an apprenticeship with the established director Kajiro Yamamoto. He directed his first film, *Sanshiro Sugata*, in 1943.

Kurosawa was, like his friend Satyajit Ray, fundamentally a humanist film-maker, but he was also a great visual stylist. His films are marked by a painterly quality and he had an unmatched talent for staging fights and action set-pieces. His work is marked as much by Western as by Eastern influences, so it is fitting that his films should have been reappropriated by Hollywood and European directors: his samurai movies, including *Seven Samurai* (1954), provided the source material for Sergio Leone's *Dollars* cycle and John Sturges's *The Magnificent Seven*, among others.

Shortly after the release of his first colour film, *Dodes'Kaden* (1970), Kurosawa attempted suicide. He recovered to make three further masterpieces, *Dersu Uzala* (1975), *Kagemusha* (1980) and *Ran* (1985), which was helped financially by the intervention of George Lucas and Francis Ford Coppola. It was in the long pre-production periods on these last films that he made detailed preparatory sketches in his trademark style—which owed a clear debt to Van Gogh and the Impressionists. His passion for Van Gogh was particularly evident in his penultimate film, *Akira Kurosawa's Dreams* (1990), in which the elderly director meets Vincent, played by Kurosawa-worshipper Martin Scorsese.

A sketch for 'Akira Kurosawa's Dreams' (1990), in which Martin Scorsese plays Vincent Van Gogh

Design for 'Kagemusha' (1980)

Design for 'Kagemusha' (1980)

Janet Leigh in the shower sequence from 'Psycho' (1960)

Alfred Hitchcock (1899–1980)

First inspired by German Expressionist cinema, Hitchcock quickly developed his signature style of suspense film-making. His films returned again and again to the same psychological territory—fear of authority figures, overbearing mothers, false accusations (with innocent men drawn into desperate situations by malign fate)—and incorporated elaborately staged set-pieces and extended takes. They also included his own often cheeky cameo appearances.

For all his willingness to discuss his technique and philosophy of the craft of movie direction at great length, like some populist Eisenstein, he professed (as would Woody Allen decades later) a distaste for the actual process of film-making. Allen attributed his own feelings to a discomfort in dealing with actors and continual disappointment in the results compared to the image he had of the film in his head. Hitchcock felt, or claimed to feel, that rendering the action on celluloid was almost redundant, since he had already created the films in the elaborate storyboarding sessions that preceded each production. Although he usually employed a professional storyboard artist, and when he contributed his own sketches they tended to be hastily prepared and very rough, Hitchcock was a gifted draughtsman and, as his preparatory sketches for *The 39 Steps* (1935) show, he could produce atmospheric work of high quality.

He left school in his early teens and went to work for the Henley Telegraph and Cable Company. He also took night classes in life-drawing at the University of London and received a rudimentary education in the history of black-and-white illustration. When this came to the attention of his employers he was moved to the advertising department, where he churned out images over the next few years. In 1920 the American company Famous Players–Lasky opened a film studio in north London and Hitchcock went to work there, initially unpaid, supplying title cards for silent films. He was eventually made head of titles. He directed his first film, *The Pleasure Garden*, in 1925, and over the next fifty years an extraordinary run of suspense masterpieces followed, including *The 39 Steps* (1935), *Notorious* (1946), *Strangers on a Train* (1951), *Rear Window* (1954), *Vertigo* (1958), *North by Northwest* (1959), and *Psycho* (1960).

Above and opposite: some of the few surviving preparatory drawings for
'The 39 Steps' (1935)

Takeshi Kitano (b. 1947)

After what seems to have been a miserable childhood, in which he and his siblings were subject to their father's violent outbursts (his father would later be the basis for the central character in his 1999 film, *Kikujiro*) Kitano dropped out of university and became apprenticed to a comedian. He joined up with Jiro, another young stand-up comic; they styled themselves 'The Two Beats' (hence Kitano's stage name, Beat Takeshi, which he still uses as an actor) and became a cult success in Japan with their outrageous, often obscene stage act which in time they brought to television.

In 1982, the director Nagisa Oshima cast Kitano against type as the brutal Hara in *Merry Christmas, Mr Lawrence*. In Japan his fame as a comic affected him adversely, with audiences reputedly hooting with laughter at his every appearance on screen, despite the violence of his character. His next sideways move was equally dramatic, when he emerged as a gifted director on his first film, *Violent Cop* (1989).

It was an accident which led Kitano to take up painting. On the night of August 2, 1994, after finishing his role in *Johnny Mnemonic*, he had a few drinks and went for a ride on his new motorbike. He crashed, fracturing his skull and cheekbone. He admitted later he wasn't sure where he was going that night, or even whether or not it had been a suicide attempt. 'I even thought my brain structure might have been changed and that it might make me more artistic,' he said later. 'It even convinced me to start painting.'

He made a successful return to film-making with *Kids Return* (1996), but his masterpiece came in 1997 with *Hana-Bi*, in which he also plays the leading role as Nishi, a retired cop who alternates between acts of casual but extreme violence and tenderness in caring for his sick wife. Kitano had been planning this film before his accident, but his brush with death clearly informs its mood. Many of the paintings he made during his convalescence are woven seamlessly into the film, presented as the art work created by Nishi's wheelchair-bound former partner Horibe. There is something perfect about these dreamy images in which flowers meld with animals, dovetailing with the film's emblematic title, which consists of the Japanese word for fireworks broken down into its constituent parts: *hana* (flower), *bi* (fire).

Two of Kitano's paintings which feature in his film 'Hana-Bi' (1997)

Above: a cartoon angel which appeared in
Kitano's 1999 film, 'Kikujiro'.
Opposite top: Kitano's failed attempt to copy Van Gogh's
'Sunflowers', which he turned into a visual joke.
Opposite bottom: another painting used in 'Hana-Bi'.
The snow is made up of thousands of copies of the Chinese
pictogram for snow; the symbol at the centre means suicide.

Mike Figgis (b. 1949)

Mike Figgis has been taking photographs for more than four decades, a passion made all the stronger by the possibilities of digital photography. As well as being an obsessive note-taker and filer of his notebooks, sketches and other art works, Figgis takes his camera everywhere he goes. The result, aside from serving as an alternative diary, is an exceptional body of work. He spent much of his early childhood in Kenya, returning to north-east England at the age of ten. The upper-class accent he had picked up in colonial Africa set him apart from his peers and he sought refuge in, among other things, photography. Around the same time he fell in love with music—jazz, blues, and rock and roll—and began to play trumpet and guitar. Rejected by the National Film School, in the 1970s Figgis joined the People Show, an avant-garde musical theatre group with which he stayed for more than a decade and where he was able to write, direct, act, compose and perform. Also during this time he played with a number of jazz bands. In 1980 he formed the Mike Figgis Group, and staged various theatrical shows relying heavily on music that he composed and film footage that he directed.

Figgis made his debut in 1988 with *Stormy Monday*, a stylish, Newcastle-set neo-noir which showed a sureness of touch both in the film's visual style and his ability to handle a star cast. His first Hollywood film, *Internal Affairs* (1990), again proved his talent for handling actors, drawing from Richard Gere possibly his finest and certainly his most unsettling performance. The next three films suggested he was still struggling to fit his talent for erotically charged examinations of the human psyche into Hollywood-style movie-making. *Liebestraum* (1991) was a low-key thriller, *Mr Jones* (1993) a disappointing reunion with Gere, *The Browning Version* (1994) a rather straightforward Rattigan adaptation. But for his next film Figgis stripped the budget to a minimum and shot on 16mm. The result was *Leaving Las Vegas* (1995), the masterpiece of his career so far, with fine performances from Nicolas Cage as the doomed hero and Elizabeth Shue as his hapless lover.

From then on, Figgis has become ever more experimental, with the dazzling split-screen experiment of *Timecode* (2000), and *Hotel* (2001) both exploiting the potential of digital video technology.

At last, some sleep after 3 days
without. Thursday 4.30 pm
Middlesex Hospital.

26/11/92.

Previous page: Los Angeles Police Department (LAPD)
officers arresting suspects, Los Angeles, 1990s

Above and opposite: pen sketches of a friend, Steven,
dying from Aids at the Middlesex Hospital, London, 1992,
and of Figgis's mother at his father's funeral, 1976

Redheugh MAY 24th 76.

Satyajit Ray (1921–1992)

As his friend Kurosawa had done for Japanese cinema, so Satyajit Ray was responsible for establishing an international interest in Indian cinema in the 1950s. He achieved this with his serene, wise and assured debut *Pather Panchali* (1955) which, alongside *Aparajito* (1956) and *Apur Sansar* (*The World of Apu*, 1959), became known as the Apu Trilogy—one of the greatest works in world cinema. Again like Kurosawa, in childhood Ray had seemed destined to become a professional artist. He received years of training and achieved some success as an illustrator.

He was born into a well-off Bengali family in Calcutta, and in 1940 he bowed to his family's wishes and agreed to attend Shantiniketan, the university run by Rabindranath Tagore, who would inspire Ray throughout his career: he adapted several of Tagore's stories for the cinema and produced a documentary to mark the centenary of Tagore's birth.

At Shantiniketan, Ray was introduced to Eastern art—Japanese and Chinese as well as Indian. He enhanced his studies by travelling through the country, scrutinizing and sketching traditional Indian sculptures, statues and shrines. He also visited nearby villages to make sketches. This introduced Ray to the humble ways of life that he would explore in his first films.

After university, Ray returned to Calcutta in 1942 and joined a British-owned advertising company. During the next decade (which included a six-month stay in London where he furthered his cinematic education), Ray worked regularly as a freelance illustrator, designing book jackets and posters. He was also a film critic, which is how he came to meet his idol Jean Renoir. He had dreamed since childhood of breaking into movies, and it was while working on the designs for a new edition of Bibhuti Bhushan Bandyopadhyay's novel *Pather Panchali* that he became passionate about making it into a film, which he did, coming close to bankruptcy in the process. As his fame grew—and he continued to direct films up to the late 1980s—Ray would still draw illustrations, regularly providing the covers for the children's magazine *Sandesh* that had been launched by his father.

A watercolour from 1942, after the Japanese master, Ogata Korin (1658–1716)

Above: Ray's wash-sketches for his first film 'Pather Panchali' (1955)

Ray's woodcut illustration for a 1944 edition of 'Pather Panchali' by
Bibhuti Bhusan Bandhopadhyay, the novel on which the film was based

Peter Greenaway (b. 1942)

Greenaway grew up in Wanstead, east London, and after Forest Hills, a minor public school in Essex, went to Walthamstow Art School, which he later described as 'a breath of fresh air—the novelty value lasted for years, and there I tried to make some sense of an accidental discovery—Bergman's *The Seventh Seal* (1957). That film changed everything.' The other seminal film in his development as a director was Alan Resnais's *Last Year at Marienbad* (1961), and if Greenaway fits into any tradition it is that of the 1960s European auteurs, Bergman, Resnais, Godard, through whose work he gained his education in cinema.

This education continued through the 1960s, when he found work at the British Film Institute (BFI) and then at the Central Office of Information, where he picked up experience in film-editing. For years he made small, self-financed, experimental films, until the critical success of *The Falls*, in 1980, led to *The Draughtsman's Contract* (1982), the film that most obviously owes a debt to Resnais. With his template established, he continued to turn out playful, obscure, erudite, and always controversial films at the rate of roughly one every two years.

The central tension in his films is between the human capacity for, and attraction towards, chaos, ugliness and violence, and the ability or desire to impose order on the world through elaborate taxonomy or game-playing. His films are filled with arcane jokes and references and are often broken down into discrete segments—sometimes numbered, as with the dark and and ludic *Drowning by Numbers* (1988), or colour-coded, as in the case of his gross-out masterpiece, *The Cook, the Thief, His Wife & Her Lover* (1989). So while his films all contain sex, death, decay, violence, and characters who are either ciphers or loathsome and sometimes both, this is all set within a meticulously realized structure containing a sense of order and attention to detail that is equally crucial to his paintings, sketches and 3-D assemblages. The actor Tim Roth summed up Greenaway's obsessiveness when he said, only half-jokingly, that during the making of *The Cook, the Thief, His Wife & Her Lover* the only significant direction he received was to move a couple of inches this way or that to restore the essential symmetry of the composition.

'Gaming Board', 1968 (oil on wood)

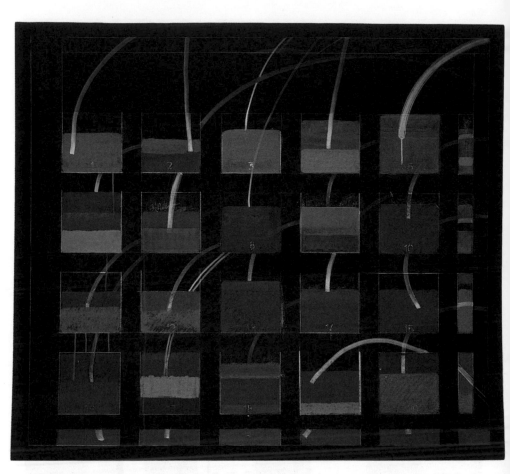

'Icarus Falling into Water', 1997 (mixed media on card)

'The Frames', 1981 (mixed media on card)

John Huston (1906–1987)

Before his directorial debut, *The Maltese Falcon* (1941), the film that confirmed Humphrey Bogart as a tough-guy star, Huston had been making a good living as a screenwriter, notably for Raoul Walsh's *High Sierra* (1941) and Howard Hawks's *Sergeant York* (1941); later he would script Orson Welles's post-war thriller *The Stranger* (1946). The collaboration with Bogart was the most important in Huston's long career, and together they would turn out *The Treasure of the Sierra Madre* (1948), *Key Largo* (1948), *The African Queen* (1951), and the underrated oddity *Beat the Devil* (1953).

Although the 1960s began well with *The Misfits* (1961), the pessimism of the film was appropriate, with its three stars (Clark Gable, Marilyn Monroe and Montgomery Clift) all close to death and its director set for a dismal run throughout the decade. His career was reborn with *Fat City* (1972), and remained on a reasonably even keel (the notable low point, in 1981, of *Escape to Victory* notwithstanding) for the rest of his life.

But things could have been very different. After a serious illness as a ten year old, he was all but bedridden for several years. He emerged with a determination to live an intellectually and physically full life. At fifteen he was introduced to the sport of boxing for which he shared a passion with his father, the actor Walter Huston, who would later co-star in *The Treasure of the Sierra Madre*. Soon afterwards Huston developed an equally strong passion for painting. 'Nothing,' he wrote in his autobiography, 'has played a more important role in my life.'

He was fascinated by the Cubists, and by the American school of Synchronism. He enrolled in the Smith School of Art in Los Angeles but was soon disillusioned with the aridity of the teaching and what he saw as the pointless discipline of the life classes there. Within months he had dropped out of art school and fallen in with a group of like-minded artists in the Art Students League. He continued to paint throughout his life. Huston had studios in each of his homes, notably St Clerans in Galway, Ireland, a house that also contained much of his art collection, ranging from Paul Klee paintings to his impressive hoard of Pre-Columbian art.

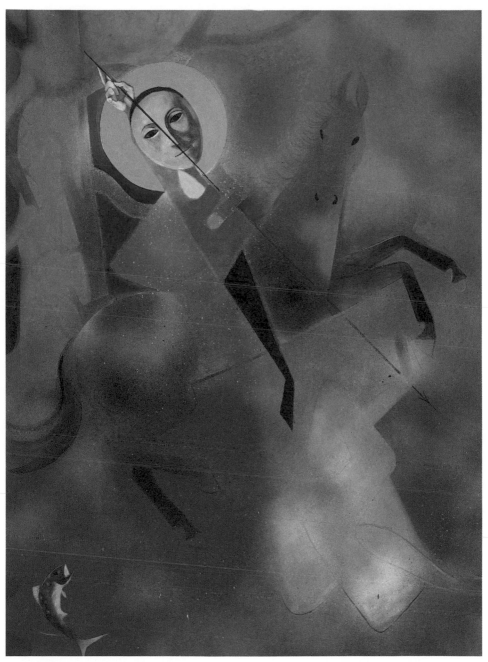

'The Spirit of St Clerans' (1960s)

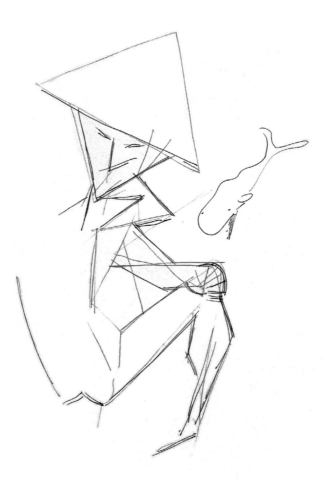

Above and opposite: extracts from John Huston's
sketchbook, 1956, the year he was making 'Moby Dick'
(pen, pencil and coloured pencil on paper)

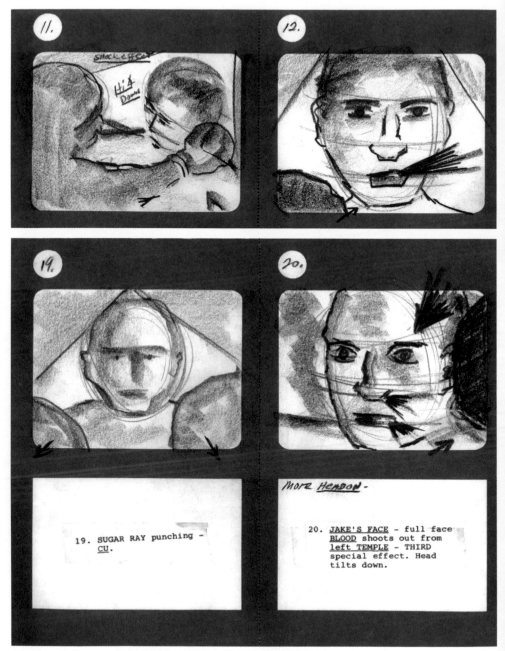

Storyboards for one of the fight sequences in 'Raging Bull' (1980)

Martin Scorsese (b. 1942)

Scorsese's twin passions as a child and adolescent were the cinema and the Church and for many years he planned to enter the priesthood. But the movies won out and he studied film at New York University, where by the time he graduated he had made a number of short films. Through the 1960s he worked as an editor and also directed his first feature film, *Who's That Knocking on My Door?* (1968), a labour of love starring Harvey Keitel, who would become, along with Robert De Niro, one of Scorsese's favourite actors.

He got his big break, as did Francis Ford Coppola and Peter Bogdanovitch, under Roger Corman, who assigned him to direct *Boxcar Bertha* (1972). The film was a modest success, but a key moment came when Scorsese screened it for his idol, John Cassavetes, who praised the style but pleaded with Scorsese to go for more personal material. Heeding that advice, Scorsese dusted off an old idea of his based around the characters who had populated his own neighbourhood of Little Italy, in downtown Manhattan, in his youth. *Mean Streets*, released in 1973, co-starring De Niro and Keitel, made Scorsese's reputation and established his trademark themes—men, often violent men in crisis, with religion generally in the background or foreground—and a signature directorial style, involving flashy, imaginative visual flourishes, long or otherwise complex takes, and pervasive pop music on the soundtrack.

While occasionally working on more mainstream material, Scorsese turned out a succession of great films, including *Taxi Driver* (1976), *Raging Bull* (1980), *The King of Comedy* (1983), and *Goodfellas* (1990), all of which bear his personal touch. Many have been script collaborations—Scorsese and Nick Pileggi co-wrote *Goodfellas* and *Casino* (1995)—or written wholly by others, most notably Paul Schrader, who wrote *Taxi Driver*.

Throughout his career Scorsese has carefully storyboarded his own films. With their urgent, primitive stylelessness, these storyboards may stretch the definition of art; indeed they may look uncomfortably like extracts from (*Taxi Driver*'s) Travis Bickle's illustrated notebooks. But they show Scorsese's innate understanding of the medium and his talent for framing shots and building sequences—in the examples featured here, sequences that have been etched forever into the minds of a generation of film-goers.

T fires A4 shot Turns to go past
Old man - blood spurts from hand

T- goes up the in pan with him.

He turns to fire at old man —
16 closer on T. as he aims.

old man - blood spurts out - T. Turns to fire.
17. Close on old man as he speaks & climbs up the in

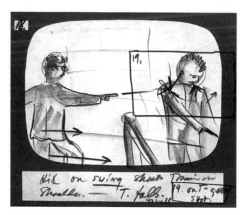

Hit on swing shoots Travis on
Swallow. T. falls 19. on T- gun
Swallow shot

.38 goes flying down stairs —
Old man - blood spurts

Some of Scorsese's detailed storyboards for 'Taxi Driver' (1976)

21.

Mafia man - Fires - [MOVE IN]

Not shot in this shot

22.

Travers falls against wall - gun slide
comes out - he fires -

22. All again
slide up

23.

Mafia man hit by gun - Then r. gas thru door -
PAN LEFT OR SWING AS herbs 20

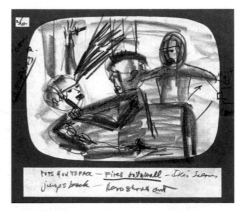

26.

PUTS GUN TO FACE - Fires into wall - Ikes seems
jumps back   Hand shoots out

31.

Bob clos into couch - Reacts to Cop -
puts Hand to Head etc. - always broke -

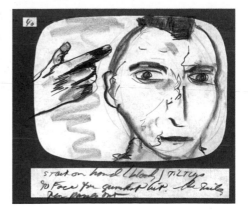

40.

start on hand (blood) TILT up
to Face. You gun drop hit. He smiles
then raises out

GRANTA

THE HANDBAG STUDIO
Thomas Keneally

Leopold Page (right) with Thomas Keneally

The Handbag Studio

In Los Angeles in late October of 1980, I was feeling the strange, malign electricity the Santa Ana winds bring to the city. The heat and challenge of the wind swept along Wilshire Boulevard as I went out to shop for a modestly priced briefcase in Beverly Hills. Passing exorbitant Rodeo Drive on my left, one block from the hotel, I saw, stretching away south, a street that seemed to have normal shops, and family cars bearing the normal scuffs of suburban use. Malls had not yet subsumed the business of such centres as this, and people seemed to be busily parking and seeking out the usual things.

In those days there were only two or three flights a week back to Australia. Australia was not yet a glamour destination, and only a few brave American travellers joined us natives on the planes to the far southwest Pacific and my vast native continent, which some people still confused with Austria. I was not due to leave for Sydney until the following night. I had time to shop.

I had not gone far along South Beverly when, opposite a Hamburger Haven, I encountered a store named the Handbag Studio. Its goods looked out at me through the glass, past banners which declared the Handbag Studio's Fall Sale. I looked in through the glass. Kidskin, cowhide, pigskin, snakeskin, crocodile.

I hesitated. I had always been a cautious shopper. But the proprietor soon appeared at the door. He had a stocky Slavic look, and resembled the great character actor, Theodore Bickel—a touch of Tartar in the cheeks, a barrel chest. He was impeccably shirted and jacketed, and an Eagle Scout pin nested in his lapel. There was a glitter of fraternal amusement in his eyes. Even then, I believe I perceived that he had dealt in markets beyond my knowing.

He said, 'So it's 105 degrees out here and you don't want to come into my air-conditioned store. Do you think I'll eat you?'

'I was just looking for a briefcase,' I said defensively.

'Ai, ai, ai!' he said. 'I have the best, young man. Hong Kong and Italy. The best!'

With these assurances, I entered the store. There aren't too many stores like it any more. Few as intimate, as individual, as uncluttered. Items given the individual respect of their own separate display.

'I have a good case,' I told him earnestly. My wife and daughters had given it to me. But one of its hinges had gone, and the other was tearing too. The storekeeper respected my sentimental attachment, but pointed out though that such an accident was unlikely to befall what he was offering me. 'You just can't put everything in them. They're not a truck, you know!' His broad eyes glimmered. He introduced me to his salesman, a man named Sol. They both had the same sort of Eastern European whimsy, but you could see at once Sol's was of the melancholy rather than the exuberant strain. As we chatted, the proprietor, with the eagle in his lapel, said, 'I must compliment you, sir, on your beautiful British accent.'

'Not British,' I told him, with an automatic Fenian twitch imbued in me by Irish grandparents. 'Australian.' It was true that the Americans, largely ignorant of the bad odour in which our accent was held by the respectable British, unconditionally liked our nearly vowel-less, nearly diphthong-less English.

'So then,' he asked me, 'how did a gentleman like you bust your hinge?'

I explained that I'd been at a film festival in Sorrento in Italy. The Australian film industry had revived in the 1970s, with directors such as Peter Weir, Bruce Beresford, Gillian Armstrong and Fred Schepisi. I had even 'acted' in Schepisi's first film, *The Devil's Playground*, and then, in 1977, Schepisi had made a novel of mine, *The Chant of Jimmie Blacksmith*, into a film. I'd played a small part in that film as well, and since Schepisi himself could not go to Sorrento for its biennial film festival, which was devoted that year to Australian cinema, I was invited to go as his stand-in.

They accommodated us in resort hotels along the Mediterranean coast, a festival load of people who had already established themselves and would go on to great renown—Bruce Beresford, the director; Barry Humphries, alias Dame Edna Everage; Judy Davis; Sam Neill; Bryan Brown; Ray Lawrence. We were still, both as a film industry and as a nation, unaccustomed to serious attention in northern European cultural centres, and enjoyed being the *plat du jour*. The Italian press took each film with a heady seriousness, and we all ate many servings of sumptuous Neapolitan cuisine. But my efforts to stuff all the Italian souvenirs I brought back had busted the bag: one of its two hinges at the back was coming away, ripping fabric with it.

I told all this to the proprietor, whose name was Leopold Page. I had begun by calling him Mr Page, but he told me this was a name that had been foisted on him at Ellis Island. He told me to call him

Leopold; in a short time, I took to using the diminutive, Poldek. Poldek would later explain to me that his true family name from Kraków, that beautiful Galician city, had been Pfefferberg—pepper mountain. I would come to think it a name that suited his exuberance, his feisty goodwill.

'Do you know some friends of mine?' Poldek asked me. He mentioned various Eastern European names from Sydney and Melbourne. No, I hadn't had the honour to meet these people, I said. 'They're Jewish friends of mine,' he explained. 'From Kraków and other places.'

As we talked, Poldek showed me a simple lock-up shining black briefcase, with nicely patterned skin. It was spacious and many compartmented. I said I'd take it. I was grateful that the shopping had been uncomplicated and unexpectedly pleasant, and in between chatting, the deal-making had probably taken no more than two or three minutes.

I gave Poldek my credit card, and he put Sol on the phone to call the numbers through to the credit company. As minutes passed without the card being accepted, Sol kept making doleful faces at us. Poldek told him, 'Well, keep trying, Sol!'

'I'm trying, I'm trying. They won't talk.'

'Ai-ai-ai, give me the phone!'

'You want the phone when no one's on the line?'

'What do you mean *no one's*?'

'I mean they went away to check the card. I mean there's nobody on the line,' said Sol, rejecting all assistance. So Poldek turned to me again, and showing he knew the map of the world, asked me how come I was in California on my way back from Italy to Australia?

I had a book out in the United States, I told him. The publishers, while I was at least in the northern hemisphere, had invited me to come over from Italy to the USA to do a short book tour. Poldek asked me the name of the book, and I told him, and he said, '*My God!* Sol, is that not the same book I just read a review in *Newsweek*?'

'How should I know what you read?' asked dyspeptic Sol.

I might have doubted Poldek's claim, except that there *had* been a review in *Newsweek*. I confirmed it with the false modesty of the astonished author.

'And now, sir, what is your name again?'

Thomas Keneally

I told him.

'Sol, Sol,' he called to his hapless assistant, parked on the phone. 'This guy's a good guy. Cut ten dollars off that!'

Sol grimaced beneath his moustache, and made a *Don't blame me!* sort of gesture with the hand that did not hold the phone.

Poldek confided to me merrily, 'Poor Sol. He had a tough time in the war.'

I was by now such a cherished fellow in the eyes of Mr Leopold Page that he called his son Freddy to come over from the wholesale warehouse and meet me. Turning up a few minutes later, Freddy proved to be a muscular American boy, impeccably dressed for business, and of less pyrotechnic temperament than his father. Poldek turned back to me. 'But what am I thinking? You haven't met my beautiful wife, Mischa.'

At the phone, Sol gave a further doleful shrug. 'They say they've got to call Australia. There's been all this Australian credit card fraud, they say.'

'Give me the phone, give me the phone,' insisted Poldek in his jowly basso. 'You shouldn't say that sort of thing in front of a gentleman.'

Sol handed the receiver to him with a gesture that said, 'Go ahead, big shot!'

'Hello,' said Poldek. 'What is your name? Barbara. Barbara, darling, you sound like a beautiful woman. I know you have your job. But this man in my store is a gentleman all the way from Australia! Do you want to kill my business, Barbara? I know you don't. But do I need to put up a sign saying, AUSTRALIANS, KEEP AWAY! Yes, I know you're doing your best. But my customer has an appointment to go to? Can you help him along? He's a writer and his schedule's tight. Don't do this to him, Barbara, darling. Make it quick is what I beg. I'll put you back to Sol now, darling.'

He handed the phone back to a mournfully gratified Sol and, as Freddy the son stood by, Poldek took me aside, towards the curtain which led into the store's back room.

'Here's what I wanted to point out... I know a wonderful story. A story of humanity man to man. I tell all the writers I get through here. Sitcom guys. Reporters for the *LA Times*. I get famous producers or their wives. Did you know Howard Koch? Howard

134

Koch wrote *Casablanca*. A really nice guy. You see, everyone needs a handbag, everyone needs an attaché case. I tell everyone I know the greatest story of humanity man to man. Some listen—an article there, a news item here. A nice young man, executive producer of *Simon and Simon* at Paramount...he does what he can. But it's a story for you, Thomas. It's a story for you, I swear.'

Every writer hears that sentence. People without an idea of how long a book takes to write pass on the tale of an amusing uncle or aunt, along with the strange addendum: *I could write it if I had nothing else to do.* The suggestion is sometimes passed on tentatively, sometimes with the sincere expectation that the writer will answer, *Wow!* That he will drop to his knees and embrace this jewel of a story. That it will take him a few weeks' leisure to produce the finished manuscript.

But I had never heard the words pass the lips of a soul so vivid, so picaresque, so full of life, as Poldek.

I said, 'What is it?'

He said, 'I was saved, and my wife was saved by a Nazi. I was a Jew imprisoned with Jews. So a Nazi saves me, and more important saves Mischa. So although he's a Nazi, to me he's Jesus Christ. Not that he was a saint. He was all-drinking, all-black marketeering, all-screwing. Okay? But he got Mischa out of Auschwitz, so to me he is God.'

Freddy was listening to this with a minor nod. It was the family story, as central as a book of the Pentateuch. 'What's happening with those crazy Mastercard people, Sol?' asked Poldek.

Sol made a despairing gesture. 'Not a word.'

'Okay,' said Poldek. 'Stick with it, Sol.' And to me: 'Come back into the repair shop, I'll show you.'

The light in the room behind the store area was factory-dim. A slim, well-dressed woman in advanced middle age was working at a long repair table covered with expensive handbags with broken clasps or hinges, and with pliers and receipt books. 'Mischa darling!' Poldek boomed. She looked up with a faint frown, like a wife used to having her husband's extravagant enthusiasms imposed on her. Poldek introduced me to her. A beautiful guy, he said I was. I was a writer and he'd been telling me about Schindler.

This was the first time I heard that name.

'Oh,' she smiled. 'Oskar. Oskar was a god. But Oskar was *Oskar* as well.'

She gave the sort of smile I would get used to from people who had been under Oskar's control in one or other of his two camps. The smile of those somewhat baffled by a phenomenon.

'A big guy, beautiful suits,' she said. 'He was very tall. Poldek and I were in his camp.'

'But your husband tells me you were also in Auschwitz?' I asked.

She admitted it with a nod. 'I was. It was an accident. They sent our train the wrong way. I was thirsty and reached up to the window of the cattle truck to break off ice, and saw the sun was in the wrong place for us to be going south to Schindler's place. We were going west. Oswiecim. Auschwitz. I hated to tell the other girls in the truck. It broke their hearts!'

Freddy, the good son, said, 'But Oskar got you out, Ma.'

'The best journey of my life,' she said. 'Out of Auschwitz and we turned up at Brinnlitz at dawn, a freezing day and we see Oskar standing on the platform in a little hat...a... Poldek, help me.'

'In one of those Tyrolean hats, you know, with the feather on the side.'

'Yes, a Tyrolean hat. There were SS all about, but we had eyes just for him. He was beautiful. And he told us there was soup.'

'Otherwise,' said Freddy, '*I* wouldn't be here, would I, Ma?'

'Exactly right, Freddy darling.'

Poldek said, 'And I wouldn't have had my darling Mischa. She is so cute this lady. Too clever for me. She was meant to be a surgeon.'

'I'm a surgeon on handbags,' she reasoned. 'And I love it here. Beverly Hills people—some are huffy, you know—but mostly so nice.'

'Come and see what I have here,' Poldek said. He led me towards two filing cabinets that lay at the back of the storeroom as he and his wife settled at top voice the issue of a Bel Air woman's handbag and who would deliver it. Poldek stopped walking and sounded bearishly reasonable. 'Mischa, I have the gentleman here. He's a very famous writer. In *Newsweek* I see his review. If you can call Mason's and get them to deliver it straight to...'

'Poldek, they only deliver retail. You know that. Where's Sol?'

'Sol's on the phone with some Mastercard *nebbish*. Besides, he's a lousy driver.'

'I'll get it there, Pop,' said Freddy. 'On the way home.'

'Could you, Freddy darling? You see, Mischa, what a fine boy we made.'

And Poldek parted his lips and made a kissing noise first towards Freddy and then towards his wife. He opened the two filing cabinets, selecting documents—a piece on Oskar Schindler from the *Los Angeles Examiner*, copies of postwar speeches by former Jewish prisoners made in Oskar Schindler's honour, carbon copies of letters in German, and documents partly yellowed, old enough for the staples in them to have rusted somewhat even in Southern California's desert climate. There was a notice of Schindler's death in 1974, and the re-burial of his body a month later in Jerusalem. And there were photographs of scenes from a camp.

As Poldek pulled out documentation from this drawer, and then another, opening and shutting with gusto, he went on commentating.

'This guy Oskar Schindler was a big master-race sort of guy. Tall and smooth and his suits...the cloth! He drank cognac like water. And I remember, when I met him the first time, he was wearing a huge black-and-red Nazi pin.'

He rifled through a folder full of photographs and pulled one out, and there was his younger self, very sharp in his four-cornered Polish officer's cap, a stocky boy, the same confident, half-smiling face as he now directed to me. 'You see, there! I was Phys Ed Professor Magister at the Kosciuszko Gymnasium in Podgórze. The girls loved me. Later I got wounded on the San river fighting Nazis in Poland. My Catholic sergeant major saved my life and carried me to a field hospital. I never forget. I send his family food parcels. Then, after Hitler gave half of Poland to Stalin, we officers had to decide to go east or west. I decided not to go east, even though I was Jewish. If I had, I would have been shot with all the other poor sons of bitch in Katyn Forest.'

Back in Kraków as a prisoner, Poldek had used a German-issued document, which had been issued to enable him to visit his soldiers in a military hospital further east, to bamboozle a barely literate German guard, slip out of the railway waiting-room yard and catch a tram home to his mother. 'And in our apartment here's this big guy, handsome, and he's discussing with her that she'll decorate his apartment at Straszewskiego Street. That's how I first met this Oskar Schindler.'

By now, Sol had appeared in the doorway of the repair room. 'They came through. The card's okay.'

'Thanks God,' said Poldek. Thanks God was a common exclamation of his. 'Now, would you like the briefcase wrapped, sir?'

'No,' I said. 'I'll carry it with me.'

Leopold turned to his patient son. 'Stay with the store a while, Freddy. I'm taking Mr Thomas up to make some photostatic copies.'

'Where will you get photocopies this time of day on a Saturday, Pop?'

'The Glendale Savings. They owe me.'

At Poldek's instructions, I left my bag at the store for the time being. I could carry the copies we got made back to the hotel in it. We crossed the road and made for the Glendale Savings Bank on the corner of Wilshire. Arriving there at a brisk pace, we queued a time in front of the busy Enquiries and Transactions counter of the bank. Poldek apologized to me for the crowd. At last we reached the counter and a young man attended to us. He called my friend 'Mr Page', confirming that Poldek was indeed well known at this branch. Poldek handed over his considerable pile of papers. 'I need photostatic copies of these, please.'

The young man's eyes looked blank. 'Mr Page, you can see it's a very, very busy time.'

Leopold did what he would always do when thwarted. He stepped back and raised his hands in a gesture invoking forces greater than this mere transaction.

'So I have lunch with the president every second Tuesday, and you don't have time to give me a few lousy photostatic copies. Is this what you want me to tell your boss? This is an important gentleman.' He pointed to me. I had begun the morning as a furtive shopper and was now the centre for the gaze of many customers. 'He is a famous writer from Australia, and he is here for only one day and a half.' Clearly, the photostatic copies needed, under the pressure of history, to be done *now*.

The young man, cowed by Leopold's portentousness, said it might take a little time. As I watched the clerk pass on the problem to even younger and even more flustered women, Poldek stepped aside with me to await the copies, and filled me in on more of his history.

Mischa was deported from the Lódz ghetto with her mother Dr Lewenstein, founder of one of the first cosmetic institutes in Poland. Mischa had, even earlier, been a medical student in Vienna, and had seen the Führer's triumphal entry into Vienna, but came home to Poland when war began. 'She saw the son of bitch, and then he ruined her life. This is how I come to meet a beautiful girl like Mischa. And smart. I mean, we were from a good family, my sister and me. But my God, Mischa's parents had brains you wouldn't believe. The Nazis shot her mother later. Why? She had a brain and she was a Jew! It's a wonder they didn't shoot her twice.'

He had longed for Mischa, he said, but another Jewish ghetto dweller and former officer had a prior interest, and an officer and a gentleman did not try to court a comrade's girl. But the other man relinquished her and Poldek set out for the Lewensteins' little room in the ghetto to persuade the mother, who considered him a braggart. It took many hours of relentless talk. And then the mother was shipped away and never seen again, as he had explained.

And so he chattered on. After Schindler's camp had been liberated by a Russian officer riding a donkey, he and Mischa came west into a Displaced Persons Camp, and he worked for the United Nations Relief and Rehabilitation Agency. He had a uniform given him by an American officer, and indeed one could imagine some officer, surveying the lines of edgy, fearful former prisoners, and seeing something undefeated in Poldek, and putting it into uniform.

Mischa and Poldek came to the United States in 1947 and rented a room in some terrible New York tenement, way downtown. Poldek saw another Polish refugee repairing handbags in a little temporary store on the pavement. He got talking to the man, and watched him at work, and went home to tell Mischa they were now in the handbag business. They did well enough in New York to move out to California in the 1950s, to start importing, and to own a few outlets, like the one I had wandered into.

The young bank clerk had returned to the counter with the photocopies. He waved to Poldek that they were ready. 'I'll pay for these,' I offered.

Poldek said, 'Are you mad, Thomas? I give this bank all my good business.' He accepted the copies from the young man and took his hand for a brief passionate clasp, as if they were both about to go into battle together. He waved to the fraught female juniors who were catching their breath further back in the office. 'Young ladies! (Aren't they beautiful Beverly Hills girls, Thomas?) Thank you, darlings.'

I went back to my cool hotel room with the wad of photocopied papers in my new briefcase. I switched the television to that day's Notre Dame game—I don't remember who they were playing, but I did know vaguely that my grandfather's brother, a great-uncle who settled in Brooklyn, had a son named Patrick Keneally who had gone to Notre Dame on a football scholarship, and this was enough to imbue my viewing with a tinge of partisanship.

With the sound low, I began reading the papers Poldek had given me. They were instantly engrossing. There was a speech that one of Oskar Schindler's Jewish accountants, Itzhak Stern, made in Tel Aviv in 1963, about his experience of working with, as well as for, this Nazi factory owner. There were a number of other such speeches translated into English from Schindler survivors from all over Europe and the United States. Then there were a series of affidavit-like testimonies from a range of former prisoners, Poldek and Mischa amongst them. There were many documents relating to Plaszów concentration camp, on the northern edge of Kraków, which was run by an SS man named Amon Goeth from whom Oskar got the labour for his first camp, Emalia, in Kraków. It was when the Russian advance of 1944 led to the closure of Plaszów and Emalia that Oskar had gone to the trouble of founding another camp, near his home town in Moravia, where his own profitable black marketeering and the ambiguous deliverance of Jewish prisoners continued.

And so I came across the typewritten list of workers for Schindler's camp in Moravia, *Zwangsarbeitslager Brinnlitz*—that is, Forced Labour Camp Brinnlitz, which was theoretically under the control of a mother-camp, the infamous *Gross-Rosen*. The list was hundreds of names long and searching through it I came upon the names of Leopold and Mischa Pfefferberg. Mischa was prisoner 195 on the list, was recorded as having been born in 1920 and was marked down as a *Metallarbeiter*, a metal worker. Leopold Pfefferberg, another *Ju. Po.*—Polish Jew—was number 173 and a

Schweisser—welder. He had not used a welding iron until then, but was confident he could learn.

This document, seen by the television glow of a football game, representing an acre of safety in the midst of the huge square mileage of horror of the Holocaust, would achieve an international renown as Schindler's List. The list was life, I would one day write and Ben Kingsley would say, and all around it lay the pit.

I found as well a translation of the speech, taken down by two of Schindler's secretaries, made on the last day of the war, addressed to prisoners and to the SS garrison of Schindler's camp at Brinnlitz. The sentiments expressed by the tall *Herr Direktor* of the camp were extraordinary, with Schindler telling his former labourers that they would now inherit the shattered world, and at the same time pleading with the SS guards who had been ordered to exterminate the camp to depart in honour, and not with blood on their hands. Poldek would tell me that while Schindler gave this finely balanced speech, the hairs were standing up on people's necks. Schindler was playing poker against the SS garrison of his factory-camp, and all the prisoners knew it. But it had worked. The SS drifted away, and left the factory and compound of Brinnlitz, and fled west towards the Americans in Austria.

I was not the only customer to the Handbag Studio to have been fraternally ambushed by Poldek. In the early 1960s, when Oskar was still alive, the wife of the renowned and controversial producer Marvin Gosch had brought her handbag into Leopold's store for repair. No doubt with many loving poutings of lips and praises of Mrs Gosch's beauty, and with the handbag as hostage, Poldek had insisted that she set up an appointment for him with her husband. For a while Mrs Gosch found this eminently refusable, but Poldek's powers of perseverance and undentable charm wore her down. Poldek told me that when Marvin Gosch invited him to MGM Studios for an interview, the producer at first chided him for being so importunate with his wife.

'You must forgive me,' said Poldek, 'but I am bringing you the greatest story of humanity man to man.'

Gosch had been a Broadway producer in the 1940s, had produced, improbably, *Abbott and Costello in Hollywood* (1945), and most recently had tried to make a film about Lucky Luciano. Hearing the Schindler tale from the lips of a survivor, Gosch was enthused and got together a team including the screenwriter Howard Koch, famous for his involvement in the screenplay of *Casablanca* and for having been blacklisted during the McCarthy era. His best-known credits included *Sergeant York*, *Rhapsody in Blue*, and the telemovie about Orson Welles's famous broadcast about Martian invasion, *The Night that Panicked America*.

Gosch and Koch began to interview Schindler survivors around the Los Angeles area. Both of them wanted to meet Oskar too, who was at the time largely broke apart from contributions from his former prisoners. I would later see in Poldek's storeroom archives a photograph of Gosch, Koch, Poldek and big, bear-like Oskar, sitting around a table, conferring. Oskar's small Frankfurt cement works, funded by the Joint Distribution Committee, a Jewish charity based in New York, had gone broke in the severe winter of 1962–63, so that the idea of film rights must have seemed then like rescue. Gosch, Koch and MGM decided that they must ultimately take Poldek and Oskar to meet and gather information from Schindler survivors in Tel Aviv and Jerusalem. Poldek became de facto archivist for all that was gathered, for every testimony and every document he could corral.

In the reasonable hope of prolonging Oskar's life, or imposing a more reasonable shape on it, Gosch wrote to him, 'I hope the fact that you have taken an apartment in Frankfurt does not mean that you are carrying on with too many women. (One is enough! Remember, dear friend, we are no longer as young as we used to be!)'

Eventually MGM bought the rights to Oskar's story for $50,000. Poldek would later claim he made a paternalistic decision to take out $20,000 from Oskar's film deal for Mrs Emilie Schindler and send it to her—I have no reason to believe he was lying—and that he took the remaining $30,000 to Oskar. Poldek and Mischa flew to Paris from Los Angeles, Oskar flew from Frankfurt, and they all met in the Hotel Georges Cinq.

Poldek's version of what happened then was credible only if one had met Poldek and at least heard tales of Schindler. In 1963, when $30,000 could support even a halfway frugal middle-class family for six years, a sane man might have taken the weekend to decide what to do with such a windfall. And, unlike the Glendale Savings, the

Paris banks closed at midday anyway, and Poldek did not meet up with Oskar till afternoon. Poldek and Schindler began to track down the names of bank managers. They found one in Clichy. They turned up at the poor man's door as he prepared for his weekend. They asked him to reopen his bank and cash their cheque. At first he said no, but then, according to Poldek, gave in to their persuasion and came back to the city centre to give them their money. Then Poldek and Schindler set off down the Champs-Elysées where Schindler shopped in front of a *chocolatier*'s store that had an enormous heart-shaped box of chocolates in the window. This was, clearly, not a box for sale—it was the *chocolatier*'s trademark. But Schindler, with characteristic exuberance, could not see the distinction. 'I would like to get that for dear Mischa,' he said.

Even for Poldek, this was too much.

'You don't have to, Oskar. This is display. You don't have to get this for Mischa. It was enough what you did in 1944.'

But Schindler entered the shop, and to the bemusement of its employees, demanded the enormous heart-shaped box in the window. He paid for it, and took it back to Mischa in her hotel. Mischa did not know what to do with this avalanche of chocolates. But since Oskar was delighted with the gift, so must she appear to be.

MGM never managed to make the film, and the story remained unknown to the wider world. The haul of documents Leopold had put together for MGM were what preoccupied and fascinated me that Saturday afternoon. At about five o'clock Poldek called to invite me out for dinner that night with him, Mischa and Schindler's former lawyer Irving Glovin. I agreed, a little nervously, like someone who was being moved too fast. I told him that I was fascinated by the material for all sorts of reasons. But I doubted I could write it. I was not a Jew. I was a kind of European, but from the rim of the earth. *Après nous les penguins*, I sometimes said in bastard French. My father had served in the Middle East in the Second World War and had sent back Nazi memorabilia—Afrika Korps *Feldwebel* stripes, Very pistols marked with the swastika, a Luger holster similarly stamped—just like the ones the Nazis wore in the Saturday afternoon pictures in the Vogue Cinema in Homebush, New South Wales.

Still, I remembered the Saturday evening when Aunt Annie

minded my little brother, and my mother and I went to the show at the Vogue—at the time, this was the most sophisticated possible activity on my limited horizons. It was May 1945, my father still away and, as far as we knew, about to be shipped to some location in the Pacific's ongoing war. And there on the screen was the newsreel footage of Buchenwald and Bergen-Belsen, liberated by the horrified Allies. There were the corpses thin and rigid as planks, stacked like so much timber. I could remember our combined shock in that western suburb of war-remote Sydney.

All this was the barest of qualifications to write the book. But I began to see that Oskar and his Jews reduced the Holocaust to an understandable, almost human scale. He had been there, in Kraków, and then in Brinnlitz, for every stage of the process—for the confiscation of Jewish property and business, for the creation and liquidation of the ghettos, and the building of labour camps, *Arbeitslageren,* to contain labour forces. The *Vernichtungslageren,* the destruction camps, had cast their shadow over him and, for a time, subsumed 300 of his women. If one looked at the Holocaust using Oskar as the lens, one got an idea of the whole machinery at work on an intimate level, and of how that machinery had its impact on people with names and faces. A terrible thing to say—but one was not defeated by sheer numbers.

I had a recklessness in me that made me open to writing the story. It took more persuasion. For my natural timidity sat cheek by jowl with the challenge and richness of this tale. There were lots of issues to iron out—above all, I needed artistic control, as essentially as former prisoners must have the right to offer corrections of fact. But I had not, as some readers would later kindly see it, fought my way to the centre of a maze to emerge with one of the essential stories of an awful century. I had stumbled upon it. I had not grasped it. It—and Poldek—had grasped me.　　　　　　　　　　　　□

In memoriam, Leopold Page (1913–2001)

IN LANA TURNER'S BEDROOM

Gaby Wood

North Bedford Drive, Beverly Hills

It was because it was night-time and raining that I decided to drive up to Lana Turner's old house in Beverly Hills. The crime had taken place forty-six years earlier, on a stormy Good Friday. This was Ash Wednesday, and if I went now, who knew, maybe I would get some sense of the atmosphere that night, when Johnny Stompanato was murdered.

At 9.20 p.m. on April 4, 1958 Cheryl Crane, Lana Turner's fourteen-year-old daughter, stabbed her mother's lover in the stomach. Johnny Stompanato was a suave, well-known gangster who had escorted other stars around town and had once been Mickey Cohen's bodyguard. Two weeks earlier, Stompanato and Lana had had a violent fight because she refused to take him with her to the Oscars (she had been nominated for the first time, for her role in *Peyton Place*). On numerous occasions he had threatened to disfigure her or harm her family if she left him—he had visited her in London on the set of her most recent movie and reportedly had such a clash with her young co-star, Sean Connery, that Scotland Yard had him deported. That Friday night the arguments escalated to such a degree that Cheryl, hoping to protect her mother, ran down to the kitchen to get a knife. She stood outside Lana's bedroom door, and when the door opened she saw Stompanato behind her mother with his arm raised, as if to strike her. She ran at him, and he fell. Lana didn't see the knife. She only saw the stab wound in her lover's dying body.

This is what Lana and Cheryl told Clinton Anderson, the Beverly Hills chief of police, when he arrived an hour and a half later. Anderson said their stories matched exactly. In the 1980s, Lana and Cheryl both wrote memoirs; their stories still matched. But let's go back to 1958: in that hour and a half before Anderson arrived, the two women were joined by six other people, not counting the corpse. Cheryl called her father, Stephen Crane, who ran a restaurant nearby (Crane was Lana's second husband; she would eventually marry eight times). Lana called her mother, Mildred Turner, because she couldn't remember their doctor's number. Mildred Turner called the doctor, and the doctor, on pronouncing Stompanato dead, suggested to Lana that she call the most celebrated criminal lawyer in Los Angeles, Jerry Giesler. Giesler was nicknamed 'the magnificent mouthpiece'; he had got Errol Flynn cleared of two rape charges and Bugsy Siegel cleared of murder. He arrived with a private eye, Fred

Otash, who was a former vice cop and fed stories to *Confidential* magazine on the side. By now the house was surrounded—by medics, policemen and neighbours in bathrobes—but one last person made it into the bedroom before Anderson: James Bacon, a journalist who slipped through by pretending he was the coroner's assistant.

Not only was the room a little crowded, but two crucial things happened in that hour and a half which made the facts unverifiable—and which have preserved the mystery in people's minds ever since. The body was found quite a way from the door with very little blood around it (that is, it had most likely been moved), and the knife was found in the bathroom, covered with smudged and unidentifiable fingerprints.

There was gossip from the start—that Lana made Cheryl take the rap in order to avoid the death penalty and save her career, that Lana found Cheryl and Johnny in bed together—and given that so many people want a piece of the celebrity puzzle, how can we know who to believe? Turner had a word for people who were obsessed with her: Lanatics.

'We get a lot of people knocking,' said the woman who opened the door to the house on North Bedford Drive. 'I usually don't let them in. Some of them are really crazy—people write letters to Lana Turner here saying they're in love with her, and they don't even know she's dead.'

The place was a broad, white, colonial-style mansion, set back from the road by a crescent-shaped driveway (it had been built for the actress Laura Hope Crews with the proceeds from playing Aunt Pittypat in *Gone with the Wind*). Large drops of rain fell from dizzying black palm trees, and a newspaper lay drenched on the ground.

The woman led me into the hallway. 'Here's the kitchen,' she said, sweeping her arm through a doorway to the left as if showing off a piece of real estate. 'This was just redecorated recently. The murder weapon's still in the house somewhere.'

'What do you mean?' I said. 'It was taken in evidence, wasn't it?'

'Yeah, but when they'd finished with it they gave it back. I mean, it belonged to my stepfather. This is his house. It was his knife.' Her stepfather, who was now dead, had rented the house to Lana Turner.

It now belonged to the woman's mother, and she had been living there for a while with her children.

There was a strong smell as soon as you walked in—a woody, smoky-sweet, cigar box smell. A large nineteenth-century oil painting hung on the wall in the hallway, and there was a suit of armour standing in the corner of the living room. Mixed in with this antebellum feel were traces of other times—the one I was looking for (the white leather bar stools Lana had sat on while drinking her inalienable vodkas, the make-up mirror with a lightbulb frame that stretched along an entire wall) and the present era that had all but recorded over it: a child's lunch box deposited at the foot of the stairs; two girls, the woman's daughters, watching TV on Lana's old bed ('a bedspread went missing you know, and never came back,' said the woman, who was not yet born then, about the famous crime). The chaise longue, visible in crime-scene photos next to the corpse, had been reupholstered in dark pink damask and moved to another corner.

I asked why her stepfather hadn't changed more of the decor after the murder. 'Well, it was his furniture,' she said, in the casually proprietary tone she'd used when speaking of the weapon. 'She only lived here for a few months. Why would he change anything?'

I stood in that room as one who has been party to a failed seance. The subject was slippery; there was no knowing Lana Turner now. She was dead, and worse—she was a fiction. I don't mean that she never lived—only that she lived as if she were in a movie.

L ana Turner was a poor girl from Idaho who moved to Los Angeles with her mother after her father had been murdered in a gambling incident. She was famously, and apocryphally, 'discovered' in Schwab's soda fountain when she was sixteen. She became 'the sweater girl' then—a name she earned by wearing thinly lined bras beneath her jumpers—and died in 1995 at the age of seventy-five (or seventy-four, depending on whose version you believe) having spent the years in between living up to what she called her 'trademark' faculties: her platinum hair, her glossy pout, her pin-up's legs. Cheryl Crane recalled that she never saw her mother without make-up. Her roles reflected her life to a stunning degree—or perhaps it was vice versa—the drinking, the marriages, the mothering, the murders. There was always a touch of the simulacrum about her; she might stand for every star who ever changed her name or her looks—others were better dissemblers, but part of Lana Turner's fleshy vibrancy was that her roots, so to speak, were always showing.

After Stompanato's death there was a coroner's inquest instead of a trial, and Cheryl was found guilty of 'justifiable homicide'. She was made a ward of the court until the age of eighteen and released into the custody of her grandmother; the District Attorney announced that she had never had a 'real home'. The inquest was nationally televised, and Lana, who testified for over an hour, was widely said to have given the performance of her life. As a result, her career picked up again, and she was at her best playing a histrionic actress for Douglas Sirk in the aptly titled *Imitation of Life*.

One of the most curious things about her is how she built such an iconic career out of so little talent. But to say that she was a bad actress is to miss the point: overacting was naturalism to her. The morning after the inquest the *Los Angeles Times* ran an editorial sympathizing with Cheryl and what was thought to be her helpless hero-worship of Lana: 'In an unreal world,' it read, 'unreality is the only substance.'

'We don't talk to strangers [in Hollywood],' F. Scott Fitzgerald has his narrator say in *The Last Tycoon*, 'And when we do, we tell them lies so well rehearsed even we don't always recall if they're true.' The woman at North Bedford Drive told me that Lana had lived there for a few months and that the murder weapon had belonged to her stepfather. In fact Lana moved in only days before the murder and moved out the morning after the inquest—she lived there for less than two weeks; and she had bought the knife with Stompanato earlier that day—the coroner found the price tag still on it. But the woman who told me these things was reciting family lore, not misleading me. Telling tales is perhaps a more useful phrase than lying: stories are what Hollywood is made of, and the fact that there may be no final documented truth in this one only makes it more fitting—makes it all the more telling a tale. The producer Robert Evans put it this way: 'There are three sides to every story,' he wrote, 'yours…mine…and the truth. No one is lying. Memories shared serve each differently.'

Some idea of how information about the Stompanato murder has Chinese-whispered its way through the past half-century can be gleaned from this snippet about a crucial aspect of the crime: why there was so little blood around the body. Fred Otash's ghostwriter told Lana Turner's hairdresser that Otash had told him that Jerry Giesler had told him to 'get the hell over here' because 'the bed looks like somebody butchered a hog in it'. They then, reportedly, cleaned up the mess and mussed up the fingerprints. Is this 'evidence'? Of a sort. It's not that you give up on the facts, exactly, only that other kinds of information begin to sidle up to them, creating a new democracy of evidence.

At North Bedford Drive, I became preoccupied with sensations—the smell of the house, the sound of the rain, the colour of the night. These things were merely subjective and yet, in a story such as this, full of smudged-over evidence and snatches of gossip, they claimed an equal footing. In fact, they held unsuspected promise; you could no doubt learn a lot about a person by following their scent.

Eric Root, a friend who claims Lana asked him to tell everyone that she killed Stompanato, has a story in his memoir about Turner's perfume. She wore Tuberose by Mary Chess, a scent Cheryl Crane also remembers being something of a signature with her mother. The perfume was first sold in 1930, and by the time Root met Turner in 1971, it was rather hard to come by. He did some research and arranged for several bottles to be sent to her from New York. Lana, he says, wouldn't stand for any other smell in the house. If you came to visit you were not allowed to wear perfume or aftershave (unless it was a tiny dose of Old Spice, which her great love Tyrone Power used to wear). So one day Root came sprinkled with something he thought she would like. 'What in the hell is that god-awful stuff you have on?' she reportedly asked before he was even in the door. Root was ordered to have a shower and let the maid wash his clothes before he could stay. He did as he was told, and once he was clean he answered his hostess's question: 'That was Tuberose, by Mary Chess.' Turner didn't question the reason behind his transgression, or over-identification. She simply put her foot down: 'No one wears that around here but me. Got it?'

When I arrived back at my hotel I did what private detectives do in thrillers: I checked behind all the doors, in the closets and under the beds. I looked at the heavy velour curtains and was gripped by the fear that someone was behind them. I changed rooms. Then I realized what was troubling me. Unlike the famous bedroom I'd just visited, hotel rooms had a way of erasing their past inhabitants. More people had done more things in each one of the identical rooms around me than had ever passed through Lana Turner's bedroom, and yet there was not a single trace here of any of them—not a gram of cigarette ash, not a spill or a stain or a record of any kind of mood. The scene of a famous suspected cover-up was in fact much less covered up than Room 425 was every day. Yet it still would not yield what I felt were facts. I supposed that what I was afraid of was also what I was after: Lana Turner would always be a shape behind a curtain to me, hidden somewhere behind, or within, the deftly woven fabric of Hollywood. □

TWO OR THREE THINGS I DUNNO ABOUT CASSAVETES

Jonathan Lethem

SAM SHAW

John Cassavetes and Gena Rowlands on the set of 'A Woman Under the Influence' (1972)

Two or Three Things I Dunno About Cassavetes

A man and a woman are walking out of a movie theatre. They'd opened the paper that morning and saw that it was playing—a single showing at that run-down, shabby movie theatre where nobody goes. They rushed in and bought tickets, an afternoon show on a weekday. Sat down in those broken seats, the two of them the sole couple in the crowd. Though crowd's not the word for it, the place is empty apart from a few guys sitting by themselves, the type that go to obscure movies in run-down theatres on weekday afternoons. The man and the woman don't care, they're excited, so. Lights go down, movie plays, lights go up. Now they're walking out of the theatre.

They've just watched a movie by John Cassavetes. I'd say it doesn't matter which one, but I know you know I don't mean one of the bad ones we try not to talk about, from near the beginning or near the end of his career or, even, right, the not-great one, that one he wrote and directed and which stars his greatest actress, his wife, but he didn't think much of, nor for that matter, do you. The man and the woman have just watched one of the great ones. You know the movies I mean, the ones that change your life. One you never forget where you were when you saw it first or how it felt to see it, one that made you think *What the hell was that? I need to see that again! Who is this Cassavetes?* No, they watched that one they'd heard so much about—the one about the family, the friends, the siblings, the performers, the one about the man and the woman.

'You okay?' he asks.

'Sure, yeah, I'm fine.'

'Nothing wrong?'

'Nope.'

'Because I couldn't help noticing there was a lot of fidgeting, squirming around in your seat, heavy sighing going on in there. So I was wondering if something was wrong.'

'Okay, sure, but I'm fine, thanks, I'm great.'

'So, wasn't that amazing?'

'I guess so.' She gave a sort of heavy sigh now, if you were watching for that kind of thing, which he was.

'You didn't love it?'

'There were a lot of incredible things in it.'

'Incredible is one word. That movie was all about my life and everything I feel.'

'I was a little impatient.'

'I can't fathom that and I think you were watching it wrong.'

'A lot of it seemed like, I don't know, actor's exercises, these endless frenzied reiterations that don't really go anywhere.'

'It made you uncomfortable.'

'I love you but it made me tired.'

'You resisted it.'

'I love you but I'm sorry, I didn't resist it.'

'Well quit saying you love me because if you don't love that movie you don't love me because I am that movie, that movie is me.'

'You're nothing like that movie.'

'I am inside and if you could see who I really am you would know.'

'Lower your voice.'

'I don't have to.'

'We swore no more yelling on the street.'

'I'M NOT YELLING ON THE STREET I'M JUST TRYING TO UNDERSTAND HOW YOU COULD SAY THAT MOVIE WAS LIKE ACTING EXERCISES! DON'T WALK AWAY!'

'I just can't be around you right now.'

'You don't need to say that please don't say that hey wait come on don't walk so fast—'

'Lady, are you okay?' The guy who says this, a large guy who must have been in the doorway of the restaurant, is upon them so quickly they're both startled and jostle into each other as they halt. The woman pushes herself away from the collision and stumbles for a second, back against a dumpster on the sidewalk and the large guy steps between the man and the woman and puts his hand up like a traffic cop and says again, 'You okay?' The woman just shakes her head, no, yes, keeps walking. Big guy walks with her, rolling his shoulders a little like a boxer in his corner, a kind of warning of physical force for anyone watching from behind. The man stands staring at their departing backs, his arms outstretched though nobody's seeing him—well, maybe loads of people, now that he's bothered to notice that the whole street's full of gawking faces, a couple of homeless people tsk-tsking him—but not the woman or the big guy she's walking with. Those two, they just keep going.

Two or Three Things I Dunno About Cassavetes

I'm writing against resistance here: the feeling I'm about to sully music with language. I've always thought that writing about film, another narrative art, was a hundred times easier than writing about music—but writing about Cassavetes feels harder than writing about music. Writing about Cassavetes feels like vocalese: putting lyrics to passages of jazz improvisation. Though he's as consuming an obsession as I've got, and though my writing happily infiltrates my love of other film-makers (and is infiltrated by my love of film), I've kept Cassavetes set apart.

I'm not religious. I'm a miner, tunnelling through a cultural ore. A happy worker, and one free, I'd imagined, of taboo. Yet in considering Cassavetes my unearthings have opened under my feet. I've plunged into a cavern full of gleaming icons, and when I reach out to touch them, I hesitate: my hands look awfully grubby.

Maybe the man and the woman saw *Faces*. Anyway, I just saw that one again and like the first time I saw it, I can't quit thinking about it. *Faces* is in one sense nothing more than a flash-frozen record of the condition of the marriage of its two main characters, Richard (John Marley) and Maria (Lynn Carlin). The film presents Richard's night out away from home and what Maria does when he's away. In another sense, *Faces* is a voracious ribald mugging of its viewers' defensive assumptions, assumptions about how much a film is allowed to make them feel about men and women and daily life and the expression of passionate impulses in a marriage or in a house or in a nightclub or in America in 1967. It's also a shattering formal essay in compression and explosion, a mix of sensory overload ('I dream of Jeannie with the light brown hair! I dream of Jeannie with the light brown hair! I! Dream! Of! Jeannie! With! The! Light! Brown! Hair!' chanted, sung and bellowed until you wish to scream) and deprivation: deprivation of the ordinary consolations available to an audience here wrenched into bewildered complicity, forced to stumble in the reeling footprints of the seemingly intoxicated performers. *Faces* refuses to consent to the viewer's wish that it at least annoy by giving *too much* or *too little*—it seems intent on annoying by both measures at once.

I've called Richard and Maria the main characters, but there are no minor characters in Cassavetes. Take McCarthy, played by Val Avery. McCarthy's the one who's trying to get over with tender call girl Jeannie (Gena Rowlands) when Richard shows up at her pad. He's the guy who admits to Jeannie that he's bewildered by his own son, a six-foot Dartmouth man in tennis shoes.

If McCarthy's not a minor character, it's partly at the insistence of his own hunger: he desperately regards himself as a player. The guy just wants a night out. Wants something he can't quite put his finger on, nor can we, but it comes in the package of Gena Rowlands. His eyeballs bulging with needs and their denial, his teeth bared in sardonic self-loathing, McCarthy's gonna get what he wants if it kills him, if it would kill him even to name it. In fact, we can see that Jeannie's already halfway promised herself to Richard, that she's readying herself for a rendezvous with Richard even as she wriggles out of McCarthy's grasp.

When McCarthy and Richard face one another it will be with the horror of mutual recognition, a doppelgänger dream out of Poe or Nabokov, two married guys, two businessmen, mirrored even in their acne-scars. (How rare, that facial confession of adolescence, for an actor! How specific that this director chose two pockmarked guys for these parts!) Only their respective styles of broken-hearted swagger distinguish them, only hair-splitting degrees of difference in the hierarchy of the suburban damned.

McCarthy doesn't have any inkling he's not the main point here. No, he's the star of his own show. He's given an episode of such merciless poignancy that any lesser version of this story would be stolen forever, and *Faces* nearly is: in it, McCarthy has blundered his way into Jeannie's boudoir. He and Jeannie have left behind in the living room another couple, who carry on with the insane cavorting that has dominated the film to this point, the rituals of drink and song which seem a barely sufficient stand-in for all human yearning, for sex and conversation, possibly for food and air and water. But McCarthy wants more. He wants contact. And he's granted it, contact and a bit of grace, even. Jeannie embraces him in tender silence as he spills it out: 'Oh, boy, what a life… What have I got after all these years? A big house, a kooky wife, and a kid who wears sneakers. I like you, Jeannie. I want you to like me for myself, I'd like to make love to you and know that you like me for my charm, my wit…'

Jeannie says nothing. Nuzzles him slightly. Her gift of listening is what she's got for him. It'll do, barely. McCarthy has by now gathered that she's not lending him more than an ear, tonight. So, in a 'you can't fire me, I quit!' spasm he wrenches himself out of the sacred moment, back into the living room, back into the drunken whirl—but not before dishevelling his own hair and untucking his shirt to simulate the grope scene he's now ashamed wasn't unfolding behind those closed doors. He's showing off for his buddy and the second girl, pretending he scored, at the small expense of whatever shreds of Jeannie's respect he hasn't already trashed.

McCarthy isn't half done yet. When Richard shows up, McCarthy'll insult him, put him in a headlock, and then forge a wheedling, backslapping, faux-friendship with him even as Jeannie's kicking McCarthy and his friend and the other girl out the door. I'm going to leave McCarthy here, though, where I treasure him most, prepping himself in the mirror on his way out of Jeannie's bedroom, mussing his hair, putting on a boorish jocularity to protect himself from himself, from his confession of sensitivity. If you're like me, you love him. That's the mystery: I don't find I want to push McCarthy any harder than he's pushed himself. I want to console the guy.

Cassavetes mostly wrecks ordinary systems of cinematic identification with his characters. In terms of tone, he refuses to commit to comedy or tragedy, faux-realism or absurdist farce. In terms of technique, he almost completely avoids point-of-view shots, the primary language of alliance between viewer and screen actor. He withholds reassuring cues usually given to characters worthy of our sympathy—the confirming glances of irascible and deferential character actors, the petting of the heads of dogs and babies. At times he even withholds vast realms of pure information: who's married and not, who's whose brother or sister, whether or not someone's a girlfriend or a prostitute, or what the outcome of a fundamentally worrisome event (worksite accident, shooting, one-night stand) might have been. He keeps the viewer on his or her cognitive heels, boxing with a flurry of contradictory material.

Still, Cassavetes creates a cinematic experience impossible to describe except as 'personal', 'emotional', 'indulgent', 'torturous', or 'demanding'. Despite thwarting our sloppy, easily awarded sympathies, nobody's ever slandered the films as 'cold', 'distant', or 'objective'. What Cassavetes has done, really, isn't to wreck identification, but to displace it. Our sympathies are moved from the characters back to ourselves. Well, not really ourselves—more to some unspecified place somewhere in the Bermuda Triangle between ourselves, our customary sense of what film is allowed to do, and Cassavetes's own implied presence as director.

The anecdotes from Cassavetes's sets endlessly underline his own titanic personal presence—his beckoning, cackling, tearful presence behind the lens, often just inches from the astonishing behaviour he'd elicited from his performers. His sound men routinely had to erase his own voice from the soundtracks, where it had intruded as he exhorted and provoked the actors to locate and deliver more of their own essential responses to the material. So, the exhilarating ultimatum Cassavetes presents is to invest so deeply in his own perilously negotiated viewpoint (as witness, catalyst, exorcist, as grumbling parent and conspiratorial sibling to his actors) that we're forced to abandon the maps and protractors we'd not even noticed we ordinarily keep between us and an encounter with a film.

'Conversation!' Nick Longhetti, played by Peter Falk, commands in *A Woman Under the Influence*. 'Weather! Ordinary conversation!' He's howling like an impotent Prospero in the storm of liquefied emotion that is his family's life, begging for a taste of the small talk or pleasantry he imagines will verify the normality—and sustainability—of his domestic arrangement. Earlier, at a spaghetti dinner, he attempts to plug the gap himself with an anecdote, a speech module so inept that it verges on poetry: 'You go for months, you don't see any kids, suddenly you see strollers, kids everywhere. Must be something in the air.'

Nick, against the evidence that his wife Mabel (Gena Rowlands) presents in every vibrant, paradoxical, transitive, absurdly responsive cell of her body, can't accept that life is so fundamentally up for grabs, that one moment tumbles upon the next with no sense of accountability to its predecessor, that every social code is in for constant renegotiation, like the stakes at a poker table where the dealer's called a game of Infinity-Card Draw. But also, Mabel sleeps with other guys. This is, weirdly, one of the least remarked-upon aspects of this much remarked-upon film: Mabel's slept around. We can plunge again and again into the ambiguity of Mabel's and Nick's distress yet somehow flinch (with Cassavetes's consent, since he drastically underplays the revelation) from the brunt of Nick's rage at betrayal. Just when these films have taught us to distrust the obvious, they'll tease us for overlooking it.

But Nick's crazy too. He's screwed it all up, failing to call Mabel and simply tell her he's stuck working all night and will miss their marital 'date' (in preparation for which the kids have been shipped off to his mother-in-law's). Boorish at best, Nick's formed an allergy to soothing speech, an addiction to jolting Mabel with Popeyeish outbursts. We've yearned, as viewers, to leap through the screen and throttle him more times than we can count. So whose side are we on? Those poor kids? Is that how little foothold we've got here?

We resort to Charlie Parker, the blues, jazz, Beatnik poetry, 'If you don't know, man, I just can't tell you,' Miles Davis with his back to the audience (Tom Charity: 'There's a correlation with Bebop here. Like Charlie Parker and Miles Davis, Cassavetes could take a standard tune and turn it inside out...'), Jackson Pollock, Norman Mailer's *White Negro* and the cult of 'Hip', all the restless-in-the-Fifties anti-verbal (even if conveyed verbally) romanticism that can seem in retrospect so mannered and indulgent but was in its moment an act as necessary as a drowning man's thrashing to the surface for a gulp of air. If the word *uptight* had never existed, and the world to which it alludes was unrecorded elsewhere, the fabulous evidence of the many species of *uptighteosity* catalogued in *Faces* alone would make the term a necessary invention of social historians wishing to decipher the consciousness of the middle of America's last century.

Hey, he's film's Bob Dylan, really! I mean it: *Faces* is Cassavetes's 'Like a Rolling Stone'. Both of those artworks make a cascading, exuberant attack on the certainties of the audience. Both consist of a declaration of revulsion, by the authors, of their subjects—Miss Lonely, in the Dylan, and the Forsts, in *Faces*—one which evolves, uncannily, into a declaration of freedom and renewed possibility on those same subjects' devastated behalves. And both were delivered in the spirit of a deliberate formal blasphemy (by use of excessive length and excessive force) against the formats intended, in their day, to contain them. Further, the 'social criticism' which is in a different sense an underlying impulse in both *Faces* and *Shadows*—a social criticism that, as in the more or less contemporaneous art of Richard Yates, Jack Kerouac, Ken Nordine, and The Fugs, was an almost automatic, possibly even perfunctory, artistic response to the American Fifties—was as inessential, ultimately, to Cassavetes's art as 'protest' singing is to Dylan's music.

Both alienated doctrinaire former-supporters like Jonas Mekas (self-appointed guardian of avant-garde film authenticity) and Pete Seeger (self-appointed guardian of protest folk-song authenticity). Both depended on confusing or surprising their artistic collaborators with sudden reassignments to overcome recording mediums that tend to freeze out spontaneity. Even the song that unexpectedly and perfectly closes *Faces*, Charlie Smalls's unself-pitying blues 'Never Felt Like This Before', could be seen as a rough draft of Dylan's indictment in 'Like a Rolling Stone': 'How does it feeuull?' Or in 'Ballad of a Thin Man': 'Because something is happening here, but you don't know what it is, do you, Mister Jones?'

The performance rhythms of the films have gulled people into calling them 'improvisations'. It's impossible not to want to refute this with some of the extensive evidence of Cassavetes's scrupulousness as a writer (one who worked, like Henry James, by the uncommon method of dictation to a secretary). Cassavetes crafted language as exacting and persuasive—and funny—in its musical irrationality, its disguised artifice, as anything by Stephen Dixon, Grace Paley, or Don DeLillo ('What did you eat, Ma? You ate fish at Hamburger Heaven? Why would you do that?'). But however much they're made of wordage, the films evade capture in nets of language like James Brown shrugging off a cape thrown over his shoulders and rushing back to the microphone: 'I'm back! I'm back! Watch me move! Oooh! Ug! Oh, yeah!"

Halfway into *Faces*, exalting Cassavetes as a writer might seem as dubious as exalting James Brown as a lyricist. Try watching with the picture off (I have, I'd like to brag): as a purely acoustic experience, the film's pure gibberish and sing-song—compulsive, unfunny jokes (well, the nightclub comic is kinda funny), distorted repetitive song-fragments, and hideously banal male pecking-order riffs. The meaning is in the faces themselves, and the stances of the bodies as they reel through these hallways, stances of grief and longing the jokes cover and the bodies uncover. On closer inspection, though, the gibberish is pierced, as if electrified, by lines so nakedly the vessels of pure existential pain ('By the way, Jeannie, what do you charge?') ('I want a divorce!') ('I thought you were supposed to be saving my life.') that the characters shouldn't be able to walk or breathe after uttering them, let alone pull the tab on another can of beer and resume their songs.

This is Beckett or Pinter stuff, really. But it arises out of a laboratory of actorly and photographic experimentation, and is filled with homely gestures of hesitation, of embarrassment. So, the craft disguises itself as happenstance disclosure. The artists here have invaded their own privacy, we think, as they invade ours. Hence we either resent them for the intrusion or credit them with some extra-literary force. The same thing that makes it possible for some people to loathe Cassavetes's actors, and, implicitly, the director who has revealed them to us, causes others of us to sentimentally patronize them in our adoration: They're too vulnerable to be acting!

We hesitate to discuss Cassavetes's limitations or even—gasp—his compromises, as though he were some species of animal, a beautiful and tender freak set loose in our brutal human world. We kid ourselves that we're not good enough for him, which becomes a convenient opportunity to refuse to meet him totally. If we can laugh at Orson Welles for his wine commercials and *The Muppet Movie*, why do we wince at mention of Cassavetes's participation in *Big Trouble* or *Whose Life Is It Anyway?* It's as though we hurt Cassavetes by acknowledging that he lived in the world, too. Really, we're seeking safety for ourselves.

We can quarantine the disturbance he provokes in us by thinking it a report from an exotic, who speaks to us through the gates of a preserve given names like 'The Sixties' or 'Bohemia' or 'Cassavetes-land' (Jon Voight: 'Cassavetes is a place.'). At worst, the films can be taken as a childish vote for a 'free-er way of life' as easy to endorse as it is impossible or undesirable to embody.

Then again, what artist have I ever met totally? How did that become my insane standard for this art? *J'accuse*: Cassavetes is complicit here. By advertising his artworks, in interview after interview, as an ongoing act of human exploration, he raised the stakes of their reception to intolerance of anything but utter rejection or devotion. Furthermore, the bastard did so, cleverly, without claiming to have accomplished anything definite: no certainty of the value of the result, only of the project of attempting the result. (Cassavetes: 'We're making a picture about the inner life and nobody really believes that it can be put on the screen, including me, I don't believe it either, but screw it.') The effect resembles the 'nobody allowed but acolytes or heretics' posture of the leader of a cult group (and cults are strengthened by heretics as well as acolytes). Albeit in a much better cause, the films scream *Believe or leave, but don't make me justify myself!* This may just be another way that Cassavetes loaded the stakes. He forced his actors to work without coherent instruction in order to throw them to their own emotional resources. He shot vast amounts of footage, including scenes he probably never intended to use, then edited versions of the films that were five and eight hours long. He withdrew versions of his films that were more 'entertaining', in favour of final cuts that were more ambiguous or confrontational. (Peter Bogdanovich: 'He wanted to be in a struggle.')

It's easy to be dissatisfied by other movies after watching Cassavetes, and easy to invest in the role of adherent who wishes other film-makers had Cassavetes's adamancy, his rigour, his fluency, his generosity. Yet there's a pratfall to be made in imagining all films ought to be like Cassavetes's, or imagining that the films would retain the meaning we cherish without the indifference with which they were originally met by the majority of viewers or potential followers. (In truth I'm often pained to see traces of his influence in the work of other film-makers.) Do I want to live in a world where every songwriter wants to be Bob Dylan, or every story writer to be Raymond Carver or Donald Barthelme (to speak of two different versions of Cassavettian purity— Carver's authenticity through austerity, Barthelme's freedom through silliness)? Thanks but no thanks. These freak-geniuses derive their energy and meaning from their brilliant commitment to excesses that would become limitations in other hands. They, and Cassavetes, need a world of more typical art the way a shadow needs a wall.

As with many people who made art that said the world hurt, the world hurt Cassavetes's art, and that world-hurt invested itself in characters like *The Killing of a Chinese Bookie*'s Cosmo Vitelli and *Opening Night*'s Myrtle Gordon, two people capable of failing to connect or inspire, two people capable of inducing and experiencing disappointment, possibly even boredom. If we're going to give ourselves entirely to Cassavetes's work, we'd better be willing to be disappointed in it, and to disappoint it. Sometimes I want to watch something else.

Though there are no minor characters in the films of John Cassavetes, there are dented souls littering the edges of the stories. Some of these are given unforgettably colourful turns (and names), like Zelmo Swift, the obnoxious, bellowing suitor in *Minnie and Moskowitz* (played by the same Val Avery that incarnated McCarthy, in *Faces*), or Billy Tidroe (played by Leon Wagner), the hapless victim of Mabel's excessive adoration at the spaghetti dinner, the one who can't sing or dance, no matter how much she exhorts him. See those movies twice and Swift and Tidroe become odd tokens of a Cassavetes-connoisseur's pleasure, however badly they've been exiled from the centre. Others are more disturbing. Eddie (Charles Horvath), the American Indian construction worker in *A Woman Under the Influence*, has the misfortune of getting in the middle of Nick Longhetti's bad mood on the construction site the day after Nick has Mabel committed to the booby-hatch. He's sent tumbling down a sandy grade by Nick, whose hand on a guide-rope has been made unsteady by his rage. We learn that in the fall Eddie has broken 'every bone in his body', though when we see him back at work, six months later, he's more or less intact. (How has anyone ever gotten away with calling these films plotless?) You could miss it on first viewing, but there's a whole Eddie-the-Indian movie tucked inside *A Woman Under the Influence*.

Lenny (Leonard P. Geer), in *Love Streams*, might be my candidate for the most subtle of Cassavetes's incidental roadkills. Here, Sarah Lawson (Gena Rowlands again), in a gesture of severely bizarre empathy, buys her brother Robert Harmon (Cassavetes himself) a household menagerie of pets, acquiring them in one swoop from a vendor of fowl, goats and miniature horses. She also buys a dog— Jim the Dog, he's called. Jim's got a caretaker, a human friend named Lenny, and Jim and Lenny are plainly inseparable, the deepest of cross-species friends. We feel no doubt they shouldn't be parted. But Sarah buys Jim the Dog. Suffering a divorce herself, she berefts Lenny of his canine pal. Lenny, like Zelmo, like Billy and Eddie, may stand for Cassavetes's awareness of the sometimes bruising nature of a

Jonathan Lethem

brush with charisma, possibly even his own, however eccentric and well intentioned.

It's no mistake that Cassavetes distrusted himself as an actor. We distrust him, too. The two films that tend to persuade even Cassavetes-sceptics that he's some kind of great director, and which strike devotees (I mean myself) as 'most perfect' or 'least flawed' (and the best entry point for newcomers) are two in which Cassavetes doesn't appear, even for a frame: *Faces* and *A Woman Under the Influence*. The films in which he's got the biggest roles are usually only favourites of those already 'converted' (I mean myself): *Husbands* and *Love Streams*. He always casts himself as, if not a villain, then largely a person of dangerous charm and ungenerous reserve, one who indulges in the feints and masks that other, more heroically Cassavettian characters usually try to see through and strip away. The films are a long war on self-congratulation, and the characters Cassavetes plays are losers, barricaded by guile from what matters most, facing questions they've made themselves too clever or persuasive to answer.

One of the last scripts Cassavetes worked on was provisionally titled *Husbands II*, and questions he never fully answered beat like a pulse in the male characters most easily taken for his stand-ins. Perhaps the purloined letter of Cassavetes's life work is his own terror of loneliness and boredom and superficiality, right there at the locus of so much vitality and inspiration, so much 'being around him was like being in a Cassavetes movie' malarkey. I'm not knocking his marriage. We all adore his marriage. But he spent his days in Los Angeles, and he was The Director. The only actor in a Cassavetes film who doesn't have the privilege of being directed by, disarmed and charmed and embarrassed and transformed by, of being called on his shit by, the direction of John Cassavetes, is John Cassavetes. His character's goodbye-wave at the end of *Love Streams* has been seen as a dying man's farewell to his audience, but that character's isolation in the final shot strikes me as more than a little like Humphrey Bogart's, at the end of *In a Lonely Place* (one of the most Cassavettian films in the classical Hollywood cinema): barred in a prison of his own personality, watching a last chance at life walk out the door. Maybe Cassavetes cast himself as a man of ingenious and tragic masks because he felt like he was getting over.

I'm old friends now with the woman who took me to my first

Two or Three Things I Dunno About Cassavetes

Cassavetes movie, though we were new friends at the time. This was more than ten years ago, when I was about to turn thirty, and my first novel was about to be published. I liked to think of myself as having already completed my basic education in film, and, as a writer-much-influenced-by-film, as having long since assembled my array of primary influences (I still like to think of myself that way. I was so much older then, I'm older than that now.) She was only in her early twenties, but she knew to drag me to see *Faces*, at the Red Vic, on Haight Street in San Francisco. She'd already seen it, and was wordless with excitement. I wanted an explanation in advance, having heard that the Cassavetes films were nothing more than a series of actor's exercises, but she refused to offer one.

It knocked me out, of course. I left the movie theatre wrestling with what seemed to me then to be an overwhelming insight, though from this vantage it appears to be not much more than the first level of resistance peeling away from what would become my consuming obsession with Cassavetes's films: that life had been revealed to be so much more like a series of actor's exercises than I'd ever understood before. This epiphany seemed to me profound enough that I knew I would have to change my life, or at least my art, to account for it.

It was sometime in this period that the same woman broke up with her boyfriend and, in the process, made an obscure gesture in which I became faintly implicated: she took his television and VCR hostage and hid them in my apartment. I remember using them to watch Preston Sturges's *Unfaithfully Yours* (another Cassavettian film, come to think of it). Presently the woman and her ex-boyfriend reached an accord, on terms unknown to me, and she collected the television and VCR and returned them to him.

When, a few months later, my first novel was published, she wanted me to know how excited she was for me. So she told me a story: she'd seen my novel for sale in a bookstore, also on Haight Street, one of the few places that was carrying the book. I asked if she'd read it. No, she explained. In her excitement for me she'd attempted to shoplift it—had gotten it into her purse, and gotten herself halfway out the door—and then been caught, reprimanded, and let go. Now she was ashamed to go back to the bookstore. She left it at that, but she knew—and I knew she knew I knew—it was the most flattering story she could tell me. □

Over 100 authors
from the 4 corners of the world.

October 20-30, 2004
Toronto, Canada

Focus on Danish literature as part of
SUPERDANISH: Newfangled ~~Danish~~ Culture

For more information on all our programs
and to subscribe to our free email newsletter visit

www.readings.org

INTERNATIONAL FESTIVAL OF **AUTHORS**
⊙ **Harbourfront centre**

LITTLE DURGA
Shampa Banerjee

Durga looking for her kittens

The story of Satyajit Ray's struggle to make one of the world's best-loved films, *Pather Panchali*, is well known: his commitment, his lack of funds, the shooting that started and stopped, his belief that India could be depicted a new way, though he had never made a film before. He took his story—and that of the other two films in what became the *Apu* trilogy—from a novel of the same name by a fellow Bengali, Bibhuti Bhushan Bandyopadhyay, which describes the travails of a poor Brahmin family in rural Bengal. The title means 'Song of the Road'. Apu is the family's only son and the hero of the story. He has an older sister, Durga, and for a few weeks of my life I was her.

I don't know when I first met Satyajit Ray. I have faint and unreliable memories of him climbing the stairs to our home in Calcutta, of him standing tall and cramped in a public bus. He was my father's friend, Manik *kaka* (Uncle Manik) to me.

I remember, Manik *kaka* didn't approve of my 'formal' name (like all Bengalis, I have two, the second one kept for the family), and I secretly agreed with him. I liked the sound of my other name, Runki—my mother had found it in one of her childhood stories, the name of a river that existed only in the writer's imagination. I was Runki in the credits of *Pather Panchali*.

I was five and a half when my first shot was taken in the village of Boral. I don't suppose I was expected to remember anything at all of what followed. Yet I do, probably because it was all so extraordinary, so unexpected, that even a child could comprehend its significance.

I was going to the local kindergarten, and none of my friends there had ever had anything to do with shooting a film. I must have felt important. My mother was a stage actress, but only on the 'amateur' stage, as part of the Indian People's Theatre Association, a progressive national cultural group which drew many talents from all parts of the country. So I knew something about the world of make-believe. Acting in films, however, was not quite respectable for the Bengali middle class. But for my father's persuasion, my mother would have remained in obscurity. With the family's active support, my gentle, quiet, beautiful mother became Sarbojaya, Durga's and Apu's mother in *Pather Panchali*, a stern and unyielding guardian of her children's well-being in a poor and struggling rural household. I believe the transformation survived as a duality within her, or maybe it dredged up the strength and pride she would otherwise have kept hidden.

I was a city child and it was thrilling to travel to a village with a group of grown-ups. We went by taxi, an ancient Dodge (I think), with deep, worn seats and lots of leg space, and driven by a Sikh, Bachan Singh. With his turban and beard, he seemed to me a man of great resolution, as he bravely left his familiar city behind to tumble and toss his way across the broken road that took us into Boral. I usually stood in the back, comfortably wedged between my mother's knees and the back of the driver's seat. Manik *kaka*, with his long legs, sat in front.

This was the early 1950s, when India was young and the heart of rural Bengal only a step away from the crowded, sinful city of Calcutta. A village like Boral was still not unlike the Nishchindipur of the film—set fifty years before. It nestled among rice fields, fruit orchards and fish ponds, where it was periodically ravaged by malaria, droughts and monsoon rains, and held together by the invisible bonds of a small feudal community.

Bansi *kaka*, Bansi Chandra Gupta, the art director, had rebuilt an old, abandoned home as a film set in the most ingenious way. The kitchen, which stood apart from the main house, was strangest of all. Its walls were so very thin. I tapped on them and got a very odd sound, nothing like a solid wall at all. But it seemed real enough, with the earthy smell of mud and the rough, sweeping, circular lines where the mud was smoothed over with cow dung.

Subrata *kaka*, Subrata Mitra, was the cameraman, with large hands, long fingers, and nails yellowed with nicotine. There was a familiar smell of his hands, whenever he held his little black light meter near me, which he did often enough, as natural lighting was what they depended on most of the time.

No one wore any make-up. But we women had to wear our nose studs. I looked forward to Bansi *kaka* bringing out his little collection of stones—mine was the bluest of blue—and the heady smell of Durofix as we stuck them on our noses.

Other than the blue stone, my only costume was a small sari, made of rough handloom material, which my grandmother had bought for me from a rural bazaar during one of our yearly visits to my great-uncle in Bihar. My hair was clipped short mercilessly each day before shooting—for 'continuity'—at the Jai Hind Saloon, just down the road from our Calcutta home.

I was horribly shy of Manik *kaka*, this tall, commanding presence with his thick wavy hair and deep grainy voice. He seemed incredibly romantic to me, even though I was five. If he talked to me, I would curl up and try to hide my face. Not surprisingly, the only dialogue I have in my two reels of the film is one shrill cry: 'Aunty!'

My mother always said that Manik *kaka* had a way with children. He would whisper to them and they would do whatever he wanted for his films. I don't think I remember ever seeing him actually playing with children. But I know he didn't treat me like a child when he asked me to do something. And if I couldn't do it, he would find another way.

When little Durga was supposed to watch hungrily as Aunty Indir enjoyed her morning meal—balls of rice kneaded to a mash with her gnarled hands—Manik *kaka* wouldn't let Mother give me my lunch (rice and buttery mashed potatoes) on time. She kept complaining as the day wore on, and we all kept waiting, I thought, for the light again. By the time the shot was taken, Mother was convinced I was dying of hunger. As for me, I remember being more disappointed by the fact that I couldn't do what Manik *kaka* asked me to do. 'Can you gulp?' he asked, and gulped himself, bobbing his Adam's apple up and down. I tried, but it was a pathetic attempt, more a plain swallow. 'All right,' he said, 'just keep staring at Aunty's right hand as she eats, follow its movement, up to her mouth and down to the bowl again. Can you do that?'

He also gave me a length of silver thread to wind and unwind around my finger—not a purposeful activity in itself, but it made me feel less of a fool, while I stared at food—food for the camera—that I knew was quite unpalatable in reality. There were long waits during this shot. Bored, I started tapping my foot against the wall. When they were finally ready for the shot, I immediately controlled my errant foot, but Manik *kaka* had noticed the movement. 'Go on,' he said, 'don't stop.' I can't remember whether that little detail stayed in the final version. But I remember my surprise at his noticing something so trivial.

I don't know how much I understood of what he was trying to do, but I picked up an enormous amount of basic information, not all that easy for my age. I understood the long waits we had for the light to be just right. We also had these large sheets of silver and gold foil wrapped on frames to use as reflectors. 'Silence!' Manik *kaka* would shout each time the shooting began again, and the clapperboard would come out of nowhere for a second to clamp its jaws sharply shut like a baby crocodile. When it was my turn to visit Sarbojaya's labour room with Aunty Indir and smile at the baby Apu, I found, instead of my mother and a real (but borrowed) baby, only the cameraman struggling with his heavy equipment. That was what I had to smile at. It was somehow only a little eccentric. I knew we were all acting in a film.

On another day I was led to a big earthen water jar filled with straw, with its bottom knocked out to make a large hole. It lay on its side. On the other side of the hole was Subrata *kaka* peering through his camera. 'Put your hand into the mouth of the jar and smile,' said Manik *kaka*. Could there be anything more absurd? Much later, when I saw the film, I realized that in that shot little Durga was actually looking for her kittens in the jar.

I was blissfully unaware of the struggles and heartaches of the two years that Ray had to wait to complete the film. But once it was released in 1955, the film took over our lives.

In Calcutta, *Pather Panchali* appealed to the intellectual and the ordinary alike. Grandmother took our daily help, Sajani *didi*, to see the film. Sajani *didi* came from a remote village in West Bengal where, the only surviving child in the family, she had been married to a guava tree—a ruse to prolong her life. When I knew her she was pretty and dark and living with a boring older man in a neighbourhood slum. The world of *Pather Panchali* was much more familiar to her. She loved the film. The jury at Cannes also loved the film and gave it the prize for 'the best human document'.

It was exciting to go from one reception to another. At one of them the guest speaker crashed through the floor of the makeshift stage right in the middle of his speech. Each time they would show the film after the speeches, and although we knew it by heart, we laughed and cried with the audience. Foreign delegations came and went, red-nosed, bleary-eyed, patting me on the head and giving Mother silent, unaccustomed hugs of appreciation. Nothing like this had ever happened before in India, nor ever will again. This was

Ray's great first film, which changed Indian cinema for all time and gave the world a new insight into my country.

As for the people who were there when it all began, the film controlled us. It's difficult to describe the intensity of something that now seems merely amusing—the acute embarrassment in my awkward growing years, of fingers that pointed, voices that spoke in whispers: 'That's Durga, you know, from *Pather Panchali.*' Things didn't change much with time; Bengalis like to cling to their institutions. And just to make matters worse, there were two Durgas and I also had to explain, 'No, I'm not the girl who dies in the film. She was the older version of me.'

I was the less memorable one. I groaned inwardly when anybody mentioned *Pather Panchali* and my small part in it. I still do.   □

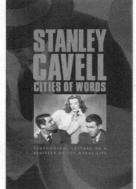

TWO YEARS IN
THE DARK
Andrew O'Hagan

Two Years in the Dark

I've been homesick all my life: I felt homesick growing up and I feel the same way now, not unhappy, not aggrieved, but never entirely at home either, not as people are in the world of *Meet Me in St Louis* or *The Lavender Hill Mob*. If being congenitally homesick is a modern condition then it's one that the cinema might have been invented to address. But I don't suppose the condition is very modern: Homer and Plato were always looking for an ideal home.

Nationalism couldn't do it, not for me. I had this teacher once who liked to wear a tartan tie; he marked me down for saying that patriotism was just another kind of gangsterism. 'And what gang do you belong to?' he asked.

'The cinema-goers,' I said.

The teacher took mints to ease his eternally sore throat. 'Then you're on your own, sonny Jim,' he growled. 'Watching movies is a homeless activity and it never fed a family or won a war.'

My father wasn't always at home, but when he was he felt homesick too and he sought to pacify himself watching the films that came on television. I couldn't avoid the feeling he watched them as a way of living yet another life, and later I felt he used them to give shape to a notion of his own childhood. It was in his nature to stress his disadvantages, so films starring the Dead End Kids, or luckless and likeable young men just keen to get their hands on some dough, met with a very subjective-seeming approval from my father's armchair, when he was there to fill it. He spoke of James Cagney as if Cagney was somebody he knew personally and could trust to stay the same. He liked films where the characters came from rough backgrounds, because he did; he liked films where tough men were impatient with women, because he was. My mother, on the other hand, liked sad films, ones in which people never got to be with the right person, and she spoke of certain actors 'playing a good part', or of famous films that were 'as old as tea'. I think she felt it was all right occasionally to suffer if people more glamorous suffered too: that was the beauty of sad films and the promise they made to you.

My mother told me people used to mistake her for Kim Novak. She said there was a man once who came to her house—she was fifteen, he was a saxophone player, and they called him The Man in the White Suit, after the Ealing comedy of that name—but she was waiting for my father to finish his National Service and she stopped seeing the man. Years later, whenever the film came on television I would look over and smile at my mother. She would smile back, understanding in an instant that movies and real life have secret things to do with one another and that only the hard-hearted could fail to see it that way. When everybody else was gone my mother and I would sit together watching old films, the smell of peeled oranges hanging over the room; me on the carpet in overwashed pyjamas, sitting cross-legged, aged ten, saying there was something very evil about *The Birds*.

It was beguiling to live in a country, Scotland, that didn't look enough like itself to be a location for its own movies. We watched *Brigadoon* and didn't recognize a blade of grass; we watched *Greyfriars Bobby* and reasoned that Edinburgh must be the capital of Disneyland. I remember consulting a film book and discovering that Arthur Freed decided to shoot *Brigadoon* in Hollywood because nowhere in Scotland looked Scottish enough. That was pleasing to my sense of place, but I knew the matter angered other people, those who objected to the way imaginations could create insults when unloosed from their responsibility to honour reality. It seemed to me that a beautiful, artistic line had been drawn, a permissive line along the ether: 'Reality is not what it is,' wrote the poet Wallace Stevens. 'It consists of the many realities which it can be made into.'

'Films are disruptive of what matters in a country,' said my English teacher in the tartan tie, 'for people live and breathe here and pay their taxes.' Mr Campbell was losing hope: he touched his glasses with a nicotined finger and scowled like Lee Marvin in *The Man Who Shot Liberty Valance*.

I wasn't always so annoying as a child, but I did have an advanced sense of the importance of torturing teachers, so I handed him a piece of paper ripped from a jotter. The paper featured a stripe of words copied out by me in forbidden green ink—more Wallace Stevens: 'You can imagine people accustomed to potatoes studying apples with the idea that unless the apples somehow contain potatoes they are unreasonable.'

Campbell poked me with the finger. 'You will end up in the loony bin, sonny Jim,' he said. 'You will. Or I will.'

Movies are a kind of poetry. I felt that very strongly watching *Jaws* the only time my father took me to the pictures. The poetry was my father being so frightened, the lemonade warm, the cinema dark like a place in the mind, Dockhead Street and the town outside abandoned to blown-about litter, and the people in their rows swaying as one body into the action on screen. But the movie itself was poetry too. The town of Amity gearing up for the Fourth of July; the town's mayor rejecting all calls to close the beach after the first shark attack; the police chief being slapped by the black-clad mother of a boy who died; and later, the three hunters stranded in the middle of the sea on their broken vessel, singing 'Show Me the Way to Go Home', and the shark returning to get them with our hearts in its mouth.

The greatest Scottish film-maker was Bill Douglas. His imagination worked differently from Steven Spielberg's—more like Satyajit Ray's, or Jean Vigo's—and it seemed second nature to him to make reality at the same time more than it was and more like itself. I got to know him before I was twenty, and his patience appealed to me; he seemed to have terrific values as a film-maker, and was an artist even when doing nothing more exacting than boiling the kettle for a cup of tea. He was born in a former mining village called Newcraighall, outside Edinburgh, a place he would commemorate in a trio of short films about his childhood, little miracles of memory, light, and argument. He lived most of his life in London and I went to see him when his cancer was bad, in a tiny flat up a lane in Soho. The flat was dark and the walls were hugged all round with cinema books—Chaplin, Mae West, Orson Welles, Truffaut. Next to the books were dozens of machines and boxes, early cinema artefacts: magic lantern slides, zoetropes, diorama, shadow-shows, objects that seemed as if they'd just come out of the hands of the Lumière Brothers.

I asked him what cinema needed now.

'You mean film-makers?' he said.

'Yes.'

'They need funding,' he said. 'And better critics. You can't make films for an audience of one. Things are rough outside and talent needs looking after.'

In 2000, the *Daily Telegraph* invited me to become their film critic. I thought the offer was timely, and could imagine a happy symbiosis between watching actors for part of the week and spending the rest of it working on a novel about performance and celebrity, so I said yes. There began my two years in the dark.

Critics are sometimes said to be as good as their period, and I'd like to be able to say that I took up my position during a great flowering of world cinema, that my term coincided with the weekly emergence of celluloid wonders guaranteed to set the old prose dancing like Nijinsky, but that was slightly more than far from the case. I have considered the matter quite closely—incorporating a recognition of every manner of deficiency, including my own—and still I have to conclude that I wrote about film during a period so fundamentally morose for the form that it makes me shudder to think about it. When I look back on my weekly diet of movies I almost pass out with misrecognition. Did I really sit down with a notepad and high hopes for so many of those films?

People employed to write about film are like cinema punters in one respect: in a time of deluge they will cling to anything buoyant that passes their way. It took me about two weeks, however, to realize that this reviewing stint would offer no golden period for me, no time like the 1940s or the 1970s, when great work was being produced by young and developing talent or by great directors approaching their zenith—a time that might automatically bring zip and moral purpose to the weekly effort of writing a column. Not a chance. Even Graham Greene's time reviewing films for *Night & Day* in the 1930s—watching Shirley Temple in *Wee Willie Winkie*—represented a period of Renaissance splendour next to the schlock I was seeing. A better critic must certainly have the talent to shrug in the face of inanity and make merry at its expense, but I found myself half zonked by the nonsense we watched, and I saw myself hunting for excuses, seeking regular comfort in the almost-good, and fearing all the while that the experience could end up ruining my love of the movies, my belief in their grandeur and my hopes for their hospitality. True love can bear no trespasses, and by the end I felt embedded in the trenches of Golden Square, watching life's spectacular dream of excellence grow stale and dull.

Stepping into a viewing theatre in Soho, or anywhere else, is like going into a private ward at an NHS hospital: people come and go with their white early-morning faces, imbibing fancy coffees while reluctantly switching off their mobile phones, waiting for the curtains to be drawn and the new life to begin. Most of the film critics had long since forgotten that this was the best job in the world: some grandstanded, some half slept. The majority just quietly lived in fear that someone might come and sit next to them. There were few friendships and even fewer smirks: most of the national newspaper critics lower themselves into their seats of a Monday morning in the manner of a greatly egotistical pianist sitting down to play the *Goldberg Variations*, and laughing (even at a comedy) could seem the lonely practice of spoiled novelists and famous visitors from the BBC's *Newsnight Review*, people who didn't see all the week's releases but who popped in for a look at some predetermined Film of the Week.

Their general morbidity made me dislike the national press screenings, so I'd often go in the evenings instead to screenings for film distributors and cinema staff, people who didn't think they'd be annihilating their critical integrity if they laughed at a gag or let out a sigh. Naturally, there were exceptions to this behaviour among the big critics: Philip French of the *Observer*, and maybe two others. Philip has been going to those screening rooms for over thirty years. He is a good enough writer not to waste his time swatting fly-by-night colleagues; he has seen hundreds come and go, some very promising, some hopeless, some lasting years, and others only weeks, like Richard Williams, the *Guardian* writer who first followed the veteran Derek Malcolm, and who found those screenings almost immediately unbearable.

'Philip,' I'd whisper, leaning over the chair. 'Who's that old actress with the deck of cards?' Philip would incline his head back a smidgeon and stick a mental jotting in your top pocket.

'K-K-Katy Jurado,' he'd say. 'She was the maneater in *High Noon*. Lovely actress. A bullfighter, you know.'

But that kind of niceness didn't come with the popcorn. The late Alexander Walker of the *Evening Standard* was a rather dyspeptic old bird, a flossy-haired, disappointed-seeming man who would peck the projectionists out of their nests if the movie began a minute later than advertised. He had a handsome connection with his readers, which is no small thing, but he seemed to hold his entire profession in low regard, mumbling about friends in higher places and giving out very wastefully on his pages about the government's funding of British film.

Andrew O'Hagan

Generally speaking, and despite the horrors, it is only on very special occasions that movies manage to be as depressing as the publicity material deployed to promote them. The film's tag line could have been written by Nora Ephron—'What Do You Give the Man Who Has Everything To Lose?'—but the production notes are routinely written by, as it were, Sasha and Rupert, two ambitious young people recently arrived in Soho with appalling spelling and bridges to burn. Film publicity people stand at the very point where the film industry's free-falling anxiety comes thudding into the earth: millions of dollars down the line, the final, defining effort is thought to lie with them, and they become desperate to deliver good reviews to their bosses. Of course, hit movies don't require good press to be successful, but the people who make movies care about not being dismissed as moneymakers, and smaller movies which need a push are often dead without the critics. You would see it on a human level: the publicity officers ringing you up to ask you what you thought of the movie.

'Oh, Sasha. Please don't ask me that.'
'Everybody is really excited about this film.'
'I'm sure.'
'Oh come on. You won't say how good you thought it was?'
'Nope.'
'Any chance of making it Film of the Week?'

Packs of publicists would haul you to screenings in a diamond-encrusted sleigh if they surmised a film was about to be ignored or demoted, but it's a sorry life, and they would get their revenge, turning haughty as soon as they had a sure-fire hit on their hands. 'What's your name again? No can do. You missed the screening? I'm sorry. I just can't do anything for you. What paper do you write for again? All the evening screenings are packed, I'm afraid. It's a masterpiece. Everybody wants to see it. Wait a minute: there's a screening tomorrow night at the Scarborough Film Festival I can squeeze you into.' That was their afternoon of glory and revenge; the next week, of course, they'd be back on the phone offering you back-rubs, saying they'd never worked on anything so powerfully moving as *Teen Pants 6*.

I didn't forget my belief in film poetry. I only felt it routinely return to a subterranean place after the first ten minutes of every film we watched, and some days I felt the ghost of Bill Douglas leaning over the proceedings, saying, 'It's tough outside. You have to look after talent.' When people made terrible movies I'd try to remember the great difficulties involved, the economics of the thing, the good intentions and even the hunger for art that must have existed at the beginning of so many of those projects. How did it go wrong? I wondered about charisma, nationality, storytelling, nostalgia: what rich failures made those movies turn out so bad, and what cultural moment were we living through that made the badness so familiar?

Orthodoxy may be the grave of invention, but it is also the mainspring of profit. Nearly every film I saw in the year 2000 was a version of something else—a previously successful movie, a best-selling book, or formulas that studios had been working to death since the days of D. W. Griffith. *Angela's Ashes* enlarged to infinity one's understanding of the word trite. Fifteen minutes into *Joan of Arc* I was calling out for the firelighters. *Stigmata* constituted an excellent advertisement for the short-term benefits of self-harm. *Bicentennial Man* made me wonder if Robin Williams had lost the power of speech. And all this in a single fortnight, a couple of weeks that would have been immeasurably improved by the box-office success of Michael Winterbottom's *Wonderland*, also released. We all liked that film, we all gave it the top spot, but not many people went to see it, though cinemas are said to be taking more money than ever before.

As the months passed the screenings became slightly painful to me. I started waking up in the middle of the night and sneaking downstairs in search of class acts: Charlie Chaplin in *The Great Dictator*, Ray Liotta in *Goodfellas*, Marilyn Monroe in *Bus Stop*, Tom Courtenay in *Billy Liar*, Richard Dreyfuss in *Close Encounters of the Third Kind*. Those nights on the sofa would turn me into myself again, restoring my capacity for wonder. I'd get up in the morning remembering my favourite lines about film (Ernst Lubitsch: 'The job of the director is to suggest two plus two. Let the viewer say four.' Stanley Kubrick: 'Bad films gave me the courage to try making a movie') and everything would be great up until about five minutes into a screening of *Kevin and Perry Go Large*, when I'd realize, once again, that no loss can be more painful than the loss of one's illusions.

Film critics can be urbane or passionate, but they can seldom be both, unless they're Pauline Kael. I admire the way some writers are married to their tone, finessing the world's troubles away with sweet jokes and winning cracks whilst allowing nothing to make them angry, as if getting angry would constitute a mortifying dive into bad taste. But nothing ever changes as a result of that kind of reviewing: its entertainingness, in fact, depends on the idea that the writer is agnostic about cinema and its darker purpose, and that the critic's job is not to call for change but to regard things merely as they are. There's no right or wrong about this, there's only style, and it wouldn't do if every film critic was André Bazin and every film the occasion for philosophical broadsides of the untickled kind.

Well, I got angry now and again. It's in the genes. I just wasn't invariably in the mood for another round of Have Fun With Culture; too many of the films were obnoxious, though even I, looking back, can see that one is not always required to use a flame-thrower to swat a fly, especially if the fly is Russell Crowe. Maybe I'm too young in the head and haven't spent enough time in Los Angeles or psychoanalysis, but I think it's quite important sometimes to hate things, not be amused by them, or loftily tolerant of them, but to want to cut off their oxygen supply and mash them into the ground, thereafter to plant something lovely in their place. I don't know that I lose my reason, but I do sometimes lose my temper. And the sameness of the terrible films just bugged me. Maybe a bad novel is just quieter, a bad gallery hanging almost private, while terrible movies starring Russell Crowe seem to come bounding towards you from every space in the culture, leaving you no choice but to reach quickly for the elephant gun and fire. It's hard to be truly urbane when there's a stampede on, and grace under pressure, as even Hemingway understood when being stoned by the subjects of his articles in the *Kansas City Star*, is not the only priority when trying to take the lid off a story. Fight fire with fire, I say, but also be grateful for those like Dilys Powell or Anthony Lane, the imperturbables, who have made it their business to thread green carnations down the muzzles of the cynical.

Over two years of reviewing I watched some patterns emerge: The Richard Curtis Film, for instance, doused in confetti and lifestyle philosophy, offering bad writing and stammering actors in low-octane settings. Then came the new British gangster films, which weren't sub-*Get Carter* so much as sub-*Lock, Stock and Two Smoking Barrels*, with red-faced characters rumbling around the lanes of Essex dropping their aitches and letting off shotguns. At one point there seemed to be several of these a week, before they were replaced with a rash of British films about freckle-faced lads from Tyne and Wear who couldn't afford to buy football boots. For reasons not very close to my heart, the badness of these films was more upsetting than the badness of *Nutty Professor II*, which managed to be undistinguished in a way that didn't really matter at all. I had thought I didn't mind if British films were no good—the way the French seem not to mind that their rock music is no good, or the way Scottish people seem not to mind being hopeless at cricket—but I found in the end that I did mind, and that my column was becoming a resignation letter in weekly instalments. One week, when a new print of Ken Loach's *Kes* was released, I gave it the premier spot and the headline said MOVIE OF THE WEEK. MADE IN 1969.

The editors at the *Telegraph* never flinched; they ran what I wrote without altering my views or questioning my sanity, though one of them nearly faxed herself to the moon when I praised Michael Haneke's *The Piano Teacher*, a film about female masochism starring Isabelle Huppert and set in Vienna. But the editors never noticed, as the letter writers did, the extent to which my experiment in column-writing was becoming a *cri de coeur*. The process of seeing so many bad films was vexing: it made me begin to agree with my old teacher with the tartan tie, asking myself why anyone would make movies when they could be building houses. That's a sort of death that is, but I did think it several times, watching some toothy actor bow-wow to his colleagues in an American golfing charade called *The Legend of Bagger Vance*.

Reading the letters that came to my office was teaching me that people could be patriotic about films as much as about anything else, and many readers felt emotionally entangled with the cinema's current releases. I found my readership to be lively and intelligent, and my editors insisted the column was popular, but, as usual with newspapers, the letters that arrived tended to be from people more emotional and more political than the average punter. That was fair enough, but it told me my judgements were pricking the skin of many readers, as though my commentary on the life suggested by modern film was also a secret and hurtful commentary on their own choices and their own values.

I liked *American Beauty* for its quirky acting, maybe its photography. However, what I didn't like was something that critics didn't reveal—its smug, nasty slagging-off of marriage, heterosexuality, conventionality. Its maker is out-gay David Geffen. I'm fed up of going to the flicks and having left-wing, liberal, feminist, anti-Christian messages forced through my ears into my brain.
A reader from Warwickshire

I'm not ancient, I'm fifty-five, but I've been around long enough to see some wonderful films and I have been a film fan since I was six years old when apparently my favourite film of the year was Jean Renoir's *The River* which still holds a place in my affections. I'm no killjoy, I can cope with a bit of sex and violence on screen if the plot merits it and I have nothing against computer generated images when they work.
A reader from Somerset

How on earth can you praise the film *U-571*? Historically, *U-571* is a LIE. Incredibly, this seems just fine by you. Andrew O'Hagan where o where is your sense of British patriotism? Your lost grandfather must be spinning in his briny grave. Mark this well: if we are stupid enough to accept this rubbish then we can certainly expect to be fed further such tosh.
A reader from Kent

As for Mr Lindsay Anderson, in the early 50s I had the misfortune to work in some cutting rooms where he was also editing one of his own films. His banging on about the British Film Industry then was on the same lines as the remarks you quoted in your article, along with a lot more leftist propaganda. As for his films, could you please tell me which were box-office successes—let alone pleased the average audience. I have seen four, and each time the cinema was nearly empty.
A reader from Bedford

I am fifteen years old and I hope you don't disregard this letter
because of my age but I want to comment on your article about
Pearl Harbor. I don't know what audience you were watching this
film with but it certainly wasn't the same as mine. At the end of
the film when I turned to the person I went with and we discussed
how much better it was than we were expecting we saw an old
woman who was left in her seat with tears in her eyes.
A reader from Devon

My readers wanted films that confirmed their sense of what they
knew, films that didn't set out, however entertainingly, to interrogate
their sense of moral reality, but rather—like popular paperbacks
about the inner life of blokes—to offer a light-hearted, tear-jerking
reassurance, and to rub balm on our modern quandaries. The toy
world of Richard Curtis featured a London as real as the Scotland
of *Brigadoon*, only more insipid, less artful in the deployment of
comforting lies. I'm sure I tried to like some of those films, and in
a way I admired my readers' certainties: it seemed no accident to me
that most of the letters I received came from a place called the Home
Counties, for most of their authors truly believed in the firmness of
the ground they stood on, and they dearly loved to be entertained
by films which said 'it was ever thus'. Any love letters I received were
written in green ink of course, by mad people, like the person I was
at the age of ten.

M ost of all I hated the Cannes Film Festival, and I almost had
to be dragged there in an iron mask. By way of
encouragement, one of the feral publicists told me the actor Tim Roth
wanted to kill me, while another one, altogether sunnier I feel, told
me Ralph Fiennes wanted me to run for prime minister. Cannes is
the publicists' Valhalla: for fourteen days their hysteria is allowed to
run your existence, and life by the opal sea is a run of heavily policed
red ropes and graded passes. I decided to ignore all that, and get
drunk from first thing in the morning until late at night, accepting
the occasional invitation to nearly drown at the prow of some
producer's yacht. I found a bar I really liked, far from the Croisette
and its horde of shouting distributors, and I sat there reading a
paperback and looking at the water. Whatever time was left I spent

in the dark watching over-touted movies—the pick of the Nepalese Underground, the latest Dogme, an unutterable event starring the moany pop group All Saints—and the columns I filed were like exasperated haikus. One time, after about a week of hiding in the bar and the cinema, I came to a lunch at the Hôtel du Cap where liposuctioned people were diving off the rocks. I was unusually happy for Cannes: I'd just filed a loving review of *Moulin Rouge*, I'd had a few shots at the bar, I was wearing a brand new linen suit, the actor Jared Leto was sitting at the table managing not to sound very thick, and I was on my way to winning a bet with a movie mogul about the winner of the Palme d'Or. (I never win anything, but I knew the French would love Björk warbling her way to the gallows in *Dancer in the Dark*.)

When it started raining the hotel guests complained to the manager, and I began smirking into cloud-forms of pastis, dreaming of Dorothy Parker, wishing the Côte d'Azur could be attacked by a swarm of killer bees.

I couldn't take Cannes seriously, and it couldn't take me seriously either, which proved to be an added bonus. I supported the films I found that were good, but I kept out of the press conferences, politely refusing all calls to write giant features saying such-and-such was the new *Citizen Kane*. Most things were the new something, mind you: but not that. The film industry is full of people who fear they might not have a job next week, and that plays havoc with their sense of proportion. They all turn up at Cannes in the sweetness of May, lovesick for their own product, but altering where they alteration find, and many go home with a very different feeling about the stuff they brought over. One film company's success is another one's failure; somebody doing well in one quarter means that somebody must get fired in another. It's a horrible world really, packed with fear and lying and delirium. But by far the most delirious of them all, to my mind, is Miramax, the company owned by two brothers who look like they only leave horses' heads in the beds of the people they care about.

Miramax spend so much promoting their movies—securing attention, baiting for Oscars—that it shocks them when they discover pipsqueaks unwilling to play. But I found the company meretricious to an inordinate degree. During my two years writing about film, it was their output that I found most consistently objectionable, partly because the company is so pretentious, acting as if they are saving world cinema from collapse and upholding great quality, when in actual fact their bigger movies are just bloated with a familiar Hollywood cretinism. I was going along quite merrily with my dislike of them when suddenly all my bemusement turned unbenign: I just couldn't live with the terribleness of their films any more. They seemed so spiritless and decayed, so painfully absolute in their cynicism, that I knew I would have to pack in the job because of my feeling about them. I even started bringing the company into my reviews of non-Miramax movies, referring, via the perfectly charming film *Amélie*, to Miramax as 'the film company now in charge of "European cinema", with the likes of *Chocolat* ("French"), *Captain Corelli's Mandolin* ("Greek"), and *Life Is Beautiful* ("Italian").'

I'm not at all interested in being 'scathing' about people's work, but sometimes, when the subject matters to you, the choice is either to speak up or compound the problem. So I stand by my anger in relation to these films, which were presented at the time as if French, Greek and Italian cinema had never existed. There was indeed something unnatural about the badness of *Captain Corelli's Mandolin* in particular, something which opened up a new seam of cultural stupidity, and I felt that nobody was seeing it, nobody was thinking. Miramax had tried to sell these as art-movies, as something very much opposed to the mushy entertainments around them, and while people were buying into that fallacy a notion of true quality was being degraded. That's what I felt. Miramax had, from time to time, supported genuinely good movies, so why was their big money now going into the perpetration of brainless Frenchified crimes like *Chocolat*? When the hoopla was on, it could seem that all the magic of cinema had become a trick, and *The Shipping News* brought me out in hives for the last time:

> Movies are all about illusion, and the greatest illusion of them all is the illusion of quality. This is Miramax's stock-in-trade. It takes stories that seem a bit classy—*Captain Corelli's Mandolin*, *Shakespeare in Love*, *Chocolat*—and turns them into cultureless pap, affected little movies which are grand in their own way, and which win Oscars, but which are actually meritless escapades fine-

191

tuned to dupe the public. Miramax has given the world a host of clichés about European culture—naughty French priests, macho Greeks, hoity-toity Englishmen, zany Italians—and has reduced human complexity to a bunch of hopeless stereotypes bursting with sentiment. Yuck. I hate Miramax. It is the cinematic equivalent of coffee-table books and slim cuisine: full of big type and hidden sugars, but popular with those who want a taste of culture with a minimum of effort.

The public relations professionals had been pushed too far. Why were they being mugged on a regular basis by this pest who refused to come to lunch? What was eating him? Who was he anyhow? An icy lady from the Miramax office called my editor and asked if the *Daily Telegraph* had a problem with Miramax, 'or was it just him?'

'Him,' said my editor, Sarah Crompton. Then she defended me, saying I had every right to my opinion, and no Miramax did not have an automatic right to reply to reviews. People were free to dislike their movies and free to say so.

I was rung later that day by a British director who said she had been asked to sign a letter in support of Miramax for publication in the *Daily Telegraph*. Another person then rang to ask me if I'd come on the *Today* programme to discuss my 'criticisms of Miramax in the light of what they argue they have done for the British film industry'.

'To discuss what?' I said.

'Well, they are furious. They say the British film industry would be lost without them.' I said I would happily come on the programme to discuss the films only. I had written as a film critic, and not as an economic analyst. It was irrelevant to my case what the Weinsteins had done for British industry.

'But that is their argument.'

'They're entitled to it,' I said, 'but I'm only willing to discuss the state of the actual films themselves, not the business surrounding them.' It seemed obvious to me: if somebody doesn't like your book, there's no point in going on the radio to tell everyone what you're doing to keep people in jobs in the publishing industry. You defend your art, if that's what you're inclined to do, otherwise you take it on the chin and shush.

SAVE UP TO £50!

Each quarterly issue of *Granta* features a rich variety of stories, in fiction, memoir, reportage and photography—often collected under a theme, like those shown overleaf. Each issue is produced as a high-quality paperback book, because writing this good deserves nothing less. Subscribers get *Granta* delivered to them at home, at a substantial discount. Why not join them? Or give a subscription to a friend, relative or colleague. (Or, given these low prices, do both!)

GRANTA 'ESSENTIAL READING.'

OBSERVER

ORDER FORM

I'D LIKE TO SUBSCRIBE FOR MYSELF FOR:
- ○ 1 year (4 issues) at just £26.95   £13 saving
- ○ 2 years (8 issues) at just £50   £30 saving
- ○ 3 years (12 issues) at just £70   £50 saving

START SUBSCRIPTION WITH ○ this issue ○ next issue

I'D LIKE TO GIVE A SUBSCRIPTION FOR:
- ○ 1 year (4 issues) at just £26.95
- ○ 2 years (8 issues) at just £50
- ○ 3 years (12 issues) at just £70

START SUBSCRIPTION WITH ○ this issue ○ next issue

MY DETAILS (please supply even if ordering a gift): Mr/Ms/Mrs/Miss

Country   Postcode

GIFT RECIPIENT'S DETAILS (if applicable): Mr/Ms/Mrs/Miss

Country   Postcode

04FBG86

TOTAL* £_____ paid by ○ £ cheque enclosed (to 'Granta') ○ Visa/Mastercard/AmEx:

card no: __ __ __ __ __ __ __ __ __ __ __ __ __ __ __ __

expires: __ __ / __ __   signature:

* POSTAGE. The prices stated include UK postage. For the rest of Europe, please add £8 (per year). For the rest of the world, please add £15 (per year). DATA PROTECTION. Please tick here if you do not want to receive occasional mailings from compatible publishers. ○

➡ **POST** ('Freepost' in the UK) to: Granta, 'Freepost', 2/3 Hanover Yard, Noel Road, London N1 8BR. **PHONE/FAX:** In the UK: FreeCall 0500 004 033 (phone & fax); outside the UK: tel 44 (0)20 7704 9776, fax 44 (0)20 7704 0474 **EMAIL:** subs@granta.com

The next day, a letter duly appeared in the *Telegraph*, written by the British film producer Stephen Woolley:

Andrew O'Hagan signed off as film critic with the *Telegraph* in a most dramatic way by attacking Miramax for making predominantly chocolate box movies, an accusation both grossly misinformed and misleading. Any American studio is destined to have patchy output and cyclical years. Their diversity does embrace lavish drama, *Shakespeare in Love*, *Chocolat*, *Life is Beautiful* etc.

But in addition their horror genre, Dimension, covers movies like *From Dusk to Dawn* and the highly successful *Scream* series. They have scored hits with comedies, and more heavyweight dramas like *The Talented Mr Ripley*. They co-produced Larry Clark's *Kids*, our own *Trainspotting*, Todd Haynes's *Velvet Goldmine*, Quentin Tarantino's *Pulp Fiction* and the recently released *In the Bedroom*. They are currently involved in producing Scorsese's epic *Gangs of New York* and continue to take risks with cutting-edge filmmakers who have somehow escaped O'Hagan's notice. Like Alexander Walker's one-man campaign against state funding of British films, O'Hagan's article reveals once again, not how meritless Miramax Films may be but sadly how our film critics are generally confused, myopically naive and simply ignorant when it comes to matters of film production and finance.

The letters editor sniffed a fight and asked me to respond. I said we should just leave the last word with Mr Woolley. His letter was his letter, it made some good points, and I'm sure he had a dozen good reasons for writing it.

Fiction writers create worlds in which different shapes can be reconciled—apples and potatoes—and the imagination is liable to conduct its own conversation with reality. But that is less true of life, where reality makes firm demands and where the imagination is often curtailed—sometimes by parents, sometimes by governments, sometimes by critics, and always by economics. In that sense modern cinema is closer to life, following a cult of the familiar, and the novel begins to appear like a shimmering mirage in the heat of the desert. Given the way I started, with my teachers and their teachings, I never

Andrew O'Hagan

thought I'd come to argue one day for the subtleties of cultural nationalism. But that indeed is what my argument with Miramax amounted to: I regarded them as totalizers, American businessmen who too often deal in rendering cultures banal and foreign, who prettify and flatten and make exotic a Europe whose traditions and languages they don't understand but merely find useful. Something weird and unaccountable had happened to people's values along the way. An imaginative British film producer thought you couldn't set out to criticize the art of modern film without showing an understanding of the vagaries of 'film production and finance'. That is where we had come to. That is what had happened.

So there I was, resigning, sending my snobbery back to the place where it had started. My day was done: I'd exhausted myself and learned to hate the movies. I haven't said much about the films I liked, but there wouldn't be much point as very few of them lasted in my affections. Over those two years I saw only two truly great films: *Ratcatcher*, directed by Lynne Ramsay, which hardly anybody went to see, and *Lord of the Rings*, directed by Peter Jackson, which nobody missed. I didn't step inside a cinema again for six months.

The cinema near the town I grew up in was called The Regal. It was beautiful, grand, and was owned by Harry Kemp, a man with well-combed hair who walked through Saltcoats with an aesthete's florid complexion. He was a small-town impresario, Sergei Diaghilev in a Glasgow overcoat, dry-cleaned, camel-coloured, and he brought movies to the people as if he were delivering the prints straight from his friends in Hollywood itself. I thought of him the night I returned to the cinema as a punter, in Montreal, during a book festival that took place in an ice storm. The cinema was a multiplex serving cartons of Sprite the size of Lake Ontario, but when the lights dimmed it was just like The Regal, a venue filled with the ghosts of laughter and surprise. Before journeying into the film I quickly glanced at the seat beside me, recalling a father's fear of sharks and his son's tireless amazement at the ways of the depicted world. □

"IF YOU L♥VE FILM, YOU MUST JOIN"
Quentin Tarantino

The National Film Theatre offers the richest and widest range of films screened anywhere in the UK. Join today and receive:

• 1 free film ticket
• £1 off all tickets (excluding The Times *bfi* London Film Festival)
• Advance priority booking and monthly programme booklet
• Discounts and offers on a range of film-related products

Annual membership is just £24 (£15 Concessions)
To join call 020 7815 1374 or visit www.bfi.org.uk/nft

bfi ●NFT   NATIONAL FILM THEATRE SOUTH BANK LONDON SE1
www.bfi.org.uk/nft

NOTICE-BOARD

NATIONAL POETRY COMPETITION

National Poetry Competition 2004

THE POETRY SOCIETY

First prize £5,000, second prize £1,000, third prize £500 plus ten commendations of £50.

Judges: Ciaran Carson, Elaine Feinstein, Simon Smith, Denis MacShane.

Entry fee £5 for first entry, £3 for subsequent entries. Free second entry for members of the Poetry Society

Closing date: 31 October 2004

To enter please visit www.poetrysociety.org.uk or send an A5 SAE to PoetrySociety (NPC0402), 22 Betterton Street, London WC2H 9BX

THE SOCIETY OF AUTHORS

The Society of Authors Grants

The Society is offering grants to published authors who need funding to assist in the writing of their next book. Writers of fiction, non-fiction and poetry may apply. The grants are provided by the Authors' Foundation and the K. Blundell Trust.

Closing date: 30 September 2004

Full details from:

website: www.societyofauthors.org
email: info@societyofauthors.org

or send an SAE to The Awards Secretary, The Society of Authors, 84 Drayton Gardens, London SW10 9SB.

CITY UNIVERSITY LONDON

CITY City University London SHORT FILM COURSES

City University offers a wide range of short evening courses for **film enthusiasts, film makers** and **writers**. Courses can be studied over one, two or three terms and are taught by professionals.

• **Film enthusiasts** can take courses that discuss the art and production of film, from the early silents to contemporary realism.

• **Film makers** can make a short film in 16mm or digital format, as well as learning about working in the film, documentary and television industries.

• **Writers** can take courses that include writing for film, television, theatre and radio.

For a prospectus containing details of all these courses, ring the Department of Continuing Education on 020 7040 8259 or view the website at: www.city.ac.uk/conted/cfa.htm

To enrol for a course, ring 020 7040 8259 or enrol online via the website.

STAY UP LATE
Jim Lewis

It was an April Sunday, and Los Angeles was trapped in a heatwave that had descended a fortnight previously and refused to lift, drying up lawns in the Valley and sending weekenders to the beaches south of town. Half reclining in the back seat of a hired car on her way in from the airport, Ruth had seen them all passing her in the opposite direction, a steady flow of slow-moving traffic, and she'd glanced down at the overcoat that she'd worn to the airport in New York, a simple reminder that she was somewhere else, she wasn't home, and it was hot outside. She was in town for just a day or two, to meet with a man about money. There was a documentary series for public television that she hoped to have underwritten, and the man—his name was Willard Altschul—was a consultant for a corporation that might or might not be willing.

The car pulled into a hidden drive above a bend in Sunset Boulevard, dropped her off and disappeared, leaving her to gaze at the tropical trees and bougainvillea growing luxuriantly over the grounds. The Blue Star: what a strange hotel, she thought. What a strange way to spend a spell, in this quiet, terraced compound. Her secretary had picked the place, because she'd read an article about it in a fashion magazine—a glamorous stayover, they said, for the style trade from New York, and movie stars who no longer lived in the city. Why not? Ruth had thought. Why not a real hotel, for once, rather than one of those bland, grey blocks they build for business travellers? A real hotel.

She checked in, unpacked and took a short nap, waking just as the sun was setting. She took dinner in her room, and then she set out, wandering through the empty halls and down to the lobby, which was silent but for the slight sound of the warm breeze through the open windows. If this is Hollywood, she thought, it isn't so much. Maybe it's only by being entirely gone that they can get the movies made. And who had they left the city to? Nobody. Nobody at all. She walked out to the pool and sat in one of the deckchairs, watching the steam rise and hover a few inches above the water; she passed no one on the way. Coming back through the lobby it had been the same: she knew that she was surrounded by guests just like herself, people conducting business, talking to friends on the telephone, watching television; but something about the layout of the half lit halls, the dark grey carpet, the darkness of the recessed casements, made it possible to believe that the building was abandoned, and that the occasional sounds she heard, a muffled thump or a soft murmuring, were not evidence of paying customers like herself, but merely the building's own wheezing and popping, the faint, helpless noises it made in its restless dotage.

The desolation of the place left her disorientated. When the elevator stopped of its own accord on the fifth floor, she got out and started into the hallway, and the doors shut and the thing was gone before she remembered that she was staying in room 608. She sighed and stood there for a few moments, and then started for the stairs at the far end. Down the darkling hall she went, and halfway along she heard music ghosting through the walls. It grew louder as she continued, until she came to a door; behind it a stereo was playing some odd kind of rock music. Well, it wasn't rock...the lower half loped along, a rhythm that was clearly meant for dancing, but not any dance that she could do. There were some horns repeating, trumpeting as if they were announcing an endless entry into heaven; and beneath, behind it all, she heard a child giggling. She stopped to listen. A little girl, a delightful sound. It ended. Was it on the record? No, she heard a motion behind the door, and then the giggling continued, running up beneath the trumpets; but there was never anything spoken, nor anyone else's laughter, just that solitary gladness, alone in the room with the music. For some time Ruth stood there, listening at the door, until she heard the elevator bell ring, and she quickly turned and hurried to the stairwell before anyone could come down the hall and discover her.

Early Monday morning she called to confirm her meeting with Altschul, but the secretary who answered the phone told her that he'd cancelled his appointments for the day, and wouldn't be available. Cancelled everything? said Ruth. But I came out here from New York. I had a meeting set up.

Yes, I'm sorry, said the other woman, all sympathy and reassurance. I can try and reschedule you for tomorrow.

Tomorrow... said Ruth. She had a plane ticket back for tomorrow evening, and she was worried that she wouldn't have time to make the flight. Could you do that? she asked. As early in the morning as possible?

Jim Lewis

The secretary agreed.

All right then, said Ruth. Thank you very much.

Later, she read the newspaper over breakfast in the garden; on the front page, below the fold, there was a story about a scandal breaking within a circle of Southern California banks, some pension funds making their way from here to there—here where they were supposed to be, there where they weren't. She read carelessly until she came across Altschul's name. He was not indicted himself, but some other members of his firm had been, and he'd been subpoenaed to give a deposition. So he had disappeared behind a screen of lawyers, not hiding but thinking, and getting ready to testify. Who knew how long it would be before she could see him?

She called her office: Oh, you might as well stay, said the head of programming. There's nothing going on back here.

Martin and I have plans for Wednesday night, she said.

Can't you call him, and tell him you won't be able to make it?

I suppose so, said Ruth.

Good, said the head of programming. Good. I'll give Altschul a call myself, and see if I can flush him out. All right?

Yes, all right, she said resignedly.

She got a new line and called Martin at his office, quickly explained her predicament and gently apologized.

Nothing to be sorry about, he said with his usual cheerfulness. I'll just reschedule dinner with the Loudons: you stay and get done what you have to get done. He laughed. I guess you're going to have a little vacation, he said. You could probably use it. Enjoy yourself.

She wanted to enjoy herself, she wanted to try, but she didn't know where to begin. It had been years since she'd driven a car, she wasn't even sure if her licence was still valid. Now she was stranded in the hotel, and she felt a little uneasy about it. This was no city for a woman like her. She believed that time kept stopping and starting again; she worried that she wouldn't feel a thing.

That first afternoon she stopped in the lobby and asked the concierge where she could find a bookstore, and he'd told her there was one up on Sunset—but too far to walk. She hadn't believed him, she thought it was just one of those things about Los Angeles, that no one walks. So she left the hotel and started out, past the empty

200

coffee shops, past the other hotels, the apartment buildings, and the comedy clubs, which were boarded up, as if there was really no point in laughing—as if it might be a terrible thing to do, amidst all that daylight. She walked and a while went by. The cars passed, burning under the burning sun. She contemplated turning back, but rejected the idea: what did she have to go back to, anyway? And she really wanted something to read, something to keep her company.

Another block, and another. The concierge had given her some landmarks to look out for, but they didn't appear, or else she'd passed them without seeing them. It was as if she wasn't really in a city at all, but somewhere else, that wasn't quite nature either: a planet without scale or distance, the sunlit surface of a commercial moon, where everything was advertised but nothing was sold. She was supposed to come to a billboard advertising a local radio station on the south side of the street, and there it was: but it was smaller than she'd expected from his description, and she thought that was the north side. Wasn't it? Which way was north? The ocean was west: which way was the ocean?

She pressed on, and sure enough, there suddenly was the store, just past a bend in Sunset, exactly where she'd been told it would be. Inside, the room was bright by the front plate glass windows, and quickly dimmed as it extended back. Here and there a clerk slipped darkly down a canyon of books, always moving away from her, like a shade surprised out of its sanctuary and fleeing back into another, safer dusk. She moved drowsily towards the back of the store, assuming that Hollywood booksellers kept their literature hidden; instead she found herself in the midst of the film section, and it was surprisingly small and serious, almost scholarly, with only a few piles of paperbound fan books on a table in front of the shelves. It was not a subject that meant much to her, but she glanced at the books for a moment: here were biographies of old film stars, a few volumes of genre celebration, the collected advice of a newspaper critic. On the corner there was a large, squarish book on a child actress, apparently a star, although Ruth had never heard of her. Gazing out from the cover was the girl herself, dressed in an old-fashioned, lacy dress, standing stiffly and smiling sweetly. She had long brown curly hair and large brown eyes, and features rare and fine: a beautiful creature, and Ruth had to admire her for it.

Somewhere in the girl's expression there was a strange sophistication, a hint that the girl knew something that other children her own age couldn't possibly understand: not sex or even celebrity—any child might have a sense of those things—but money. *Abigail Orton: The Briefest Fire* read the title.

In the photograph the child was slight and luminous, a divine thing in the making but still too young; so it was the divinity to come that intrigued her followers, the producers, the directors, the audience. When had Ruth been that young and small? Hadn't there been a year or two when she'd had a similar command? Not quite so powerful, and nothing she could use at the time, but a period nonetheless, when the whole pink world was hers. She thought about it and she was touched. Well, wasn't she supposed to be touched? Without really thinking about it, she reached down to rest her hand on the book's cover, maybe to open it, if she could find a reason to.

Just then there arose in her chest a certain sudden trembling, a jacking that she wrote off as the hormonal fluttering of her heart in its sixth decade: it wasn't the first time. Her face flushed, and she stood as still as she could while the sensation went by, as if a small hot wind had simply passed through her on its way to join the heatwave outside. She put her hands down on the table to steady herself, but again there was that whipping in her heart, her age itself briefly radiating. She was trying to think. The book was back on the table, and she was leaving the store, carrying something she had bought and blinking in the bright sunshine outside, chiding herself for having forgotten her sunglasses at the hotel.

That evening she went down to the restaurant off the lobby, but the room was crowded, and so noisy she couldn't make herself heard to the maître d'. She asked him for a table for one, and he cocked his head with a questioning look. For a long moment she stood there, staring across the tables, with all those boys and girls so well turned out for something. She hadn't seen so many people since she'd arrived, and she couldn't figure out where they'd all come from. The maître d' touched her arm to get her attention, and she broke out of her daze. Nothing, never mind, she gestured with her hand, and then she passed back out into the soft warm breeze along Sunset.

Back in her room she ordered up a meal from the kitchen, and then searched her bag, discovering in its bottom a novel, the one she'd somehow purchased at the bookstore that afternoon. It was a strange story in a strange style, the monologue of a married man driving drunkenly to meet his mistress—but once she'd begun it she didn't want to stop, and she picked at her food and turned through its pages, long after the night had begun at her window, long after the traffic below was stilled, until she reached a point halfway in the book, where she stopped, laid it down, and lowered herself into a bewildered, dreamless sleep.

The next day she decided to take lunch by the pool, and there she lay, reading a magazine and wondering why the hotel, otherwise so careful, offered such weak coffee. She was stretched out on her back, half blind in the sun as the minutes drifted by. She didn't hear, and then she heard, the little girl standing beside her.

Without introduction the child spoke. What's the name of this hotel? she said.

Ruth was startled but she answered automatically. The Blue Star.

The what?

The Blue Star, said Ruth.

But that isn't what they used to call it, said the girl, not defiantly, but with genuine puzzlement.

What did they use to call it? Ruth sat up.

Something else, said the girl. I'm not sure: Garden Something, or Something Gardens.

There was a moment of silence while they both contemplated gardens. I'm sorry, said Ruth. I don't know. Maybe you can ask someone who works here; they might know. Did she glow by day, the child? She had long, thin legs, dark hair, and pale, pale skin, almost translucent, so that it seemed tinged with a very faint blue from the arteries below. Her eyes were huge and brown, and already she had high cheekbones, already a lush mouth, so recently become wide that she hadn't yet learned how to control it, and her lips helplessly expressed little moments of emotion. The girl nodded with the kind of deference that only those who have a gift for solicitude can muster, and Ruth felt a momentary need to reach out and touch her. Instead she put her hands in her lap and held them there. It was only then, in the hesitation, that she realized the child was Abigail

Orton—it had to be—her features were too distinctive to mistake, and her air, her attitude, was perfectly self-controlled, a theatricality of the really-real. The girl stood motionless against the sun and stared. Finally she spoke again, as if making conversation was an easy favour she was glad to perform for her elders. I like your suit, she said, glancing down at the black one-piece.

Thank you, said Ruth. My daughter gave it to me a few years ago. I think this is the first chance I've had to wear it.

Oh, do you have a little girl? Abigail asked.

She's not little any more. She's all grown up now. Her name is Jane... She thought of Janey; she should call her.

Is she here?

No, she lives in Houston.

Oh, okay. So she's still here. The girl looked relieved.

No... said Ruth. Some hobbled bar was crippling the beat of reason.

Oh, okay, said the child again, and she looked down for a moment and furrowed her brow conscientiously, as if she was trying to memorize a short fact. I'm sorry, she said. But I think you'll see her again. Ruth gave her a puzzled look, and the child responded by making a face to show she was chastising herself.

It's all right, said Ruth gently.

The girl began again. Are you here on business?

Well, I was supposed to be, said Ruth. I was going to meet with a man, but... She gestured at the vapours of her purpose, and then dropped her hand. Why are you here?

I'm all done, said the child. So I have nowhere I have to be right now. So I'm here.

You don't want to go home?

Oh, no. Not any more. She reached up and twisted one of the curls of her hair in her pale, slender fingers. Is it fun, what you do?

It's all right, said Ruth. Most of the time. Sometimes I wish I was doing something else. But, you know... She didn't know whether or not she should talk to the girl as she would talk to a grown woman, so she wavered wildly, now speaking in a near sing-song, now lapsing into a knowing tone. And you? Do you like... She thought it would be unseemly to mention the movies out loud, so she settled for hanging the sentence on a shared understanding.

Oh, yes, said the child, suddenly grasping on to the kind of bright enthusiasm she might have used for a television interview. It's the most fun, really. I get to stay up late, and everyone's so nice, and they all work very hard, which is good, because it makes me work hard. There wasn't a moment of pain or boredom in her eyes, really it was extraordinary, how she projected belief and swept all unease away.

So what do you do now? asked Ruth.

I just wait. What do you do now?

Ruth shrugged. Right now, I'm going to have a glass of lemonade. Do you want to join me?

The child stood perfectly still, thinking. Finally, she said, My mother doesn't like me to be out in the sun.

Ruth was startled, showed it, and immediately wished she hadn't. Your mother? was the first thing she could think to say. Well, that was silly—as if famous girls didn't have mothers, but descended fully formed from the empyrean. Is she here?

She's near here, said the child. She's waiting over there, but she's watching. She says I have to be careful of my skin.

I have some... Ruth reached down into the bag beside her and withdrew a tube of sunblock. Do you want to put some of this on?

The girl started to reach for it and then stopped. Maybe I should go inside and get my jacket, she said. Just, in my room.

Ruth nodded, and the child started away, walking gracefully across the deck and down the path towards the hotel. An hour passed, the afternoon got up on its hind legs and stared across the city, but Abigail didn't return.

Later, Ruth stopped a room service waiter who was passing her in the hall with a silver tray on his shoulder, upon which were arranged four identical glasses of orange juice. Excuse me, she said to him. Can you tell me what the name of this hotel was? I mean, before it was the Blue Star.

The waiter shrugged as well as he could beneath his burden. Oh, yeah. I don't know, he said with the politest inexpertise. I know it was called something else a long time ago, when they first built it, in the Twenties. You can ask the concierge. He might know. And if he doesn't, there's a book about us, about this place, they sell them behind the front desk.

But there was no one behind the desk at the moment, and instead of waiting Ruth went back to her room and lay on her bed. Dressed only in a loose, thigh-length shirt, she was nonetheless damp from a perspiration that no air-conditioning could cure. She tried to read, but the type was obscured, now and again, by the half transparent image of a girl child, who appeared and vanished in luminous sections: from cheek to shoulder, from waist to wrist; and later, in her fitful sleep, in a dream too persistent to be pleasant, but too benign to be a nightmare, she heard the sound of the girl behind the door, laughing and laughing.

The next day Altschul's office called. I'm very sorry, said the secretary. Mr Altschul asked me to ask you if we could reschedule your meeting. He isn't going to be able to make it.

Can I speak to him? Ruth said quickly. Even on the phone?

I'm afraid he isn't taking any calls right now. He did say that he'll get back to you as soon as he can.

He's not in?

The secretary hesitated... He's in, but he's not taking any calls.

In a moment Ruth was angry; she held the receiver tightly and felt a word catching in her throat. Oh, come on, she said, to say something; but her tone was high and tight, controlled to compensate for her lack of control. I'm staying here at the Blue Star, I'm waiting to see him. I know he's...occupied right now, but... And here she realized that she had said as much as she could, and there was nothing more.

I know, said the secretary. This has been difficult for a lot of people.

—I don't care what it's been for other people, said Ruth, her voice quickly rising towards a temperamental panic, a madness that sounded familiar, though never as an emanation from herself. It was, she suddenly realized, the bootless complaint of an old woman, and it was so strange and terrible to hear that she instantly hung up the receiver and sat down. To calm herself she took a deep breath, but she found herself holding it until her lungs trembled, and then letting it go in a burst.

Some months earlier she had been to see her doctor. She really thought she was losing her mind. That couldn't be the way it was supposed to go; she felt like a turtle on its back. But her doctor had said that there was nothing especially wrong with her, it was just the way things worked when it was your time. He had offered her pills to replace the hormones, but she'd spent some time reading up on the therapy and finally she'd refused. It wasn't a matter of risks and benefits; she just wanted to pass into her final maturity with as much dignity as she could, and not try to remedy what age endorsed. Now she wondered if she shouldn't take the drugs, after all: was this dignity? To be losing control during a business call? Across the room she could see her reflection in a mirror above the dresser, the room light and grand between. With her hair cut fashionably short and her clothes well tailored, she wasn't so old. She didn't look that far gone. Funny, to be lucky with time. It should have been worth something more.

Well, she had her daughter, she wouldn't have traded that for all the world. And she had a man she loved; that was something. After her husband had died she'd spent so much time alone that she'd begun to wonder if one man wasn't all you got. Then she met Martin—just like that, at a party to celebrate the inauguration of a new season of classical music on television. He was handsome and charming and she liked him at once; three years had passed, and she loved him.

He wanted to marry her. She'd been bewildered when he brought it up. It was so unexpected, it hadn't even occurred to her. And did she want to marry? Again? No, never, no. Did she need a man? No, but yes, she wanted this one, she wanted his company, she liked to hear him talk, she liked the way he slept, how his hand moved unconsciously to her hip, what noise he made dreaming. She found it hard to imagine living with a man again, and marrying was the last thing she wanted to think about, but if it was important to him, she would think about it.

After lunch that day she called him. I'm still here, she reassured him. How are things there?

Just fine, he said. Going along as always. He hesitated. —I had a chance to make a small fortune for Cosima Hoffmann. A contract with the San Francisco Opera, and a record deal, the whole everything. I was going to make ten per cent of a small fortune for myself. His voice tensed slightly, and then relaxed again. But at the last minute she turned it down.

Why? asked Ruth.

I don't know, he said. She didn't like the weather in Northern California. She didn't think the money was enough. The truth is, as we all know, that she has an old girlfriend living there, and she refuses to sing in the same city.

I'm sorry, she said.

I'm sorry, too, he replied. We're not going to be able to get to Greece, then. Not this summer, anyway. Maybe in the fall.

I don't care, she said.

Okay, he said softly. But anyway how are you? What are you doing out there?

Nothing. Waiting and waiting for this ridiculous man to finish giving his depositions and grant me an audience.

Nothing glamorous? No movie stars? No one, nothing Hollywood?

No, she said. Just me, catching up on some reading and killing time.

All right, he said. I wish you were here, I'm waiting for you. I love you.

I love you too, she said, and the affirmation made her smile, even as she said goodbye and hung up the phone. But she wondered afterwards why she hadn't told him about Abigail Orton, why she kept it a secret from him, what she wanted to save, for herself and this child.

She turned on the television, set the volume down low, and calculated the time zones, the distance in hours between herself and her daughter in Houston. Janey was twenty-three, only twenty-three, living in Texas and married to a lawyer almost a decade older than she was. As a child she'd been at once wilful and self-enclosed, as if her own world was sufficient. So of course she'd done exactly as she wanted, and of course it was a conservative thing, marrying a man who only had a small portion of her imagination. It had all happened so quickly: one day she was in college, and the next she was in love. Ruth wondered if it was because the girl had lost her father at such an early age.

She'd come late to love, herself; and then there were a dozen fine years of marriage; and then leukaemia came and killed him very quickly. He used to suck on the tip of his index finger when he was thinking, a habit that Janey had picked up at the age of five, and had carried with her, unto the next generation. It comforted Ruth to think that something was always saved.

The line was ringing. —Hello? said Janey.

It's me, it's your Mom.

Oh, Mom. Hi. I was just thinking about you.

Are you busy?

No, no, Janey said hurriedly. It's almost evening, you know. I'm not doing anything. I'm just sitting in back, looking out at the yard...at the, there are these black squirrels.

But you're good? You're okay?

Sure, yeah. It's good to hear your voice.

How's Richard?

Richard is okay. He's still at the office, actually, working on something. I don't know what. She hesitated. Well, a mother knew.

What's wrong?

Nothing really, Janey said, and fell silent.

Well... said Ruth. To press or not to press. I worry about you, she said—which was not quite true, for no young woman ever needed less fussing over. But it seemed, all the same, to be the right thing to say.

Oh, there's nothing to worry about, said Janey, and Ruth could hear her frown. —Then there was a knock on the door.

Just a moment, said Ruth into the receiver. —Who is it? she called across the room.

Housekeeping, came the reply.

Where are you? said Janey.

In a hotel in Los Angeles. I'm supposed to be having a meeting with this man. But...

The door was open, the maid had stepped halfway into the room, paused, and was regarding Ruth with a questioning look. Ruth raised one finger. Hang on a second, she said to Janey, but by then her daughter had her own distraction, her front doorbell ringing at the same time, 2,000 miles away.

Mom, she said. Someone's at the door here. Can I call you back?

Of course, said Ruth. Whenever you have time, and she hung up the phone without realizing that Janey didn't have her number.

Towards evening she went to take a shower. The setting sun was bright in the bathroom, she looked at herself frankly. In her teens and twenties she'd sometimes gone without a bra, though her mother had warned her that a woman built as she was couldn't afford to allow her body to fall too far, too soon. That was the word she had used, fall, and at the time Ruth had imagined her breasts swaying down by her knees, a comical, cartoonish picture that she'd never quite been able to get out of her mind. And here she was—she gave herself a small smile—and it had happened. Well, not that far. She thought about Abigail Orton, waiting on one side of the age of fertility, while she was passing through the other side. It seemed to her somehow pleasing that they were alike in that regard, however temporarily; it was a state they shared, this freedom from, this exile from the red thing.

Now it was almost night, and she turned on the television, looking for something worldly to watch. But there was nothing but laughter; there was no news, even on the news channel, only this and that entertainment. Still, the screen was bright and the sound was soothing, and in time she was sedated. She got up and walked out on to the balcony, bearing her little daze, and stood there watching the sun settle on the horizon, all the way down by Santa Monica. The heat from the day had become trapped in the concrete of the roads and buildings; now it was being released in dark waves that settled between the soft draughts of the ocean breeze. There was a police helicopter hovering in the southern sky, doing nothing. M-I-A-S-M-A. Not a word she often thought of.

She heard Abigail Orton's name coming from the television inside—thought she heard it, barely heard it, and she hurried back into the room. But by then it was too late; the segment was over, she caught the last two or three syllables, which meant nothing to her, and the final flash of an old photograph; and then they cut back to the host of whatever show it was. She spent a few moments trying to read his expression, hoping that she could infer the tone of the story. He was...serious? respectful? He was talking about something else entirely, now, and she couldn't tell.

The next time she saw the girl, she imagined, she'd mention it. I saw you on television. I *saw* you. I saw *you*. No, she couldn't do that. It would be better to be direct and friendly, without fawning—

to treat her as the child she surely was, rather than the tiny idol everyone took her to be. That would win her, wouldn't it?

The next day passed...the next. Each morning she would call Altschul; each time she made it only as far as his secretary. Then she would call her home office in New York, and they would tell her to stay, stay as long as it would take. She had to stay...the matter had to be settled. By eleven in the morning she would be sitting in the lobby, reading a newspaper, while around her the hotel staff slipped, on their way to wherever. From time to time she would find herself waiting for Abigail to reappear; but the girl never showed. Had she checked out? Gone on to another set, to another interview?

Then one evening Ruth was standing by the front desk, waiting for the clerk to return from whatever obscure task he was conducting in the room behind, so that she could ask him for some extra ice and another washcloth. There was a stirring by the door to the garden, and a procession of adults emerged from the gloom: three men in light loose suits, two women in tight, expensive dresses. None of them uttered a word, and they seemed to be protecting some smaller object of utmost worth, a glowing thing which they had almost entirely surrounded. They moved across the lobby, and for a moment Ruth glimpsed the girl, Abigail, walking steadfastly forward with no expression on her face but that of her beatitude. One of the women must be the child's mother, thought Ruth, and she studied them as they passed to see which one of them it might be. But neither woman seemed to fit the role; one was dark-skinned, Hispanic, where the child was so fair, and the other was a little bit too young, only in her mid-twenties herself. She hadn't had time to look at the men's faces, but she watched them as they moved away from her on the dark, carpeted floor, and she noticed that none of them seemed to be touching the child, as the parent of a ten-year-old would occasionally touch her, or be about to touch her; none rested a hand on her, none reached for her. It was as if the little girl—now completely hidden again—was some powerful and self-contained personage, who received nothing from those around her, but gave and gave. The group reached the elevator and one of the women pressed the call button. In a moment the door opened and they went inside. But as they turned and waited for the door to shut again, they parted

211

slightly, and there stood Abigail. She raised her eyes, and gave Ruth a startlingly frank look, her face open, curious, lit with a show-and-tell genius. You are lovely and you are forgiven, the look said, and then she disappeared behind the bodies of her entourage, who stared out at nothing until the elevator doors closed again.

It was late at night and Ruth woke from restive dreams to sheets wet with her own sweat, an intolerable mirror of her condition. She wondered how hot the moon might be. She couldn't get back to sleep; she couldn't stop thinking and she wasn't at ease. She rose and went into the next room, and sat on the couch with her book, but the book wouldn't be read. She deserved a drink. In the room again, she started to open the minibar, looking for a vodka—but she thought better of it, dressed quickly in light pants and a T-shirt, and headed downstairs to the lobby, asking the Asian woman on duty at the front desk to have someone from room service bring her a double vodka tonic, out by the pool, and put it on her tab.

The water was blue in the black night, there was the faint suspiring of traffic coming up from Sunset, not a sound, but a sense. The pool glowed from the lights below, as if below was beyond. So much trouble, she thought. The water was lapping, the water was sipping, singing sweetly. In time there were two empty glasses on the table beside her, one more on the ground beneath her chair. She had a glass in her hand; overhead the starless sky was turning imperceptibly.

Honey, she said to Abigail, who was standing quietly on the other side of the pool, barefoot and still, her fantastic ivory face shimmering in a glaze of reflected light. It's really very, very late, isn't it? You should be in bed. You need to sleep, we all need to sleep. But...I need to sleep too, but I can't.

I have to go, said the child.

I know, that's just what I was saying— Oh. Do you mean you're leaving?

The girl nodded silently.

I'm so sorry, said Ruth. I really enjoyed meeting you... She paused, unsure of how much affection the child would be able to believe. I like you, she said at last, and felt a certain satisfaction for having said it. Not for her the strange affirmations of fandom. She liked the girl, she felt drawn to her. She could say so.

Abigail had crouched at the side of the pool; then she was sitting on the edge with her bare legs dangling in the water. If I go in, will you come too? she asked.

Ruth paused. I want to, she said. I really do. But I shouldn't.

Why can't you?

I don't know. I shouldn't.

The child kicked her legs slowly, causing small waves to ripple out into the water. I have to go, she said again, but instead of standing, she slipped off the side and into the pool, so suddenly, and with such seeming lack of thought that Ruth was startled, and for a moment she thought the girl had fallen in—she would drown—there she was, face down in her dress, below the surface. Quickly the woman stood and started for the water, reaching it just as the child surfaced again, spluttering water and then laughing. Come in, the girl said. Please come in with me.

I can't right now, said Ruth. I don't have my bathing suit...

You always say you can't, the girl complained. But you could if you wanted. Ruth felt her toes curling at the lip of the deck, her bare feet abrading on the rough surface. And she was ten years old, staring down at the ten-year-old waiting in the water below; she was ten, and then she was fifty again, and her heart was drumming in her chest. Well, why not? She couldn't decide whether to jump or dive, she bent her knees, hesitated, bent a little further and fell in, fully clothed, to the sound of the girl's candy laughter.

The pool was warmer than she had expected; she came up and wiped her eyes. —Where was Abigail? Treading water down at the deep end, with her long black hair spread out beside her. Come on! the girl insisted, and for a moment Ruth wondered what the hurry was—but she swam, in a crawl modified to allow her to keep her head above the water, down towards the deeper end of the pool. When she looked up Abigail had vanished, and the water was closed over the spot where she had been. Ruth stopped swimming and looked down through blue to a flickering form. She started forward, just as the girl surfaced again, shouting softly: Come on! Please?

She was starting to feel her drinks again; was it that dizziness, or another? Was she cold or hot? She shivered. The pool seemed to have grown much bigger in a moment or two; she couldn't see to its edges or touch bottom with her toes. On and blue it went, Abigail at a

Jim Lewis

long distance and getting longer, getting more pale, if that was possible. Wait, said Ruth. Wait for me.

But again the child sank below the surface, and Ruth was alone, suddenly lonely, and with a peculiar sense that she should be scared, but she wasn't scared at all. She wanted to be with Abigail, wherever the child was: that would be fun. But she was getting tired, maybe she really was too old for this. Where was the girl? Waving through the water; and there she was again, surfaced and laughing, calling. Ruth swam towards her, but slowly and heavily; she was almost entirely out of wind. Once again the child disappeared, and this time she was gone for a good while, time enough that the echoes of her voice died away, leaving only the sound of the water playing gently against itself. The walls of the hotel were wheeling above her, with here and there a dim light shining, and the rest of it dark. The woman felt a surge of concern, which quickly grew into a longing, and then a prolonged agony for everything she was going to be without, a crush of pain which felt, again, like ecstasy for everything from which she might be released. She paused for a moment to see if Abigail would surface at last, and then she inhaled as deeply as she could and started down, and as the pool closed over her head she began to swim with long, unlaboured strokes, down through the waves, down in search of the lights and the little girl, who was laughing and calling for Ruth to come on, to come down; and when the woman's breath expired at last, and her lungs began to fill with water, she was so far gone and travelling, she didn't even think about what she was leaving behind, except to wonder, just for a moment, who was going to miss her the most. □

GERMANY
Chris Petit

From an early age I stalked movies for clues to a life I didn't understand. As a child growing up in the 1950s, cinema was more real than the everyday and I found meaning there. I didn't know what I was looking for, but then, as now, it was predicated on the negative. Aged three I had to be removed from the Kingston Odeon for bawling, brought on by the certainty that Danny Kaye as Hans Christian Andersen was an ogre; so wise, so young. I never liked Cary Grant, Jack Lemmon, Melvyn Douglas, Laurel and Hardy, Harold Lloyd, Rock Hudson and didn't care for Glenn Ford or Tony Curtis either. I liked most women, even Doris Day, but not Joan Crawford, Jane Wyman or Bette Davis. I was enamoured of Cyd Charisse and Ava Gardner. Later, I had trouble subscribing to the auteur theory, Hitchcock in particular because of a dislike of the actors he used, except for James Stewart because he had played Charles Lindbergh in *The Spirit of St Louis*.

That films were American was a given and I grew up thinking there was nothing else. Towards the end of the 1950s I learned there was such a thing as British cinema. It seemed to consist only of films about the war, watched by me with apprehension, thinking them an anticipation of the war to which I, as a boy, would one day have to go. We grew up under the shadow of one war or another, a situation compounded in my case by a father in the army.

When I was three we went to Hong Kong and my fourth birthday in June 1953, soon after our arrival, was spent on the beach in the New Territories. I was given an inflatable dinghy, a present that made perfect sense, reward for the dreariness of a life of post-war austerity until then. The family was reunited. My father had gone ahead to Hong Kong and before that had been fighting in Korea. We went to a cinema to watch the Coronation. It was in colour. I felt no nostalgia for England. If the price of life in Hong Kong was a new sister, unwanted by me, and a fearsome Chinese amah, these I was willing to negotiate. My parents had a stereoscope with scenes in 3-D colour of the Coronation and Hong Kong views, including the tram to the Peak. Our first flat was by the sea and had a balcony and I felt at home there in a way I hadn't in the gloomy houses of rationed England where boredom was a recurring theme; I came from a generation left out in the pram, which resulted in a lifelong aversion to gardens in winter.

We moved from the high, sunny apartment to a dark ground floor in Kowloon, with bewildering memories of city chaos, aggressive digestive smells of food and drains (England had never smelled of anything), a sense of the sky being further away, and the Chinese swarm, a frightening opposite of the regimentation and uniform of army life. They spat all the time, their phlegm on pavements a source of fascination because I would never be allowed to. There was hostility in their jostling. I held my mother's hand tightly, fearing I would be swept into the arms of the Chinese.

The first intrusions of an adult world include accompanying my father to a police station where a soldier was detained after arrest for drunkenness. I was disappointed by the lack of definition or mystery to the scene: a young man in a bare room sleeping it off on a camp bed; was that all? My father took me to church, driving past the airfield where a big silver plane lay crumpled at the end of the runway, crashed and abandoned. The church was always full to overflowing for Sunday Mass. A slender young Chinese woman in a print dress fainted in a way that I found both shameful and exciting. At four I already suspected the world was not something I would come to terms with. I asked for jeans that zipped down the side, pointed them out in the market, and was told by my mother side zips were for girls. The confusion of that moment connects intimately with seeing the border to China for the first time. I understood its fortifications were part of the reason my father had been sent to Korea and wondered what where we were standing looked like to someone on the other side. I couldn't see the difference. The simplicities of life in the New Territories belonged to another time. I didn't know whether I really liked the kindergarten in Kowloon, run by a Miss Hazler, or was pretending. I sensed for the first time that I might be difficult and reacted by playing off parental affections, one against the other, always testing. I don't think anyone told me we would have to leave or why we were there in the first place.

The boat back took twenty-five days, the journey out over forty. On the voyage home I saw my first western. My father disappointed me by sleeping through what I regarded as a vital discovery. Even the gunfire failed to wake him. I liked the way people hid in the film, watching from behind rocks. Hong Kong was already a dream.

Compared to the rusty old troop ship that had taken us out, the boat home was fast and modern, and I half believed England had been transformed in our absence into the vibrant colours of the stereoscope. Failing that, films held promise, especially those in Technicolor. I wanted to live inside them, become physically transported.

My fifth birthday was in Great Malvern. I was given a Hornby clockwork train set when I had hoped for electric. It went round in a circle. Scant reward for the complexities of Hong Kong, I thought, aged five; an insult, in fact, after the culture shock of returning home to a country in a broken-down state of convalescence. The set came with a station. The station sign said Ripon. My father told me Ripon was in Yorkshire. I found the arrangement of the letters tight and sinister. It seemed to signify that life from then on would mean less. It was summer and I wore a shirt I liked and helped my father lay a garden path. I have vivid memories of my parents in Hong Kong: Father handsome in uniform, sometimes in his mess kit with scarlet jacket and yellow lapels; Mother exotic in splashy print dresses, bare arms tanned. I found them more glamorous than anyone in the movies (but it was never quite enough because they weren't in the movies). I don't remember them so well after June 1954.

We moved to Kingston upon Thames to live with my paternal grandfather, a GP. He was from Ireland and said 'fillums'. He took the *Daily Sketch*, for the racing, which I read for risqué comic strips. A drawing of a woman crawling through a desert in a bikini became fixed in my sometimes feverish imagination with the young Chinese woman who had fainted at Mass. My grandfather got a television, also for the racing. Next door lived a boy a little older than me. We agreed a preference for *The Range Rider* over *The Cisco Kid* and *The Lone Ranger* and he galloped round his garden whacking his backside. He had two half-brothers, almost grown-up, one of whom he later he murdered with a crossbow, for which he was sent to Broadmoor.

His Davy Crockett hat was a source of envy. He had seen the film too, which I never did—as punishment for misbehaviour. An aunt of mine in the United States was sending over real cowboy boots and an authentic holster. I talked them up but my heart wasn't in it because my friend was older and I knew I could never catch up. Then I was disappointed in a way that couldn't be admitted because when they came they weren't quite real enough to inhabit the world of the movies, as I believed might yet happen, and I would be exposed as a fraud.

Germany, 1957. Iserlohn, in the industrial Ruhr: a medium-sized town of undistinguished features, the only surviving evidence of its previous order a policeman in peaked cap who stood in a pulpit at the town's main intersection with a whistle to direct traffic. We were part of the occupation forces, the British Army on the Rhine (BAOR), with a BFPO address (British Forces Posted Overseas). Sunday lunch times we listened to *Two-Way Family Favourites* on the radio. My father drove an old Opel, then a Standard 10, and we lived first in part of a requisitioned old house in Am Tyrol, then at Rubensstrasse 14, a semi-detached box on a new estate on the side of a hill, quartered in order of rank, with senior officers in the road above. We took weekend picnics by the Mohne dam of *Dam Busters'* fame, the damage marked by lighter stonework showing the repairs. There was an organization called, I think, the Army Kinema Corporation to which I insisted on being taken in exchange for not kicking up a fuss about being dragged off to televisionless Germany. If England had been a regression after Hong Kong, Germany was another step back, into a strange country, darker than home, arrested by a past which everyone was careful not to mention, it being a time of economic miracles. Secretly I found this land full of the emptiness of defeat fascinating, with none of the scary otherness of Hong Kong. I went to an army school and mixed for the first time with what were called the other ranks, boys called Tommy Chatting and Roger Outlaw who had a brother, Keith, names as exotic, almost, to my ear as Jay Silverheels who played Tonto in *The Lone Ranger*.

At the Iserlohn cinema I saw *The Spirit of St Louis* and a western called *Cowboy*. It was crowded and smoky, with wooden seats less comfortable than in England. I think there were trams in the street. Little part is played by the immediate landscape or its people in my memory, apart from an elderly woman hired for the hopeless task of teaching German. The only other person is a man in a check shirt who threw a stone at me, down from where we lived on part of the estate still being built. A group of us had been baiting him. Usually I'm quite good at dodging things, but when I came to move nothing happened and I was gashed on the side of the head, needing stitches. Perhaps I half wanted to be hit, as part of a process of identification. Certainly the stone chucked took on symbolic importance in terms of failure and losing. It came to represent the start of the doubt that later turned into the main legacy of a lapsed Catholicism. I don't know anyone who says 'I don't know' more than I do.

There were rumours of marauding bands of German kids looking to beat up the English. I saw only German school children with strange satchels, like briefcases, worn on their backs, and bicycles with smaller wheels and fat tyres. They were always more serious than us because they had to work harder at school and on Saturdays as punishment for having lost the war, so we believed. We bought a German Telefunken radio second-hand, with push-buttons and a display of arresting names (Hilversum, Luxembourg) and I wondered if they mightn't have a more interesting technology. Cakes and coffee were what they were admired for, and their motorways, not that I ever saw one. We lived, holidayed and shopped apart. The British NAAFI was a dreary army stores. The real Mecca was the Canadian base in Hemer, selling superior cereals, with give-away gifts, and American comics with an immediacy lacking in English ones. I copied their drawing style: flatter and harder. English comics had a whole series devoted to the war, scoured incessantly for reference to Iserlohn, never found. A birthday party involved being taken to the Canadian cinema to see a matinee of *The Indian Fighter* with Kirk Douglas, a film that remains vivid for its opening with Elsa Martinelli stripping to bathe in the river, and a later scene where cavalry scouts returning from patrol are found to be dead, bodies propped in the saddle, their heads scalped.

Yesterday I looked at the film for the first time since then, to check the scenes as I remembered them. But none of it happens, not even remotely the way it has lodged in my imagination, both moments so fleeting they make me wonder how much my other memories of that time are exaggerated, false or wrongly remembered.

Post-war West Germany was a profitable market for Hollywood, not only with the occupying US Forces. Wim Wenders famously said, 'The Americans colonized our subconscious.' It was deliberate, starting with a 1947 directive to rebuild the country's motion picture theatres as a way of imparting information to the Germans which would influence them 'to understand and accept the US programme of occupation'. Film distribution was controlled by the Americans, with the support of the US Motion Picture Export Association, who dumped Hollywood's back catalogue—films from the 1930s and 1940s banned under Hitler—on the West German market. For future directors such as Fassbinder and Wenders, growing up after the war, these movies, voraciously devoured, were celluloid's equivalent to junk food. The first image Fassbinder saw on a movie screen was a covered wagon in a western. There was in effect no German cinema.

I became privately fascinated by German loss, far more than the ostensible object of my admiration, the Americans, who, close up, seemed too certain and extrovert, their GIs huge like giants in a cartoon compared to British soldiers, who tended to be short. The confused emotions of losing grew more interesting than the uncertainties of winning. I didn't know it then but agreed instinctively with Graham Greene's observation that success is only delayed failure. Germany was complicated, its bewitched silence more enthralling than the usual domestic ones. These were personified by a young German woman of around twenty who had come to look after us in 1955 before we moved to Germany. By then there were three of us children to take care of. My sister and I loathed her. We turned her into an object of implacable hatred.

She would have been around ten or eleven when the war ended. There was an elder sister in England, married to an Englishman, and the family was from what was then East Germany. A brother had vanished on the Russian front. The Russians, when they came, had thought flush toilets were for washing potatoes. I gathered this information piecemeal but remained stubbornly incurious because of our mutual hostility, the war never an open subject. I grew used to silences, adept at deflection, and became less communicative, resentful of not being told things I believed I was old enough to understand. In Iserlohn she broke something and crouched behind the sofa, weeping and inconsolable.

It never occurred that we were punished because of what she had been forced to endure. Fassbinder would have made a screenplay out of her story (which I no doubt repressed): the young woman with a shameful secret, inserted into an uncomprehending bourgeois family where the victim victimizes and cruelty substitutes for trauma. I have no memory of the *mise en scène* of our drama. I had started making emotional investments elsewhere: in comics, in films and life outside the house. I didn't find out until years later what the Russians had done to her and her sister, and the Nazis before them.

One thing I am certain of is no one talked about the Jews all the time we were in Germany between 1957 and 1958. I probably didn't even know what a Jew was, other than those in the Bible. As far as I know, there weren't any in my father's regiment. That we were Roman Catholic and went to church was unusual and I had begun to resent not being like everyone else (most of me wanted desperately to conform, to be super-invisible). I worried religion might cause more problems than it was worth.

In the summer of 1961, in England, I found out about the Jews, in Reigate, staying with a school friend during the summer holidays. His parents were diligent and cultural and listened to classical music and had books, including a paperback with photographs of the exterminations, which I read without anyone noticing. Through school gossip we were aware of Nazi war crimes, though not the details, and of Adolf Eichmann's trial in 1961, the exact nature of which eluded me because there were no newspapers in the feral English boarding school I then attended. In this highly censored and insulated institution boys of a certain age were allowed to carry sheath knives and there was a thriving black market in smuggled books, including one on First World War atrocity with an illustration of a serrated bayonet designed to rip your guts out.

The Nazi experience was bypassed in favour of British grit: Dunkirk, the Battle of Britain, El Alamein, D-Day, fed by a steady diet of war films. Once a fortnight, on Saturday afternoons, we sat in a blacked-out classroom and watched films shown by a man who came in a van with a projector and a stack of silver cans. First we got *Look at Life* or Edgar Lustgarten introducing crimes from the annals of Scotland Yard, one of which was called *The Case of the Burning Caravan*, followed by features that included *The Cockleshell Heroes*, *The Cruel Sea*, *Dunkirk* and *Yangste Incident*.

Some Germans were allowed to become surrogate Brits: the Red Baron and Rommel. I read *The Spies of Peenemunde*, another smuggled item. It was technical and dreary despite a lurid cover. The underground caves appealed (we were fearsome diggers, criss-crossing school grounds with a honeycomb of secret tunnels, desperate to escape) but none of us could grasp the concept of slave labour as a modern phenomenon: how could *Spartacus* equate to Germany, 1944? We found it easier to see the war as an extension of life at school, *Colditz* and *The Wooden Horse* our models. We thought the Germans were fundamentally decent and that Hitler was brilliant but mad. My father had seen him speak in 1938 and reported that he was a mesmerizing orator. He'd chucked his hat in the air along with the rest of the cheering crowd. This story always left me confused. I knew my father had worked in Germany after leaving school, in the steel industry, by then on full military footing, but I never understood why, first, he hadn't shot Hitler and second—given this extraordinary anecdote, which in my mind translated as my father having met Hitler except he was too modest to say so—the British government hadn't utilized his first-hand experience and packed him off to fight the Nazis instead of wasting him on the Japanese.

At school the Japanese were prized for being the most bloodthirsty. We had all seen *The Bridge on the River Kwai* and the book *The Camp on Blood Island* filled in the details. I felt an emotional investment because a young officer, whose best man my father had been, won a posthumous VC after charging a Japanese slit trench and throwing his wounded body in front of it to prevent them firing. (In the regimental museum in Norwich there was a school of inferior paintings depicting scenes of heroism that caused me anxious nights, as much as those of another lesser school, the nineteenth-century maritime one of shipwreck.) Our maths teacher had been tortured by the Japanese, his tongue split. We wondered if he had learned his favourite punishment as a prisoner of war, pulling us up by the ears. We weren't entirely innocent. School seemed curiously more militarized than army life in Germany. The staff, all men, clung on to their old ranks, calling themselves Commander or Captain, and the war was a form of currency in terms of banned literature and as a court of appeal. Turning conversation to the war was usually enough to get you out of trouble. We speculated endlessly and authoritatively. I inserted my identification with Germany, without much success. Germans were dismissed as losers while maps in the classrooms still showed the British Empire red.

When I remember so much else I can't recollect the name of the book on the Nazi exterminations. There were photographs of piles of dead and statistics beyond comprehension, and accounts of dispatch and process, down to the showers. I could make no sense of it. The procedure sounded plausible for its terrifying ordinariness and logic, but motive was something I could not even begin to work out because I could not relate this account to the country where I had lived, which had given no clue of this history. Having been there, I felt in some way contaminated. I wondered how I would have felt growing up German and learning this.

New German cinema came out of nowhere. It didn't of course but it looked that way, especially in the context of a washed-up English cinema. It was a clean surprise, political and stringent. The films first came to London in the mid-1970s, with a back catalogue, contributing to an impression of density, and played at cinemas like the Academy, the Paris Pullman, the Camden Plaza, the Lumière, the Electric and the Gate, when London was a good city for cinema. I spent most of the 1970s in the dark, with a job where I was paid to watch and write about movies. I vanished into press screenings and the dingy preview theatres of Soho, sometimes two or three times a day, at a time when the whole history of cinema could still be retrieved and mugged up, encyclopaedic days in which I was always a tardy student, sniffing out what might interest me and ignoring the rest. Too much had already been claimed and argued over, a pantheon established, so I lost myself in the interstices, in B-movies, in their last gasp in the 1970s, second-division French new wave, the more obscure spaghetti westerns, Don Siegel and the films of Jean-Pierre Melville and John Milius, up to a point, as well as early Cronenberg. True to childhood viewing habits, I followed the careers of actors (for the way they moved): a young Robert Duvall, Angie Dickinson, Françoise Dorléac, Lee Marvin, Lou Castel, Geneviève Bujold, Lino Ventura, Eastwood before he got his chipped tooth fixed, late disillusioned Mitchum, John Cassavetes. I retained little sense of narrative, which was always the problem when I came to make films.

The first shock of German cinema was its recognizable ordinariness, as something within one's own grasp of experience, including the anti-epics of Herzog, whose sweat and awkward enterprise were the opposite of the overstatements of Lean. Herzog, Fassbinder and Wenders fell into the category of what the great American critic Manny Farber called termite art, a purposeful burrowing with no regard for anything except the task in hand, which neatly took me back to the tunnels we dug at school (*The Great Escape*). Kluge and Straub had already announced something was happening in German cinema, but it wasn't until Fassbinder, Herzog and Wenders arrived as part of a Munich school that there was a proper sense of what. They were brattishly cineliterate, self-educated like Fassbinder, through a promiscuous immersion in movies from an early age, or from film school. All of them regarded their films in the context of other cinema. For Fassbinder it was Sirk and melodrama, for Wenders the lonesome cowboys of Nicholas Ray, with Herzog the hardest to place, as the least in thrall to Hollywood. All were defined by a grand restlessness, the urgency of making up for lost time.

Just as the French new wave had roots in the Nazi Occupation, and emerged out of an exposure to unseen Hollywood films after the war, so the Germans reacted to their American occupation. Herzog, the most exotic of the three, cited an early childhood memory that had caused him to cry with fright at the sight of a black GI with a banana, both unseen in Bavaria before 1945. As the French new wave had belonged to Cannes as much as to Paris, new German cinema was a film festival phenomenon, sustained by a generous domestic subsidy system which compensated for the years of little or no production. At festivals we became part of the same loosely connected circuit, with German cinema a model for everything that was wrong with British films.

I had grown up with a British cinema that did not correspond to my own experience in that there was little I recognized in or about it. Instead I read the novels of Patricia Highsmith for an emotional and physical terrain that I understood, her flat prose hiding deceptive levels of reserve and homicidal emotions. It took nothing to imagine getting in the kind of mess her characters did. I enjoyed the ambiguity of her books, the emotional complications, the lack of resolve, with detail (waiting for a letter) assuming the same significance as more dramatic events. Whenever I tried reading English novels or murder stories I found them strangled by class, too tinny or literary or just plain forced. I wasn't interested in what my contemporaries were doing, except in music, which was reported in lively and partisan terms, unlike cinema, with the exceptions of Raymond Durgnat and Manny Farber. Farber, a painter and the canniest watcher of films, latterly wrote with his wife, Patricia Patterson, also a painter, and they were very quick on to the Germans, especially Fassbinder, for a quality that reminded him of Fra Angelico. Through Farber I learned to appreciate Fassbinder after an early dislike. Farber looked at films in other ways than repeating the story, as most critics did, or reverting to the kind of academic theory then fashionable, managed well enough by the French but often redundant in its Anglo-Saxon forms.

In England there was almost nothing, no financial organization with the vision to fund something as remote and strange as Herzog's *Fata Morgana*, conceived as a series of tracking shots along the edge of desert civilizations and beyond, or *Aguirre, the Wrath of God*, equally hallucinatory, a mad search for gold in a jungle wilderness with Spanish conquistadores, to a soundtrack by Popol Vuh. Early Herzog was a folly of derangement, a celebration of pointless endeavour through hostile country, a perfect metaphor for the absurd (not least the absurdity of film-making), and deeply German. He was a throwback to those popular mountain-climbing films of the Third Reich—in the sense of the impossible task—skewed by the knowledge of what had happened since. In a way that bordered on madness, Herzog embraced the naivety and insanity of the Hitler years in a solo effort to restore a German visionary romanticism tarnished by the Nazis.

Aguirre starred one of the great gypsy mercenaries of cinema, Klaus Kinski. He had done a stint in English cinema in the 1960s, enlivening black-and-white B-movies, as a slum landlord or a gangster, which led to a small part as a chain-rattling anarchist in Lean's *Dr Zhivago* where his anger seemed less to do with his character's predicament than finding himself in such a bad movie. After that he turned up in Sergio Leone, shot for eating peas with a knife, and in spaghetti westerns playing to the gallery with the narcoleptic twitchiness of a Nosferatu at loose in the wrong genre, a role he would later do for Herzog, perfectly etiolated. He was driven by a vast, humourless frenzy the screen seemed barely able to contain, with a grand megalomania and the hammy conviction of a man who knows acting is more than a matter of life and death. Herzog gave a similar impression, with his bizarre, intense way of masticating words, chewed thoroughly before being spat out. 'Jah, jah, it is good to work with the hands,' he said, eyes afire, of my unlikely stint in Bavarian forestry after leaving school. It never occurred to him there was any way other than the nigh impossible, a true master of the lost cause. Herzog and Kinski shared the same crazed identification that led them to threaten to kill each other.

Herzog's films, often presented with the challenge of a remote and hostile location, were pared down by the logistics of budget and equipment, as were Wenders and Fassbinder whose early work was self-contained and determined by the hit-and-miss guerrilla tactics of any new wave. Acting tended to be earnest (Wenders), stiffly theatrical (Fassbinder) or out-there (Herzog). Wenders was rootless. Fassbinder was an invasion: a film every hundred days, year in, year out. They were rhetorical while remaining wary of rhetoric and overt manipulation. Kraftwerk said, in their mock-serious way, that after Goebbels and Hitler the postures of rock and roll weren't available to German musicians so it became necessary to develop a more democratic relationship with the loudspeaker. The films were similarly unstarry, though Fassbinder borrowed the Warhol model, forming a troupe that worked factory-style, a euphemism in many cases for slave labour and sexual tyranny. Hanna Schygulla was, briefly, the only bona fide star to emerge from the stable, giving Fassbinder his first commercial hit with *The Marriage of Maria Braun* in 1978, after more than thirty films and over a decade of work. Most new German cinema counted for little at the domestic box office, but it was for a while given a very generous subsidy, allowing careers to develop from mistakes, in a way unimaginable now.

As an aspiring film-maker stuck for a subject, I envied the Germans their past. It was there, implacable, a reference the size of an iceberg (so much submerged). The solemnity of Wenders, even playing pinball, was part of that German existential package of being able to take oneself seriously. He announced that rock and roll had saved his life and in his films thought nothing of stopping the action while he played a record. He dedicated his first feature-length film, *Summer in the City*, to the Kinks; in *The Bitter Tears of Petra von Kant*, Fassbinder played the Walker Brothers' 'In My Room'; both unimaginable in English cinema. Jukeboxes littered the movies like clues in a murder mystery. Their films were purposeful and premeditated, even in their doubt. When I interviewed Wenders's collaborator, the Austrian novelist Peter Handke, in 1979, he was gleeful over a line from a crappy German detective show: 'Perhaps there are new kinds of despair yet unknown to us.' The war and the subsequent amnesia had removed all spontaneity. Instead they quested, labouring under the same shadow while going in their different directions, lugging the baggage of the past, briefly incapable of not producing grand, displaced metaphors for Germany's suppression. It was a period of greatness that lasted no more than a few years, and none of them stuck around. Fassbinder craved being ugly on the cover of *Time* ('When ugliness has finally reclaimed all beauty, that is luxury'). He dreamed of huge riches in Hollywood during the 1980s but died in 1982. Herzog lost his alter ego when Kinski died in 1991 and he drifted into documentaries, and Wenders, victim of rock and roll's salvation, did the Transatlantic shuffle to diminishing effect.

Because films no longer contain the clues to life they once did, I barely watch them now, and when I do I find myself distracted, as in life, by what's in the background, as though that were the real, immutable subject of the film, the equivalent to the invisible cities of which Calvino wrote, its hidden meaning: the importance of the way a street looks, the furniture in a room, the way the extras have been organized, rather than what the actors are saying or doing. It's partly a legacy of the childhood desire to inhabit movies, partly inattentiveness and the wish to let the mind and the eyes wander (and wonder). Most films are designed to counter two key modern impulses, boredom and drift, the point at which I usually become interested. Out of this idle fascination I started to take photographs of films but only of the background landscapes or details, because it seemed to me that a view in a film is just as valid a part of a personal landscape as those from life. These pictures became incidental reminders of the part of film-making I enjoyed most, scouting locations, wandering around, more purposeful than a tourist, trying to match up what was on the page with something that looked the way you imagined it. I liked the recce photographs and Polaroids that got stuck on a board. The search was always surprisingly tiring (like walking round an art gallery) but

Chris Petit

pleasurable, a sense of random days. After the locations were found I was never so interested again until the editing and used to think, why can't we leave it at that?

With actors I always felt embarrassed asking them to pretend, though I knew perfectly well that's what they did for a living. Most of the time they were desperate to rehearse and I could barely bring myself to watch them. I preferred editing because it was a good excuse to break off communication with the outside world (like watching a movie, in fact).

Recently, I watched these German films again for the first time since the 1970s and understood how little part my own time in Germany had played in previous viewings, a blanked landscape. Only now have I attempted to retrieve it. Re-seeing these films, I realize how much I liked them for their background, their shallow composition and an absence of tricksiness, eschewing the jump cut for tracking shots as a way of defining space and time, and situating characters within a landscape. Of post-war movies, new German cinema seemed the most naturally photographic, not necessarily in terms of realism but as a way of recording, as a summary of the possibilities of 35mm film. It was a trait shared by Fassbinder, Herzog and Wenders, despite their obvious differences. It's the opposite of Gregg Toland's deep focus for Orson Welles, and by implication that other train set bragged about by Welles, the boy's whole bag of directorial tricks. The quest for identity and the idea of Germany are inseparable from the films, for all the overlay of American influences in Fassbinder and Wenders and the remoteness of Herzog. All shared a classical sense of composition. None was formally radical in the way that Straub's films were, conditioned more by a feeling for biography and location, a sense of poetic space. Wenders, like Fritz Lang, was always very good at moments of threshold, the significance of the doorway in the sense meant by Bachelard, who noted that to remember all those crossed was nothing short of an account of one's life.

The emotional paralysis of Wenders's work looks clearer now, its loneliness inherited from the western. His men understood each other better than they did women. Displacement became his great early theme in low-key dramas played out on the border zones of identity and often along the great divide of Germany. His cultural ticket was

230

written by that gloomy precisionist, Peter Handke, his frequent collaborator and definer of modern German angst. Handke's novella, *The Goalkeeper's Fear of the Penalty*, adapted by Wenders in 1971, was a minimalist alternative to Herzog's far-flung epics of the absurd: a journey through an Austrian urban and rural landscape whose invisible historical map was more important than any human investigation into the pointless murder that does the opposite of drive the story, turning it into an essay in distraction. The only moments of true feeling—to paraphrase Handke—come from an external source, music.

The real star of Wenders's films is his cameraman Robbie Müller who is Dutch and saw Germany with a foreign eye as Robert Frank had seen America. While in *Alice in the Cities* the film's apparent discovery is an American landscape, covered in an extended prologue, the film's real excitement is Müller's visual chronicle of the more impenetrable German Ruhr, and for me a personal retrieval of a lost world. The irony of Wenders, for all his craving to be away, was that he worked best where he felt most trapped, at home. Müller shoots Germany as virgin territory, which it was, because the terrain of early Wenders, particularly *Kings of the Road*, remains otherwise unlogged. Just as the English musicians Wenders admired tinkered with imported American models, he did the same, including *The American Friend* in which Dennis Hopper, miscast as Patricia Highsmith's Ripley, sneers, 'What's wrong with a cowboy in Hamburg?' Women tended to be glum, occasionally waspish, marginalized into improbable one-night stands. Emotional helplessness disguised ruthlessness, excused in the grand scale of things; how could it be otherwise after what Germany had done? The same emotional core permitted Fassbinder's monstrousness and the far more savage and confident heterosexual and homosexual encounters.

Wenders's talent was for itinerary rather than narrative, for places rather than the stories put in them. Given nothing to do except create an extended sequence out of the road, he comes close to genius. *The Goalkeeper's Fear of the Penalty* only discovers its proper pace, and subject, after leaving Vienna, with a long bus journey out of all proportion to the level of incident shown. This is done with a haunting authenticity lacking in more scripted moments. The best part of the film is 'The Lion Sleeps Tonight' heard on a tinny transistor radio, a sequence when all the disparate strands come briefly together into a believable whole: the goalie's past, the half-hearted murder of a cinema cashier he is running away from, and his failure of imagination make perfect sense for a moment. Seen now, *The Goalkeeper's Fear* is too full of the wrong kind of action in a way that it didn't seem at the time, as though the frame of reference has shrunk, just as a moment of false rage with Rudiger Vogler kicking in the television in a US motel in *Alice in the Cities* damages what Wenders is best at, capturing the banality of life on the road, with its lack of dramatics and the tedium of its rituals, in a way that is magical because it gives time and space to those extended moments other films pass over.

The problem was that the films became less rather than more marginal, pegged by Wenders's American ambitions and auteurist aspirations, signalled by casting movie directors such as Samuel Fuller and Nicholas Ray in *The American Friend*. *Lightning Over Water*, made during one of the transitions to America, hung around watching Ray die in a way that did no one any favours. I ended up quarrelling with Wenders's sentimentality and male bonding and thought life was more isolated than his films allowed. In that respect it was the classic, ambiguous relationship of mentor and protégé, with too many unspoken complications. He produced my first film in 1979, *Radio On*, a modification of what I admired about German cinema: weather and landscape, a taciturn romanticism, cultural climate, boredom and dreariness and an emotional soundtrack, courtesy of Kraftwerk.

Fassbinder and Wenders's early work was so full of recognizable moments of small epiphany they encouraged me to think of film-making for the first time, an option that had previously seemed impossible in terms of British finance and lack of an inspirational model. They were both good with bars and the streets outside in a way that was close to home, and there was the music, but also the pacing, the confidence to let things take their course in the time it takes to do them, where previously most films (pace Warhol) had seemed to be about ways of speeding up action.

Fassbinder's Munich I now see I recognized from my time there in 1968, just as *Alice in the Cities* reclaimed the forgotten childhood landscape of the Ruhr. Fassbinder also preferred the ordinary: any bar, any street, any apartment, in counterpoint to the extraordinary emotional upheavals going on. It gave the films a grounded authority which he would counter with theatrical lighting and stilted acting that allowed for little in the way of personal gesture or complications of continuity. The style was characterized by an acid eye, flatness and hurry, sketchy lighting and an urge to get on with the next shot, and yet the films are full of effortless sumptuousness and luminosity. He wasted no time on set, unlike Godard who doodled for hours, keeping the crew waiting, while he made up his mind. The momentum of Fassbinder came less from the story than speed of shooting, often against financial odds in the early days. An entourage of willing helpers and hangers-on meant the next film could be prepared while the present one was shot and the one before finished. Subsidies and federal prizes were fed into the system, and failing that credit cards were extended to the limit.

The German sound recordist who worked on *Radio On*, a Wenders regular, had done a day on Fassbinder's first film and quit because he could see the way things were going: tantrums, provocations, auto confessions, life manipulated so it could be raided for the work, uncertain pay cheques, tears before bedtime and the whole sexual merry-go-round, as chronicled in *Beware of a Holy Whore*— Fassbinder's 1971 account of the making of the disastrous *Whity* earlier that year—marking the end of the first stage of his career. Fassbinder's stamina was phenomenal: a film for every year of his life, more or less. The abuse was legendary, the frequent tenderness of the work matched by the monstrousness of his private life which became the raw material for his films, with anything permissible, a self-devouring process that killed him young. In his pomp, his producer required three assistants who did nothing but fly all over Europe scoring for Fassbinder's cocaine habit that grew to seven or eight grams a day. At his last Cannes film festival he spent 20,000 marks on cocaine and sold off part of the distribution rights for his next film, called *I'm the Happiness of This World*, never made because he was already in the next, in exchange for a guaranteed supply.

Fassbinder checked out for good in the early morning of June 10, 1982, in his room with its 'cock mirror', a strip around the walls at the appropriate height, in front of a videotape of *20,000 Years in Sing Sing*, the cigarette in his fist burned down to the butt, on a day the Rolling Stones were due to play in Munich.

In retrospect, I date the day of his death, exactly one week before my own thirty-third birthday, as the start of the end of my own enthralment with cinema. The momentum continued for another couple of years but my obsession was on the wane. I had managed to make two feature films, was planning a third in Paris at the time, which fell through and relocated to Berlin, followed by one more in Berlin in 1984, after which I stopped. I often wonder why. Nothing was resolved nor was anything missed: a reserve perhaps, a lack of adventurousness in my own life, and indecision about my own direction, in front of and behind the camera. I admired Fassbinder's shamelessness, the sense of transfiguration in his life, his painful honesty and sexual gangsterism, never mind that he ruined so many lives and lied whenever he opened his mouth, except when he was eating. There were no secrets or irony where I felt drawn to ambiguity, deflection and deferral, all the English vices, without any real desire to explore them in English cinema. Cinema was never a matter of life and death to me. I hadn't been saved by it or anything else, undone by English diffidence, stubborn but not combative, too easily discouraged. A religious upbringing, tepid in some respects, extreme in others, left me suspicious of self-sacrifice and subjugation. The film industry struck me as too like the army, which I'd already rejected.

I envied Fassbinder his martyrdom. His life was irrational and without responsibility, focused towards a single goal in a way I wished mine could have been. I watched him accept the jeers of a festival crowd, fists clenched above his head like a victorious boxer, unrepentant. I didn't really believe in anything, had chosen not to I realized after Fassbinder's death, so it seemed wrong to carry on. What little I had to say could be said in other ways. I was drawn to the margins and internal exile, aspired to an invisible career. I resolved to surprise myself by what I did.

Besides, I had a hunch that what Fassbinder represented was the end of something and the art cinema gravy train wouldn't go on much longer and that even those as established as Wenders and Herzog would find life difficult outside the widening mainstream. Fassbinder's death did for them too in a way. The centrifugal force they needed disappeared with him. The real energy of German cinema went with his departure, was perhaps already in the process of dissipation. Herzog's attention was no longer held and Wenders turned to angels and the later films became ghosts of themselves.

I never met Fassbinder. We were in the same room a few times. He was an actor too of course, a very good one, in life as well as on screen, his appearances calculated for effect. Slob. Gangster. Leather boy. Fist fucker. The variable weight. Then just when you had got used to that he would turn up swanning around in an evening suit with his old friend and sometime lover Udo Kier like they were auditioning for Visconti's high decadence. One year at Cannes I gate-crashed his lunch table on the beach with the film critic Jan Dawson. It was one of the years he brought all the boys. It was eighty degrees and Fassbinder wore his heavy leather jacket, a string vest and a battered grey fedora. Dawson and I were there to interview his disgraced art director and actor Kurt Raab, who had starred in a film not made by Fassbinder. Raab lorded it over the table, showing off his English, because he was the one we were talking to. The rest of them, a dozen or more—including director Daniel Schmidt, Harry Baer, sometime actor and Fassbinder's loyal production manager and general fixer, and Peter Chatel, actor in *Fox and His Friends*—sat there in a silent sulk, topped by a scowling Fassbinder. The only other woman at the table was their publicity agent. Herzog came for a while and said something to upset her and make her cry. He returned with a spray of red roses so big it was impossible to make him out behind them at first, presented them to her and made her cry all over again. The boys sulked even more. A sense of willed torture dominated the occasion, hostility towards any outsider (Dawson and me), barely suppressed hysteria and a general desire to make the experience as joyless as possible. All this I am sure was calculated by Fassbinder. We exchanged hostile looks as I left. They're all dead now, the people at that table, with the exception of myself, the publicity woman and Harry Baer. □

Great writing on Cinema
from BFI Publishing

www.bfi.org.uk/books

BFI Film Classics

"a treasury that keeps on delivering ... any film person needs the whole collection" *Independent on Sunday*

New and forthcoming in 2004 £8.99 each

Viridiana
Gary Indiana

Andrei Rublev
Robert Bird

César
Stephen Heath

In the Realm of the Senses
Joan Mellen

if...
Mark Sinker

Horizons West
Directing the Western from John Ford to Clint Eastwood
Jim Kitses

Highly expanded new edition of **the** definitive critical account of the Western and some of its key directors, first published in 1969.

Published in September 2004 priced £17.99

BFI Modern Classics

"short and sharp critical essays on acknowledged film greats that consistently strike a decent balance between piercing assessment and an invigorating read" *Empire*

New and forthcoming in 2004 £8.99 each

Groundhog Day
Ryan Gilbey

Unforgiven
Edward Buscombe

The Matrix
Joshua Clover

Withnail & I
Kevin Jackson

Nosferatu
Phantom der Nacht
S. S. Prawer

The Thin Red Line
Michel Chion

DOWN IN FRONT
Colson Whitehead

STEPHEN GILL

This is the part where we find our seats. Step on toes, suck in gut, make yourself flat as a movie screen. Is this too close? Is that coat a coat or is that coat a person? Short man plus tall man equals vaudeville when it comes to line of sight. His split ends will polish subtitles. How far away are flying cars when every seat is equipped with its own cup holder. Fight over armrests in warm little skirmishes and settle down, settle down, just in time to see previews of better movies than the one we've paid to see. Everything good was sold out.

This is the part when the movie starts and it's too early to be disappointed. Except for the well-prepared, who always keep a little disappointment handy, just in case. Still precious seconds to believe in enchantment. It's their first date and she has yet to discover that his laugh irritates her. In the getting-to-know-you stage, we meet the main characters. He always plays the bad guy, something about the eyes. Years from now he will achieve lasting fame as the host of a children's morning show, everybody's uncle. Like most of us, typecast and never chosen for the leading role. People recognize themselves in actors and recognize faces from movies that are now beyond recall. Wasn't he in, didn't she play. Tip of your tongue. So many movies over the course of a lifetime, how can we keep track. Pay attention. Little things you barely notice will be important later, will save us at the last moment, help us out in the clinch.

This is the part where nothing is as it seems. A mystery or complication has raised the stakes. A doomsday device or someone said, *I love you.* Certainly stakes have been raised, villains will require us to tap our last reserves. If anyone can pull it off, they can. Just look at them up there. His trademark smirk, her famous smile. When they were children they discovered that aspects of their faces could be parleyed into more candy, longer hugs, better toys. So well cherished and well squeezed that the stuffing spills out in places and eyes hang by threads. Who will begrudge them mansions and fans. In interviews they thank all the little people. According to tabloids he has predilections. They say she's had some work done. *Giant Light Bulb* is a magazine popular among moths. He's seen everything she's ever done and yet they are no closer than the day he first laid eyes on her. The career-making debut. Everybody needs a little attention every once in a while.

Colson Whitehead

This is the part where they have sex. They just met but they have a lot of chemistry and it has been foretold on the poster. They know so little about each other, that's what makes it so realistic. America's Sweetheart wrestles the Sexiest Man Alive over who gets the next close-up. So much of life comes down to who has the better representation. This is the scene that has everybody talking. Geriatric double entendres hobble out on walkers. Pubescent boys are sexually imprinted. Fans for life. Make a move. Find a pretext. The lack of eye contact helps considerably. Kiss me you fool. Flattery will get you nowhere.

This is the part with the montage sequence. Their love grows, pruned by expert editors. On the cutting-room floor truth lies in snippets. Take notes, everybody: maybe your relationship will blossom if you run through a field holding hands on a sunny day. Pass the JuJuBes, please. A jumbo-sized MacGuffin and a medium Coke, thanks. He likes it when the characters say things he could never bring himself to say, and he mouths the dialogue, an echo in the fourth row. She likes it when the characters exhibit emotions she has never felt so that she will know what to do when and if the time comes. Critics take notes in the dark. All he's looking for is a big-screen surrogate for his antisocial tendencies, is that so wrong. Here he comes, that's him with the axe. Fingernails scrape the bottom of popcorn containers. Palms cover eyes. Someone in the back row is screaming. The actors pretend not to hear. Chorus of shush. So immature, all this talking at the screen. Crying babies should be taken to the lobby.

This is the part where me and my crew walk towards the camera in slow-mo. Dapper and composed. In a few minutes we will outrun a fireball. After the special effects team got through with this scene, no one could know that he was just a man in an empty room. Computers these days, you can't tell what's real and what's not, a dozen extras is an army, an empty theatre is a sold-out show. Who is that sitting beside you, how solid is their companionship. That's gotta hurt. Don't try this at home, kids. The stuntman says, *I'm always falling off buildings, why can't I blow up for a change*. He was a clumsy child, so this line of work seemed perfect. She points at the screen and says, *I went to high school with that guy*. Exquisite sadness of Cop #2 as he shoves the perp into the squad car. Aren't we all Cop #2 from time to time. The likely suspects sit handcuffed in the back seat and there's bulletproof glass to protect us in case they get free. Keep telling yourself it's just fake blood.

This is the part that has them throwing stuff at the screen. Soda cups full of lukewarm fluid, bits of candy, kernels of resentment from super-sized buckets. Time for the free refill. The critics did their best, warned them about the dangers. Four and a half stars, three stars, two thumbs up or down. The more complicated the subject, the simpler the rating system must be. None of this was implied in the trailer. Hard to escape the familiar feeling that this is not what you paid for. Walk out to protest the unlikely situations, walk out to protest the weak motivation, walk out to protest the underlying assumptions of our culture. You get what you pay for. Should have waited for video.

This is the part where the villain lays out his master plan. Stand next to the globe, it will save time. He gets all the best lines and I wouldn't mind getting the number of his orthodontist. Check out the layout of the secret hideout, you'd think it cost a pretty penny, but he got that laser cannon used, and those curtains were on sale. The villain tells the hunchback, *Never pay retail*. Of course there's a hunchback. Remember this scene from commercials and savour that prelapsarian bliss. Human ambition so small compared to the immensity of the underground cavern. Must be a bitch to heat in the winter.

This is the part with the flashback that will explain it all. The back story. Faster than it will unfold over the years through my words and deeds, faster than it will be conveyed in my stingy revelations and incomplete confessions. Jesus Christ. Six writers listed in the credits and this is the best they could come up with. As if this scene could make up for all my shoddy character development in the first half. This plot is the balloon that slips out of a chubby kid's fingers and swims away. Can't follow it at all. Nature calls. What will you miss during the trip to the concession stand or restroom. The important clue or meaningful glance you've waited your whole life for. Something flickering ten feet high on the screen and impossible to misunderstand. Make a break for the exit light and sprinkle *Excuse me* and *Thank you* along the way. When she gets back, she asks, *What did I miss?*, and he whispers, *Nothing*.

This is the part with the impossible odds and the backs against the wall. Outnumbered and outgunned, out of bullets and passports and safe houses. Minor plot complications compared to the fact that you no longer love me. Screenwriters call these twists of fortune reversals but loss is one brute syllable and works for scale. All those cellos, I think the soundtrack is trying to tell us something. After ninety minutes of comic relief, the sidekick finally has something constructive to say. He says, *You can make it*. Not much, but his inflection really sells it. Pan zoom wash fade and cut, this is the celluloid jive, the lingo we use that we might see things better. What's the word for the camera direction that means, Let the camera rest anywhere except my face at this moment. Fade to black for a few seconds.

And this is my favourite part. This is the part with the final showdown between good and evil. Still time to gather my weapons before you surprise me with one last trick. Turns out this part of the country is chock full of cliffs. Weekends, holidays, last-ditch attempts, any excuse at all and people are hanging off them. Geological truth reduced to fodder for cheap suspense. Against all odds. After all these weeks, this is the part that always draws the projectionist back from his newspaper or pulp novel. Every showing he hopes that this time it will turn out differently, that this time you and I will stay down after this thorough defeat, and each time he is disappointed. Check your pockets for cavalry, escape hatch, convenient prop. What are we to do when the happy endings we trained ourselves not to expect arrive on cue to refute what we know about the world. They cheer or clap hands or become statues in the stadium seating. Yeah, right. Saw that coming. They don't make them like they used to. Still time to dry your eyes before you hit the bright light of the lobby. The jerks at the end of the row won't leave, hence this traffic jam. But wait, where are you going. This is the part where you look for my name in the credits. Wait, where are you going. I'm pretty sure my name is in the credits.   □

QUIET, PLEASE
Adam Mars-Jones

Adam Mars-Jones

I miss silence in the movies. Not silent movies—the films so called were anything but, since they relied on live music from a piano pit or an orchestra to convey mood, momentum and sound effects. What I miss in films is silence, not only as a neutral medium, or even for its powers of contrast, but for the things from which music is debarred. There are things that only silence can express.

Music in films can be as carefully chosen from sequence to sequence as wines to match the courses of a banquet—or it can be sloshed about as casually as syrup or custard over institutional pudding. Film music can be stained glass or wallpaper. The classic directors in the past who are most associated with appreciating the power of music also had a complementary understanding of silence. Music best retains its power by being rationed.

When music is everywhere in a film, audiences feel less rather than more. A case in point would be a mildly successful, mildly fizzling blockbuster from 2000, *The Perfect Storm* (directed by Wolfgang '*Das Boot*' Petersen), a story of fishermen's ordeals in extreme conditions at sea. It's sometimes hard to hear the roaring of the winds over the lachrymose raging of the orchestra. The composer is James Horner, whose most famous score was also for a marine disaster—but at least *Titanic*, in James Cameron's vision, was a romance (a romance with 1,503 real deaths used as the backdrop for a single fictional one, but a romance all the same). *The Perfect Storm* is based on a true story and aspires to tragedy, but Horner's score in its lushness and sweep is jarringly wrong. Petersen doesn't even have the excuse that the music is there to hide the weakness of the special effects—the special effects are the most impressive parts of the film. So why have music there at all? The presence of music on a soundtrack always tells us we're at a distance from the natural world (which is why music accompanying wildlife documentaries feels so tacky and suspect). Every dollar spent on the music neutralizes a thousand spent on the visual effects, the digitized mountains of water which would be awe-inspiring if they were only let alone.

The omnipresence of music in films is part of a general cultural pattern of obliterating silence, in lifts, airports, shopping centres, lobbies and restaurants. For film-makers there is the additional temptation to fill a soundtrack with pop classics and sell the film that way—but that hardly applies to a piece of product like *The Perfect*

Storm. Hollywood always assumes that the young are the prime market for almost every film, which becomes true when films rival music television in the relentlessness of hit placement. Despite regular waves of prediction, film as an art form has survived the onslaught of television and even MTV. Demographically it would be sensible (more sensible every year) to chase a senior market, for whom saturation with music becomes a deterrent. Older people may have a degree of hearing loss that is hardly noticeable in daily life but makes it hard to extract film dialogue from its inanely seething background.

When music is a constant feature of a film, the director forfeits the possibility that a moment of music will provide a pivot around which the whole film swings in a new direction. For his 1956 film *A Man Escaped*, for instance, Robert Bresson keeps music reined in, concentrating instead on patterns of significant sound inside the prison where the hero is confined—tappings on the walls, a spoon being scraped into sharpness on a stone floor, the gamelan-jangle of keys against metal railings. Roughly every ten minutes Bresson gives us the same sombre burst of a Mozart Mass, always when the hero is mixing with others in the confines of the prison. There is some talk about God among the inmates, but still the music in its organized sorrow is pitched far higher, spiritually, than the action can justify. Those few sombrely blazing bars of orchestra and chorus are more than enough to furnish the soundtrack, since when they aren't being played they are likely to be replayed in the audience's memory. Then when his hero escapes, Bresson lets loose with Mozart in the major. The blaze of organized joy at this point shifts the plane of the story from physical release to transfiguration. Bresson has made us wait ninety minutes to experience one of the simplest effects in classical music, the move from minor to major, as if we had never heard it before, and the music at this point tells us that we are witnessing not good fortune but grace.

The word 'dialectic' was quite properly pensioned off years ago, after decades of overuse, but perhaps it could be brought out of retirement to convey the way silence and music can act on each other as elements of the aural design of a film. Bresson is inescapably a director of 'art films', but much more limited craftsmen in film can achieve modestly overwhelming results. Michael Anderson, for instance, who directed *The Dam Busters* in 1954, is no one's idea of an auteur, but his use of music is highly sophisticated. Eric Coates's 'Dam Busters March' is a classic of film music but it isn't played to death, and the incidental score is carefully modulated. Passages of tension usually rely on natural sound and dialogue, with music being reserved for moments of release. Then at the end of the film the camera shows, in silence, the rooms of men who didn't come back from the raid on the Ruhr. As an account of a dazzling wartime exploit, the apotheosis of boffinry, *The Dam Busters* isn't above a certain amount of tub-thumping, but the director also knows that there are moments when it's the silent tub that makes the most noise.

Silence in this short sequence performs the function that the Mozart Mass does for Bresson—it takes the film into new territory. The camera doesn't stand in for a person, Barnes Wallis (Michael Redgrave) say, or Guy Gibson (Richard Todd), though that too would be a legitimate sequence—the victors should acknowledge the cost of their triumph to others. What is being registered here is absence. The approach is impersonal, almost documentary, though there's little enough to document in the bare quarters of these servicemen: just a travelling clock ticking on, outliving the man whose wrist-turns wound its spring. Music is absent also. Music is the sign that something has become part of culture, whereas this little sequence documents bare absence before it can be tamed into grief. Music takes the edge off, and here we need to feel the edge. The Dam Busters Silence deserves to be as well known as the Dam Busters March.

There are several current directors who could have imagined the visual side of the sequence, Steven Spielberg among them, but none of them would have dared to abstain from the stock musical cues for feeling.

Spielberg took over from Stanley Kubrick a typically slow-brewing project, only partly prepared when he died—*AI*. If Kubrick had made it, the music score would certainly have been less saccharine. Kubrick enjoyed using pre-existing pieces of music (at least once cancelling a commissioned score during editing), and used them in longer extracts than has ever been the fashion. Whether it's Bartok's Music for Strings, Percussion and Celesta in *The Shining* or Ligeti's *Musica Ricercata* in *Eyes Wide Shut*, Kubrick used substantial stretches. It's as if he set himself the challenge of absorbing the energy of the music into his visuals without cheating by chopping it up.

During the editing of *2001*, Kubrick received an advance pressing of a record by the Berlin Philharmonic from his friend Herbert von Karajan. It included music by both Johann ('Blue Danube') and Richard (*Also Sprach Zarathustra*) Strauss. He started playing it in the editing suite with no thought—to start with—of its bizarre appropriateness. If this story is true, then it seems that music was an area where the great control freak could allow himself to be seduced into spontaneity. After excluding chance so single-mindedly from his project Kubrick could let it back in at the last moment, and even enjoy playing with it.

2001 is remarkable for Kubrick's use of the present that Karajan sent. Johann Strauss's magnificently insipid waltz loses all its sentiment when it's made to accompany a sequence of docking with a space station. Richard Strauss's grand gestures seem quite modest, really, when configured as a fanfare to eternity. But the film is also remarkable for its fidelity to silence. For once in the movies, engines roaring in a vacuum make no sound. Infinity isn't given an echo just because we're more comfortable with that illusion. Music and silence, bland actors and overwhelming sets—everything contributes to Kubrick's vision of a cosmos full of grandeur and devoid of personality, full of emptiness and waiting.

A dozen years later, the advertising campaign for *Alien* warned that 'In space no one can hear you scream'. But every engine-note and explosion in the film was helpfully relayed to the audience's ears through a conducting medium that didn't exist.

Sometimes music can enter a film even later than it did in the case of *2001*. Sometimes a commissioned score fails to find favour, and must be replaced at the last minute or even later. Music shares this never-too-late property with another element of film language, the voice-over, but voice-overs are inherently suspect. They've been used so often as sticking-plaster for a bleeding narrative that their very presence makes critics narrow their eyes. It's the cheapest way to cover up defects that can't be remedied, orange pancake make-up in spoken form.

Music doesn't give the game away like that. No one watching Alfred Hitchcock's *Torn Curtain* on its first release in 1966 could have known from internal evidence that the original score was composed by Bernard Herrmann, before John Addison was called in. Hitchcock had a profound understanding of the possibilities of sound design in films, and could boast at least two technical firsts—first British sound film for *Blackmail* (1929), where the soundtrack is as inventively expressionistic as the visuals, and first electronic score, with *The Birds* (1963). His partnership with Herrmann is one of the great pairings in cinema history, up there with Greenaway and Nyman, Lynch and Badalamenti. The high point of their collaboration was certainly *Vertigo*, but Herrmann had a credit (as 'sound consultant') even on *The Birds*, where there isn't anything that could really be described as music.

There was no obvious reason why *Torn Curtain* should have led to rupture, though Hitchcock did have a complex attitude to artistic sharing, and a certain amount of history in terms of driving his most talented collaborators away (such as the brilliant screenwriter on *North by Northwest*, Ernest Lehman). It's true that Herrmann's music for the new film (which you can hear on the DVD) was dark and ominous, and Hitchcock was under pressure from Universal to come up with something more varied and entertaining. But the question of the relative power of music and silence is in there somewhere too.

The most famous scene in *Torn Curtain*—really the only sequence which is even grudgingly admired—is where the hero kills the agent who has been detailed to keep an eye on him in a farmhouse. The killing is slow, ugly, and desperately hard work. Other Iron Curtain agents are only a few yards away, so there can be no question of using a gun—it's all down to saucepans, kitchen knives, spades and finally the (gas) oven. Bernard Herrmann wrote music for the scene. If there is one 'cue' he is famous for, it's the screeching violins that accompany the showerbath murder in *Psycho*. He had come up with an extreme score before, so why not now? Hitchcock didn't use it, not because it failed as music, but because it was music. The scene as released plays in silence (the characters, after all, are desperate not to be heard at their grisly work). Hitchcock understood that music, even when it seems inflammatory of the emotions, is actually a lubricant. Certainly the scene is much harder to watch without the orchestral score. Hitchcock and Herrmann never worked together again.

That's the myth, even if it doesn't quite add up. After all, if Hitchcock was so adamant that the farmhouse killing should be shown without music, why did he get Herrmann's replacement John

Addison to score it all over again, before he finally decided? But it's a necessary myth, now that music has so largely vanquished silence.

Still, there are tiny signs of a silent backlash, and not just in art movies like Gus Van Sant's *Elephant*, where music and silence, speech and ambient noise were woven with astonishing subtlety into an aural design. For me, much of the tension of watching Peter Weir's splendid *Master and Commander* came from waiting, as a master film-maker set his story in motion, with dialogue, sound, set design and special effects all making their mark, for the moment when he remembered to underestimate his audience, and dropped in some of the sea music that has been a celluloid plague at least since Erich Wolfgang Korngold wrote the score for *The Sea Hawk* in 1940. It didn't happen. When music was eventually used it was familiar (Vaughan Williams) or more or less in period (the fiddle and cello duets between Russell Crowe and Paul Bettany). But the first forty minutes played without music. These days we have to be grateful when at least one mainstream director trusts the visual and dramatic language of film to stay afloat, without an orchestra below decks constantly pumping out bilge. Silence and music have coexisted in films in a thousand different ways in the past, and music is the loser when silence dies.

□

DR GONAD
Atom Egoyan

Philip Toubus (twelve times), aka Paul Thomas, Toby Philips, Phil Tobias, Judy Blue, Phil Toubes, Paul Tanner, Phil Tobis, Phil Toubus, Grady Sutton, Phil Tobias, Paul Tomas

Few careers fascinate me more than that of Paul Thomas. According to the International Movie Database (IMDb), Mr Thomas has acted in almost 300 films, and must hold a record for directorial credits (208).

His extraordinarily prolific career seems to have tapered off in the last year, with his last credit as director being *WMB: Weapons of Masturbation* in 2003. As an actor, Mr Thomas will have a hard time matching the thirty credits he scored in 1981, including *Swedish Erotica 1–4, 8, 11, 13–14, 17–18, 22, 25, 28–29,* and *40–41.* The IMDb states that Mr Thomas is sometimes credited as Judy Blue, Toby Philips, Tory Philips, Toby Phillips, Philip Tobias and Phil Tobus, amongst several other incarnations. Given the invariable spelling errors that must occur on certain pornographic titles (when one produces over forty volumes of *Swedish Erotica* in a single year, mistakes are bound to be made), most of these monikers seem to be some sort of variation of Paul Thomas's birth name: Philip Toubus.

It is under this name, Philip Toubus, that I first came into contact with this talented individual. He was one of the principal actors in Norman Jewison's *Jesus Christ Superstar.* Mr Toubus—who has a distinctive singing voice—played the part of Peter. Watching this film when it was released in 1973 changed my life. I had sung hymns every morning at school, and endured compulsory Bible readings, but the religious imagery meant little to me until I saw this magnificently entertaining movie. I can still remember every word of Tim Rice's witty libretto.

I particularly remember Mr Toubus/Thomas as he denied Christ three times. His look of increasing bewilderment as he fulfils Christ's prophecy struck me as something close to sublime. Years later, I would witness this same face (though decidedly less bewildered) in such films as *Dr Gonad's Sex Tails, Dracula Sucks, Nasty Nurses* and, of course, his crowning porn achievement, *Best of Caught from Behind 2.* Though Mr Thomas would go on to perform in *This Stud's for You, Cumshot Revue* and *Naughty Cheerleaders,* nothing would erase the pleasure of the young actor, in his first screen credit, denying Jesus Christ.

What went so horribly wrong (or so spectacularly right) in Mr Toubus's career? A pathologically cynical agent? A simple and almost plaintively earnest desire to stretch his wings? I have always thought that Mr Toubus would be an ideal subject for a documentary—a documentary I will never make.

I will never make this documentary because I have constructed a perfectly structured framing device for this film, and it would crush me if Mr Toubus would not conform to it. In my fantasy of our imaginary interview, Mr Toubus would deny me. First, he would deny me three times and then, by the end of the interview, he would have denied me more times than there are episodes of *Swedish Erotica* (sixty). I would intercut his denials with images from his porn career and cutaways from his denials in *Jesus Christ Superstar*. The big problem with this approach is that I have no idea what Mr Toubus could possibly deny. He certainly couldn't deny his participation in the porn. He might deny that this was a lamentable choice. But even if he were to deny this (and there's a very good chance Mr Toubus is perfectly pleased with his decisions), this would only account for one niggling denial. Certainly not enough for a movie.

So this potentially fascinating film will never be made.

As an aside, our careers almost collided at the Adult Video News Awards, a splashy event held every year to honour the best in porn. In 1997, Mr Thomas won Best Director for his work on *Bobby Sox*. A year earlier, my film *Exotica* had won for Best Alternative Adult Film (difficult to believe, but it's also there on the IMDb record under 'Awards & Nominations'). I entertain the fantasy that Mr Thomas was on the nominating committee that selected my film.

Needless to say, Mr Toubus would deny this.   □

NOTES ON CONTRIBUTORS

Shampa Banerjee worked in publishing in India for many years and wrote and edited post-production scripts in English for directors such as Ketan Mehta and Satyajit Ray. She now lives in California.

Atom Egoyan is a film director whose works include *Exotica*, *The Sweet Hereafter* and *Ararat*. He has received, among other prizes, the 1997 Grand Prix and 1997 International Critics Awards from the Cannes Film Festival.

John Fowles's novels include *The Magus*, *The French Lieutenant's Woman* and *Daniel Martin* (Vintage/Back Bay Books). A first volume of his diaries was published by Jonathan Cape last year. He lives in Lyme Regis, Dorset.

Karl French's most recent book, *Abba—Unplugged*, will be published by Piatkus in November. The pieces in this issue are abridged from his book, *Art by Directors*, which will be published by Mitchell Beazley in September. He writes a daily TV column for the *Financial Times*.

Tessa Hadley lives in Cardiff and teaches at Bath Spa University College. Her most recent novel is *Everything Will Be All Right* (Jonathan Cape/Henry Holt).

Ian Jack is the editor of *Granta*.

Thomas Keneally's *Schindler's Ark* won the Booker Prize in 1982. *Office of Innocence*, his latest novel, is published by Sceptre/Doubleday.

Jonathan Lethem is the author of six novels including *The Fortress of Solitude* (Faber/Vintage). His story collection, *Men and Cartoons*, will be published by Vintage in the US in November and by Faber in the UK in January 2005.

Jim Lewis has written three novels including *Why the Tree Loves the Axe* (Flamingo/Berkley) and, most recently, *The King is Dead* (Flamingo/Vintage).

Adam Mars-Jones reviews books for the London *Observer*. He was one of *Granta*'s Best of Young British Novelists in both 1983 and 1993.

Andrew O'Hagan won the 2004 James Tait Black Memorial Prize for his most recent novel, *Personality* (Faber/Harvest). An extract entitled 'You, the Viewers at Home' appeared in *Granta* 79.

Chris Petit is a film and video-maker and an author. His films include *Radio On* and *Chinese Boxes*, and his video work has covered weather, surveillance and the M25. His latest novel is *The Human Pool* (Scribner/Pocket Star).

Maarten 't Hart is the author of thirteen novels, most recently *The Sun Dial* (Arcadia/Toby Press). His short story, 'Midsummer in April' appeared in *Granta* 83. He lives in the Netherlands.

Colson Whitehead's books include *The Intuitionist* (Granta/Anchor) and, most recently, *The Colossus of New York* (Fourth Estate/Doubleday).

Gaby Wood is writing a book about Lana Turner. She writes for the London *Observer*, and lives in New York.